Vocal Tracks

The publisher gratefully acknowledges the generous contribution to this book provided by the Ahmanson Foundation Humanities Endowment Fund of the University of California Press Foundation.

Vocal Tracks

Performance and Sound Media

Jacob Smith

UNIVERSITY OF CALIFORNIA PRESS
Berkeley · Los Angeles · London

University of California Press, one of the most distinguished university presses in the United States, enriches
lives around the world by advancing scholarship in the
humanities, social sciences, and natural sciences. Its activities are supported by the UC Press Foundation and by
philanthropic contributions from individuals and institutions. For more information, visit www.ucpress.edu.

University of California Press
Berkeley and Los Angeles, California

University of California Press, Ltd.
London, England

An earlier version of chapter 2 appeared as "Filling the
Embarrassment of Silence: Erotic Performance on
Recorded 'Blue Discs,'" in *Film Quarterly* 58, no. 2
(Winter 2004–5): 26–35, published by University of
California Press. An earlier version of chapter 1 ap-
peared as "The Frenzy of the Audible: Pleasure, Au-
thenticity and Recorded Laughter," in *Television and
New Media* 6, no. 1 (February 2005): 23–47. Both
printed by permisssion.

Library of Congress Cataloging-in-Publication Data

Smith, Jacob, 1970–
Vocal tracks : performance and sound media / Jacob
Smith.
        p.   cm.
    Includes bibliographical references and index.
    ISBN: 978-0-520-25493-0 (cloth : alk. paper)
    ISBN: 978-0-520-25494-7 (pbk. : alk. paper)
        1. Voice culture.   2. Voice.   I. Title.
PN4162.S57   2008
808.5—dc22
                                          2007039511

Manufactured in the United States of America

17   16   15   14   13   12   11   10   09   08
10   9   8   7   6   5   4   3   2   1

This book is printed on Natures Book, which contains
30% post-consumer waste and meets the minimum requirements of ANSI/NISO Z39.48–1992 (R 1997) *(Per-
manence of Paper)*.

Contents

Acknowledgments

Many people helped me gather research materials for this book, including Shawn Wilson at the Kinsey Institute; David Diehl, Jerry Fabris, and Leonard DeGraaf at the Edison National Historic Site; John Mehlberg; and Brother Russell. Several portions of *Vocal Tracks* appeared in an earlier form in *Film Quarterly* and *Television and New Media,* and the comments of the readers and editors at those journals—in particular Ann Martin at *Film Quarterly*—added much to the subsequent development of that material. Similarly, at the University of California Press, Mary Francis, Lynn Meinhardt, Ann Twombly, and two readers offered encouragement and made thoughtful and insightful suggestions that helped me sharpen my arguments and polish my prose.

Various friends and colleagues have shaped my thinking and encouraged my work. Robert B. Ray and Sean McCloud were important inspirations in my initial transition from musician to academic. Fellow graduate students at Indiana University provided invaluable discussion and feedback, in particular Bob Rehak, James Kendrick, Jon Kraszewski, Matt Yockey, Sarah Sinwell, and Jasmine Trice. I have received much guidance from my professors, most notably Barbara Klinger, Joan Hawkins, Glenn Gass, and David Haberman; Matthew Solomon and Paula Amad, who at different times read portions of the book and made helpful comments; Greg Waller, who lent a wise ear to my problems and always offered a voice of clarity; and Michael Jarrett, who has been a generous adviser, and who not only read and commented on chapter 4, but named it as well.

This book could not exist without the enormous fund of knowledge introduced to me by Richard Bauman, whom I had the great luck of finding in the office when I applied for an independent study. Professor Bauman also introduced me to Patrick Feaster, who shared with me the wonders of early sound recording and so made this book possible. I owe much to Patrick's generosity with his remarkable collection as well as to his patient friendship as I fumbled toward historical accuracy. Chris Anderson has been an invaluable mentor and keen-eyed editor of my work and has inspired my love for historical research. James Naremore was a guiding force in my academic career from the beginning, and his clarity of thought, encouragement, and careful editing have profoundly shaped this book.

Dale Lawrence provided a perspective on issues of performance from outside the academy, but more than that, he has been a friend, interlocutor, collaborator, and mentor. My parents were more than generous with their love and support while I wrote *Vocal Tracks,* and my sons, Jonah and Henry, consistently reminded me of the life that existed outside its pages. Finally, this book could not have been written were it not for Freda, whose insight, patience, and love enabled me to find my voice.

Introduction

Imagine that you are the audience for a phonograph record in the first decade of the twentieth century. You might be listening through ear tubes at a public phonograph parlor in an urban shopping area, or at home with your ear cocked to a large amplifying horn. The first sound you hear is a voice, which speaks the following words in a stentorian tone: "The Laughing Spectator, by Steve Porter, Edison Records." After a short orchestral prelude, a male voice asks, "Say, Mac, where's your partner?" "Why, he's not here," another man answers. "But say, Professor, after I get through you'll never miss 'im. Listen." A higher-pitched male voice announces, "Hello, Mac!" The lower voice replies, "How are ya, Reilly?" "What's the matter, Mac?" asks Reilly. "You look upset!" "I *am* upset," Mac answers. "My bank busted and I lost me balance!" On the heels of this joke, you hear the laughter of an audience that seems to be attending a vaudeville comedy routine. "Say, Mac," Reilly continues, "where're you goin' for the summer?" "I'm not *goin'* for it," Mac replies. "I'm gonna wait till it comes here." The audience laughs again, but this time a particular audience member stands out from the rest: a man whose outrageous bray is so jarring that it causes Mac to step out of his stage persona and ask, "What's that?" Mac and Reilly continue with the act, but now each time you hear the audience's response, you cannot help focusing your attention on the raucous and idiosyncratic laughter of the unnamed spectator. The comedians are equally distracted: "Is that a man or a goat?" Mac asks, causing the audience to laugh all the more. Finally, Mac invites the laughing spectator onstage, where he begs the comics not to tell any more jokes. Without explanation, Mac suddenly bursts into song, singing a series of teasing questions to the spectator, who begs him to stop. As usual, the man can't contain his ridiculous laughter, and the routine ends as the orchestra does a quick final vamp.

The phonograph record you've been hearing was released in 1908, only the second decade that sound recordings were mass marketed for entertainment. Made at the dawn of an era of mass media, Steve Porter's *The Laughing Spectator* demonstrates the remarkable versatility of the voice as an instrument of performance. In the course of little more than two minutes, we have heard a spoken announcement, a comic dialogue, the laughter of an audience, and singing. Porter's voice is more versatile than it may at first appear, since he is performing the parts of both Mac and Reilly. In this Porter was part of a phonographic tradition in which performers played multiple parts of a dramatic routine. Such an act often had to be specifically identified on record company promotional material to be fully appreciated, and the brief opening dialogue with the "Professor" ("Say, Mac, where's your partner?") is meant to cue the listener to appreciate the full dimensions of Porter's vocal achievement. As we will see in the chapters that follow, this is only one way in which performers took advantage of how the modern media separated them in time and space from their audiences.

But of all the voices we hear, it is that of the laughing spectator himself that makes Porter's record such an apt way to begin a book about vocal performance in the media. Note that the laughing spectator's emergence from the crowd is very like a later landmark moment in media performance: the film in which Charlie Chaplin first appeared in the famous Tramp costume. *Kid's Auto Race*—made six years after *The Laughing Spectator*—presents the Tramp as one of a crowd of onlookers at a race, but after he notices the newsreel camera filming the event, he works his way into the center of every shot, setting himself apart from the rest of the spectators. For James Naremore, Chaplin's performance serves as an allegory about acting in the cinema, since it invites the audience to "take pleasure in the difference between acting and accident," and its humor depends on the recognition of Chaplin as an actor, as opposed to the "real" people around him—who, as Naremore points out, are performing, too (1988, 14).

The Laughing Spectator presents a similar allegory, but in this case, we *hear* an individual performer emerge from an anonymous, undifferentiated audience. As we recognize that goatlike laughter as a performance, the laughter of the crowd is made to seem "real," even though the sounds of the audience are every bit as constructed a performance as the other sounds we hear. But *The Laughing Spectator* can also illustrate how the sound media have gravitated toward the voice at the limits of language. Consider how the eponymous hero in his wordless vocalizing is able, through his unrestrained and unmistakable laughter, not only to distinguish himself from the rest of the audience, but eventually to join the performers onstage: the voice that functions as an index of the body in the throes of raw, unrestrained emotion upstages a comic performance built on wordplay. The sound media have been adept at framing expressions such as this, in the process redefining what counts as performance and allowing us to hear the voice in new ways.

Such issues have received relatively little discussion by film and media historians. One of the goals of this book is to use the media of the past century to better understand the performance function of the voice. Roland Barthes has written that no analytic science could exhaust the subject of the human voice, and it is easy to understand why. The voice can function as an index of the body, a conveyor of language, a social bond, a musical instrument of sublime flexibility, a gauge of emotion, a central component of the art of acting, and a register of everyday identity. The voice is slippery, easily sliding between these categories, sometimes functioning as a conscious expression, other times as an unintended reflection of the self. As Mladen Dolar has pointed out, one of the central paradoxes of the voice is that it is at once "the axis of our social bonds" and "the intimate kernel of subjectivity" (2006, 14). Our voices reveal our social roles, and at the same time they are intimately connected to our individual bodies and our most closely held sense of identity: Dolar compares the voice to a fingerprint, whereas Jonathan Ree writes that the voice is "as private and vulnerable as your defenseless naked body" (1999, 1). The voice's ability to operate on so many levels is an important part of its fascination as a vehicle of performance.

Considering the protean quality of the voice, it is fitting that in the following chapters we will listen to voices engaged in acting, singing, joke telling, public speaking, wiretapping, and telephone conversation. What unites these disparate types of performance is that they occur in the context of sound media such as phonograph records, film, and radio and television broadcasts. In other words, my study offers an examination of the styles of vocal performance that developed in tandem with media technologies. The voice was the first aspect of performance to be captured and reproduced in real time by a modern recording instrument, and vocal performance can serve as a gauge for the consideration of performance in the media more broadly. Another goal of this book, then, is to use the voice to understand the media better. As Thomas Edison's phonograph developed into an entertainment medium in the decades after its 1877 invention, it came to have important implications for the development of modern performance styles. For example, never before had performers been separated in time and space from a face-to-face audience. New sound technologies such as the phonograph also preserved nuances of performance such as the grain of the voice and wordless vocal expressions of intense emotion that would have eluded written scripts or musical scores.

Since my topic lies at the intersection of the voice, sound media technologies, and performance, I draw on a variety of scholarly work. Much of the analysis of sound recording has been centered on motion pictures, and one of the dominant approaches to sound in the cinema has been theoretically informed by the writings of Sigmund Freud and Jacques Lacan. The overarching concern of writers such as Mary Ann Doane, Kaja Silverman, Amy Lawrence, and Michel Chion has been the relationship between the voice and the image of the cinematic subject. Their writing tends to concentrate on the primal resonance of the voice and its function as an index of gender and identity. Unfortunately, this psychoanalytic school has tended to ignore the ways in which film texts function in larger cultural and social contexts. Another recent approach to sound theory shows an awareness of this limitation. The work of writers such as Rick Altman, Jonathan Sterne, Leigh Schmidt, Emily Thompson, James Lastra, and Lisa Gitelman has been concerned with excavating the origins and cultural meanings of the sound technologies of the nineteenth and twentieth centuries, as well as the cultural history of hearing. These approaches to sound theory have several benefits. First, by focusing on the media apparatus, they allow for the discussion of a large field of culture, including research and development, invention, and production. In contrast to much of the psychoanalytic school, these are also studies that strive to be culturally and historically specific, seeing technological objects as crystallizations of larger cultural processes and discourses. But where the psychoanalytic school overvalued the media text, these works undervalue it. Their focus is so squarely on the apparatus that one can forget that the machines were ever used to transmit human performances.

Performance has entered the discourse of media studies most often under the rubric of film acting. Film theorists have long recognized the reciprocity of message and medium in cinematic acting styles: how the close-up could capture subtleties of gesture and expression, or how editing could be used to construct performances. Though acting has always been one of the central sources of fascination for audiences and popular critics of film, however, it has often been relegated to the sidelines of academic discourse, particularly in writing associated with the study of "auteur" directors, film genres, and psychoanalysis. But cultural studies and the recent turn to historicism in film studies have renewed interest in acting (Wojcik 2004, 5–6). Diverse writers such as James Naremore, Roberta Pearson, Richard Dyer, and Pamela Robertson Wojcik have made important contributions to the study of film acting and its connections to culture, history, and technology. Their work, however, has been confined largely to film and, to a lesser extent, television. The film-centered approach has meant an emphasis on gesture, with little work being done on the techniques of and discourses surrounding the voice. This is an unfortunate lacuna, since the voice is such an integral aspect of acting and has frequently been a central topic in debates about acting technique. Further, radio and phonographic texts can provide rich and frequently overlooked case studies in modern acting. For example, the descriptive sketches found on phonograph records from the 1890s to the 1920s provide a body of performance that runs parallel to early cinema, and they can broaden the scope of the scholarly dialogue on media performance beyond the binary of stage and screen.

Besides work on acting in the cinema, my analysis of sound media performances is also informed by performance theory, by which I mean the work of sociolinguistics, the ethnography of speaking, and conversation analysis as represented by scholars such as Erving Goffman, Richard Bauman, Robert Hopper, Dell Hymes, Roman Jakobson, Harvey Sacks, and Gail Jefferson. Performance theory provides a model of close formal analysis that is grounded in cultural and historical specificity and that is centrally concerned with the social effect of form. This body of work is of particular importance for an analysis of how vocal performance is shaped by media technologies, since by becoming familiar with the nuances of face-to-face communication, we can better understand the ways in which aspects of it are mobilized or altered in mediated performances. Goffman's work in particular has provided me with a vocabulary for describing the intricate performances of everyday interaction and the ways in which these have been incorporated into media texts.

Guided by these different theoretical approaches, my study begins with two chapters that examine how recorded vocal performances have been shaped by the separation of performers from their audiences in time and space. In both chapters of part 1 I show how the phenomenon that Erving Goffman has called "flooding out" has played an important function in a mediated context and can be seen as a central stylistic aspect of modern vocal performance. Scholars such as Dell Hymes and Richard Bauman have defined performance as a mode of speaking that formally sets itself off from everyday talk, presenting itself to an audience for an evaluation of the performer's skill. Performers are accountable to and evaluated by their audiences, and so they must typically display a certain mastery. But the central feature of a variety of phonograph records, radio and television broadcasts, and amateur recordings is the performer's loss of control. Adapting Hymes's terminology (1975, 24), this is a type of performance that seeks to present a "breakthrough out of performance." These media texts are structured in such a way as to highlight a moment when a performer loses his or her composure and vocally floods out, shattering the performance frame and thereby offering a tantalizing suggestion of authentic and spontaneous expression.

Before going any further, I should say something about my use of the term *authenticity*. In work on the sound media, much has been written about the idea of sound "fidelity." Rick Altman is among scholars who have sought to dispel what he calls the "reproductive fallacy" in theoretical work on film sound, which held that sound recording technologies reproduced the original sound "faithfully, in its full three-dimensionality" (1992, 39). Instead, Altman stresses that sound recording "represents" rather than "reproduces" sound, since choices about such things as microphone placement always make the recording an "interpretation of the original sound" (1992, 40). Discussions of a recording's fidelity then, are best seen as a way of assessing its "adherence to a set of evolving conventions, like the parallel standards established for such culturally important qualities as 'realism,' 'morality,' or 'beauty'" (1992, 40). Similarly, James Lastra (2000, 152) argues that effects such as authenticity and immediacy are, like fidelity, products of "historically defined and mediated conditions." In the chapters that follow, I am concerned with *authenticity* as a culturally important convention, one that was the concern of performers as much as engineers. To create an effect of "authentic" or immediate presence, studio performers had to develop stylistic techniques that would, in Jonathan Sterne's words, "stand in for reality within the system of reproduced sounds" (2003, 285). In many of the case studies that follow, I attempt to identify and historicize vocal expressions that provided a sense of authentic presence. Contextual evidence from period documents indicates how certain performers, styles, or techniques established particularly powerful, direct, or "real"-sounding performances. Lastra (2000, 152) has encouraged us always to ask whose interests are being served when qualities such as authenticity are attributed or denied. Indeed, we shall see that decisions about what makes an "authentic" vocal performance have often been conflated with notions of race, gender, and class.

In chapter 1 I examine the recorded laugh in the mass media, focusing on early phonograph recordings and the broadcast laugh track. I present the laugh as an instance of "flooding out" and look closely at its use in a genre of turn-of-the-century phonographic recordings called laughing records. I argue that the performance of the laugh has helped bridge the gap between listener and prerecorded media texts, and it has served as an indication of authentic human presence in the media. An equally compelling early phonographic genre is the "laughing story," typified by Cal Stewart's Uncle Josh records, which can be seen as a precursor to the broadcast laugh track. These records show that the performed laugh has been associated with white, working-class "country" authenticity, from Stewart's Uncle Josh to Andy Griffith. The debate over the ethics of the laugh track reveals anxieties about the radio and TV audience, the legal and aesthetic arguments for "liveness," and the performance of authentic presence. The discourse surrounding the laugh machines that produced the laugh track reveals how these proto-sampling devices often struck both the audience and television professionals as strange and unsettling, another index of the overdetermined meaning of the laugh.

Chapter 2 is concerned with verbal performances of the erotic, a mode in which the separation of performers from audiences is of particular importance because of the way in which it changes the dynamics of risk in performance. The object of study in this chapter is a genre of early phonograph records called "blue discs"—under-the-counter erotic performances that are roughly the phonographic equivalent of the stag film. The role of sound in general and the voice in particular in the presentation of the erotic has not received enough critical attention, and blue discs provide a useful case study in that project, as well as in the analysis of the female voice in the cinema. Such records also provide a case study in how erotic performance is shaped by performance contexts ranging from the burlesque stage to film pornography. An important distinction can be made between the relative levels of risk involved in performing erotic material for a face-to-face audience and those of doing so for a listening audience that is separated from the performer in time and space. The effect of risk on performance can be gauged through an examination of blue discs, on which one finds both a mode of joking keyed to a face-to-face context and an erotics of flooding out that illustrates the emergence of styles of modern erotic performance made for a mediated context.

The work of Linda Williams has indicated ways in which films have featured a spectacular display of the body; for this reason it is useful for my examinations of uninhibited vocal performances. In her essay "Film Bodies: Gender, Genre, and Excess," Williams argues that the defining feature of film genres, such as melodrama, horror, and pornography, are the spectacles of bodies in spasm, caught in the grip of intense sensation or emotion (1991, 4). In her longer study of film pornography, Williams analyzes the visual structure of hard-core porn and describes the orgasmic "money shot" as the center of textual gravity. Williams's analysis of this dynamic is primarily in visual terms, and she even claims that there "can be no such thing as hard-core sound," since vocal performances can be faked, while the undeniable evidence of the "money shot" cannot (1989, 126). My project investigates that claim by examining a range of sound media texts whose center of gravity is a "breakthrough out of performance" much like the hard-core money shot. My study can add to Williams's investigation of performance in the "body genres" in several ways. First, I broaden the range of what are considered spasmodic performances to include the laugh, secret recordings, and flooding out in anger. Second, if Williams is interested primarily in describing the structures of visual pleasure to be found in film pornography, this study seeks to provide a close analysis of audible structures of pleasure in a range of sound media genres.

Both of the chapters in part 2 deal with the ability of sound technologies to represent nuances of vocal performance that would not have been audible to a theater audience. The microphone's ability to capture subtleties of vocal timbre and inflection faithfully opened up the possibility of new forms of performance marked by a quiet intensity and subtle shadings of inflection, suggestive of intimacy and emotional density. In chapter 3 I investigate styles of vocal acting that developed in tandem with sound media technologies such as radio microphones. Twentieth-century acting has often been discussed in relation to the cinema camera and the development of the close-up. Equal consideration needs to be given to the closely held microphone, which had an effect on acting just as it did on styles of popular singing and public speaking. The use of the microphone and the formal particularities of radio drama are important areas of inquiry because the voice and techniques of vocal training have consistently been pivotal issues in moments of stylistic change in acting. We will see that microphone technology did not dictate a single style, and that different approaches to radio acting were judged according to cultural notions of gender.

Taking as a starting point the assertion that much of the meaning of modern vocal performances lies on the level of the "grain of the voice," chapter 4 looks at recorded performances by male singers over the past century. I trace the interaction of two different vocal styles, one characterized by a rough, throaty rasp, the other by the round, clear tone of operatic bel canto singing. The throaty rasp has been associated with an African American male performance, and it can be heard in recorded performances by black pioneers of the recording industry such as George Washington Johnson, Bert Williams, and Louis Armstrong. These singers were able to create styles that could fit into dominant cultural standards of singing, while also making use of a tradition of African American expressivity. Rasp became an important aspect of white styles of vocal performance that sought to represent blackness, beginning with turn-of-the-century recordings of the minstrel show tradition and culminating in rock-and-roll singers in the 1970s. A tone that had been excluded from traditional schools of vocal training in the West became increasingly freighted with cultural meaning for white singers over the course of the century, indexing blackness, class, masculinity, and emotional catharsis.

In part 3 I turn my attention to the use of recording technology to record vocal performances secretly. Arising from the particular historical and technological context of the 1940s, this technique for capturing performance has become the linchpin of a remarkably successful genre of broadcast entertainment. Chapter 5 begins my examination of secret recording by looking at Allen Funt's "candid" format, as embodied first on radio as *Candid Microphone,* then on television as *Candid Camera,* and later in a more sexually explicit format on cable television and the feature film *What Do You Say to a Naked Lady?* (1970). The success of *Candid Camera* can be seen to arise in part from Funt's adaptation of the format he developed for radio. This went from the incitation of a victim (who was often identified as an ethnic type) and an unmediated address to the home audience, to a format that was performed live in front of a studio audience and based on what Funt called "the reveal": the moment when the gag was revealed, and the victim flooded out in surprise.

My analysis of Funt's programs enables an examination of the different ways in which performance has been structured in radio and television. In fact, one benefit of taking performance as on object of study is that, in tracing performances across different media, the particularities and protocols of a particular medium can come into sharper focus. Thus, my analysis of recorded laughter provides a means to examine links between genres of phonographic recordings and broadcast laugh tracks on radio and television; my consideration of erotic vocal performance allows me to make comparisons among stage burlesque performance, phonograph recordings, and film pornography; and in this chapter, my study of secret recording as a distinct form of entertainment enables us to better analyze radio and television programming such as *Candid Camera* and reality television. The candid format is also a productive case study for thinking about the uses of recording in terms of a historic shift away from live broadcasting, as well as in its connection to modes like wiretapping and wartime sound technologies. Funt's shows were in some ways transitional texts, hybrids of the live and recorded that experimented with both modes in innovative and influential ways.

Continuing the previous chapter's interest in secret recording, the objects of study in chapter 6 are recordings of prank phone calls, a form that was, for many years, the domain of amateur performers who duplicated and distributed cassette tapes to friends and acquaintances. Cassette technology is an example of what Annabelle Sreberny-Mohammadi and Ali Mohammadi have described as "small media," and the portability and ease of duplication of cassette tapes were a factor in the rise of prank calling as a form of entertainment. The telephone has been a difficult subject for media scholars, in part because of the fact that it does not offer up discrete texts for analysis. These recordings can offer a first step in the study of telephone interaction in a more traditional media studies mode, since they are both comedy texts and secretly recorded conversations. The most prevalent spectacle of prank recordings is the incitation of a male victim to engage in performances that have traditionally served as a prelude to physical violence. The humor of these pranks is derived from the way traditional measures of masculine status are revealed to be anachronistic and ridiculous. Besides shedding light on the performance of masculinity, prank calls enable us to study historical changes in the cultural experience of the telephone. The prank call is a performance that has, since the 1950s, been associated with contradictory cultural meanings, understood both as a form of comic entertainment and as a social problem that became a topic of urban legends and horror films.

These three aspects of vocal performance (flooding out, the increased significance of timbre and inflection, and the use of secret recording) developed in connection with sound media technologies, and they can tell us something both about how technology influences culture and about the ways in which culture shapes our judgments of technology. Ultimately, I shall argue that all three function as crucial signs of human presence in a mediated world, and, as such, they reveal the nature of performance in the modern media and the voice's role as a chief instrument in the construction of social identity. One of the ironies that will emerge in the chapters that follow is that such depth of meaning can be found in wordless vocal expressions such as the rough edge of a singer's voice, exclamations of anger, or unrestrained laugher like that heard on Steve Porter's 1908 *The Laughing Spectator*. In fact, I hope that this book will function a bit like the laughing protagonist on Porter's record: drawing the reader's attention to the often unnoticed but insistent and all-too-human sounds of the mediated voice.

PART ONE

Flooding Out

CHAPTER I

Recorded Laughter and the Performance of Authenticity

In Steven Spielberg's *A.I.: Artificial Intelligence* (2001), the android David (Haley Joel Osment) tries desperately to appear human and so win the love of his adoptive mother, Monica (Frances O'Connor). In one of the film's most affecting scenes, David and his "parents" laugh at the way Monica eats her spaghetti. At first, David's laughter appears remarkably human, making us momentarily forget that he is a robot (figure 1). But gradually this laughter takes on an eerie and uncanny quality that makes him seem less human than ever. Jonathan Rosenbaum writes that the scene asks us to consider the line between mechanical and real laughter: "The laughter of David and his adopted parents becomes impossible to define as either forced or genuine, mechanical or spontaneous, leaving us perpetually suspended over the question as if over an abyss" (2001, 36). There is nothing new about this phenomenon. Though the spasmodic and nonsemantic nature of laughter makes it seem an unlikely carrier of meaning, it has played an ongoing role in the presentation of the authentically human in mass-mediated texts, notably on early genres of phonographic recordings and the broadcast laugh track.

The sound of uninhibited laughter, produced both by performers and by audiences, was an important index of authentic presence used to bridge the gap between recorded sound and the listener. The recording studios of the phonograph industry represented a radically new type of performance space, where performers had to develop new stylistic techniques meant, in Jonathan Sterne's words, to "stand in for reality within

Figure 1. Haley Joel Osment as the android David in Steven Spielberg's *A.I.: Artificial Intelligence* (2001). Frances O'Connor and Sam Robards play Monica and Henry Swinton. Source: BFI.

the system of reproduced sounds" (2003, 285). The laugh emerged as an expression that was particularly able to represent a sense of immediacy when mechanically reproduced for audiences that studio performers would never see. Recorded genres of "laughing songs," "laughing records," and "laughing stories" show that the laugh played a central role in the introduction of recorded sound as a form of entertainment. Further, these records can be seen as precursors to broadcast laugh tracks, which I place in the historical and discursive contexts of radio, television, and an "ideology of liveness."

Paddy Scannell writes that "all day, every day and everywhere people listen to radio and watch television as part of the utterly familiar, normal things that anyone does on any normal day" (1996, 6). The laugh track is an especially mundane part of the everyday TV experience that Scannell describes. For most viewers the sound of the laugh track is intensely, intimately familiar, so much so that focusing on it takes a concerted effort. It is by definition background, a part of the sonic wallpaper, effortlessly tuned out. In this chapter I'd like to bring the background to the fore, to make that familiar sonic object strange. As I plan to show, the laugh track is part of a larger story of the recorded laugh in the history of media, and telling that story can provide insights into the ways in which people have interacted with media technologies and in which bodies and voices have been represented through them. As such, the examples I will present from phonograph records and radio broadcasts can also illuminate performances found in Hollywood films. Throughout these different media contexts, the laugh has been presented as the ultimate expression of the human—often as the result of its connection to discourses about race, class, and gender—and its mechanical reproduction has served as a lightning rod for anxieties concerning the social dimensions of mass media performance and consumption.

CRACKING UP: THE PERFORMANCE OF LAUGHTER

To begin an examination of the relationship between performed laughter and the media, consider the way in which early "talking machines" were demonstrated to the public. Interestingly, the use of the laugh to demonstrate the virtuosity of talking machines predates Thomas Edison's 1877 invention of the phonograph; it can be found in conjunction with the eighteenth- and nineteenth-century devices of Wolfgang von Kempelen and Joseph Faber. Kempelen, most famous for his automaton chess player, also designed a keyboard-operated machine in the 1780s that could imitate the vocal organs. Using Kempelen's designs, Charles Wheatstone, a leading British scientist of the time, built a talking machine in 1837. After seeing it demonstrated, an observer wrote that the machine "laughs and cryes with a perfect imitation of nature" (Feaster 2006b, 52). A decade later Joseph Faber designed a similar speaking machine that featured the torso of a "Turk" and a more convenient keyboard. The *Illustrated London News* noted in 1846 that the machine was capable of not only speech, but "even whispering, laughing and singing: all this depending on the agility of the director in manipulating the keys" (Feaster 2001, 67). Indeed, laughter seems to have become a routine part of Faber's demonstrations after 1846; the *London Times* noted on August 12 of that year that the machine laughed "with the merriment of good humour" (cited in Feaster 2006b, 68). The laugh seems to have been a particularly evocative performance, one that was used for testing both the realism and the amusement value of a talking machine.

This was still the case when Edison's tinfoil phonograph was displayed thirty years later. Early demonstrations of the phonograph often delighted audiences: the machine laughed and coughed and sneezed. Accounts of exhibitions of the tinfoil phonograph reveal that laughter recurred frequently. Take, for example, an article from the *New York Sun* on February 22, 1878, which described how Edison "coughed, sneezed, and laughed at the mouthpiece, and the matrixes returned the noises true as a die." The *Philadelphia Press* on March 9, 1878, described the following demonstration: "Laughter and whistling and singing and sighing and groans—in fact, every utterance of which the human voice is capable—was stored in that wondrous wheel and emitted when it was turned." The *New York Daily Graphic* described on March 15, 1878, how a phonograph exhibitor had "laughed to his heart's content . . . and the sounds were reproduced" (Feaster 2006a, 125).

In these demonstrations of the phonograph, as was true of earlier demonstrations of talking automata, the laugh was presented as the spontaneous creaturely expression of embodiment, a performance particularly capable of testing the limits of mechanical reproduction. The laugh in this context functioned like the "easily recognizable forms of human speech," such as rhymes or popular quotations, that Jonathan Sterne (2003, 251) argues were mobilized to "help the machine": "by the use of clichéd and conventionalized language, early 'performers' of sound reproduction helped listeners help the machine reproduce speech." But the laugh continued to play a central role in phonographic performance beyond these initial demonstrations, as is indicated by the fact that it was prominently featured in the recording industry's earliest catalogs.

George Washington Johnson's *Laughing Song*—whose chorus is a gale of rhythmic laugher—stands as a particularly dramatic case in point because its massive popularity made it an instant standard that was "closely identified with the emerging entertainment phonograph" (T. Brooks 2005, 32). Johnson's laughter was transmitted far and wide by traveling exhibitors like Lyman Howe, whose 1891 program at the Welsh Congregational Church in Scranton included Johnson's *Laughing Song* fifth on the bill (Musser 1991, 32). Tim Brooks, a historian of recorded sound, cites the report of a traveling exhibitor in New England to the trade journal the *Phonogram* in July 1892: "Johnson's 'Whistling Coon' and laughing song are immensely popular, and I presume they will always be. There is more call for them than for any other selections" (T. Brooks 2005, 34).

Johnson's records were an important part of traveling phonograph demonstrations, and *The Laughing Song* became perhaps the first blockbuster of the emerging market for entertainment phonograph records. Johnson had been performing for coins at the Hudson River ferryboat terminal when he was hired by Victor H. Emerson to record for the New Jersey Phonograph Company in 1890 (T. Brooks 2005, 26). The U.S. Phonograph Company's 1894 catalog claimed that "over 25,000" copies of *The Laughing Song* had been sold; as for sheet music of the song (which Johnson wrote himself), the figure was said to be "over 50,000" (T. Brooks 2005, 35, 40). Whatever the exact numbers, this record was certainly one of the (if not *the*) best-selling records in the country during the 1890s (T. Brooks 2004, 55).

Johnson's performances of "The Laughing Song" and "The Whistling Coon" are also notable as the first popular vocal recordings made by an African American.[1] Johnson's laugh certainly carried with it racist stereotypes of the minstrel show, as was illustrated by the comments of the early phonograph producer Fred Gaisberg, who described Johnson's laugh as "deep-bellied [and] lazy like a carefree darky" (1942, 40). In an American musical culture steeped in the blackface minstrel show tradition, part of Johnson's success had to do with his aura of authenticity: "Johnson's performance *sounded* authentic, just like the black panhandler on the street. This was far more unusual than it might seem, for in the early days of recording most artists sang in distinct, stilted, almost shouted tones, striving above all else to make the words *very clear and understandable*. When they imitated blacks, in sketches and song, they were so broad and mannered as to be almost cartoonish. But here was the real thing, a black street singer doing just what he did for nickels on the sidewalks of New York" (T. Brooks 2005, 31–32). In spite of their racist stereotypes, these records are important documents of African American recorded vocal expression, and ones that highlight both the limited stylistic choices available to blacks and their inventive and resourceful responses to those limitations.[2] In the context of my larger argument, Johnson's "authentic" blackness was performed by his laughter and served to amplify the sense of authenticity already associated with that expression.

As was the case with pre-phonographic talking machines, the laugh was a significant and powerful index of presence for the first audiences of prerecorded performances. Johnson's *Laughing Song* juxtaposes sung verses with a chorus of rhythmic laughter, but another early phonographic genre called laughing records are almost entirely the sound of unrestrained and unaccompanied laughter. These records were made by various labels throughout the first decades of the century and can tell us more about the interaction of vocal performance and media technologies.

One of the most successful was *The Okeh Laughing Record*, released in 1922. This recording did so well that it was quickly followed by two sequels called *The Second Laughing Record* and *The Okeh Laughing Dance Record* (T. Brooks 1979, 3). In the most prevalent model of the laughing record genre, a recurring, elementary narrative frames the laughter. The records begin with a very solemn performance of a musical solo (often a horn or a vocal performance). These recordings are "framed" in a very particular way: a serious musical piece is being performed, and so the listener is keyed to respond appropriately. By "frame," I refer to Erving Goffman's term for the definition of a situation that governs social events (1974, 10). The initial framing of laughing records as highbrow concert culture must be seen in light of the high prestige that classical music had for phonograph listeners in the early decades of the century. The phonograph industry made clear distinctions between its high- and low-culture products, distinctions that were physically inscribed on records: from 1903 Victor's operatic recordings bore a "Red Seal," in contrast to the "Black Seal" of popular records. Although high-culture products were prominently featured in industry ads and catalogs, it was sales of the low-culture popular tunes that had enabled the expansion of the phonograph companies: "Victor produced three times as many popular as operatic discs" (William Howland Kenney 1999, xiii).[3]

The introductory music on these laughing records establishes a classical performance with a one-to-one relationship between the musical performer and a listener. This performance is then punctuated by a fluff of some kind, an audible (sometimes barely audible) mistake that interrupts the smooth flow of the musical solo. Immediately following the mistake, a woman is heard to break out laughing. Her presence was previously hidden, and her laughter thus changes the listener's framing relationship to the recorded performance.[4]

For Goffman, laughing can be an important instance of flooding out, when "the individual will capsize" as a social interactant, dissolving into "laughter or tears or anger" (1974, 350). The most common instance of flooding out is the "unsuccessful effort to suppress laughter, sometimes called 'breaking (or cracking) up'" (351). This phrase is particularly appropriate, as it points to the cracking up of the social frame as well as to the the act of uncontrolled laughter itself. When the woman in the laughing record floods out, the one-to-one situation between listener and performer is altered, as there are now at least two audience members. The listener's role is suddenly made uncertain, free-floating. Is the listener part of an audience—or situated outside and overhearing the performance? The woman's flooding out precipitates the listener's frame reorganization: the listener has lost a certain formal connection with the performer but has gained a relationship to the laughing audience member, who has broached the ritual constraints of the situation.

As the recording develops, the musician nobly tries to continue the instrumental solo, but the laughter of the woman in the audience proves so unsettling and infectious that the performer cracks up as well, revealing his identity as a man. What follows for the rest of the record are waves of laughter from both the man and woman, each one's guffaws stimulating and encouraging the other's, interspersed by short-lived attempts by the man to return to his performance. After the performer's first mistake and the introduction of the laughing woman, the listener's role has been problematized. Now, as the performer himself floods out with laughter, *his* role is also destabilized, and the listener's further so. The distinction between performer and audience member on the recording breaks down, and as the contagious laughter stimulates the listener, the distinction between listener and recorded performer breaks down as well. All three subjects become unified in this community of spontaneous laughter: a moment of frame disintegration.

The main purpose of these recordings seems to have been the incitation of the listener's laughter, a project in which they were successful far beyond the scope of their local cultural origins. Fred Gaisberg wrote that Burt Sheppard's *Laughing Record* was "world famous," and had sold "over half a million in India alone." He provides this brief description of its reception: "In the bazaars of India I have seen dozens of natives seated on their haunches round a gramophone, rocking with laughter, whilst playing Sheppard's laughing record" (1942, 41). Similarly, Andrew F. Jones, in his study of media culture in the Chinese Jazz Age, describes this scene:

> Sometime around the turn of the twentieth century, a young Frenchman named Labansat set up an outdoor stall on Tibet Road in Shanghai and began to play gramophone records for curious Chinese passersby. Labansat, whose career up to that point had consisted in operating a peep show for Shanghai theatergoers, had recently purchased an imported gramophone from a foreign firm, Moutrie & Company. His new business gambit was simple and effective; he would ask each listener to pay ten cents to hear a novelty record called "Laughing Foreigners" (Yangren daxiao). Anyone able to resist laughing along with the chuckles, chortles, and guffaws emerging from the horn of the gramophone would get his or her money back. (2001, 53)

Jones notes that Labansat "laughed all the way to the bank," earning enough from this routine to establish China's first record company (53).

Scenarios such as these suggest that laughing records helped ease anxieties about a potentially disturbing new medium. Henri Bergson's famous essay on laughter illustrates this point. For Bergson, the comic

"consists of a certain mechanical inelasticity, just where one would expect to find the wideawake adaptability and the living pliableness of a
human being" (1956, 67). Laughter, for Bergson, functions as a social
sanction against rigid or mechanical behavior: "[Laughter's] function is
to convert rigidity into plasticity, to readapt the individual to the whole,
in short, to round off the corners wherever they are met with" (174). In
other words, whenever a person is acting rigid or mechanical, that person is not adapting to the particular moment and so is socially sanctioned by laughter.

In Goffman's terms, Bergson's definition of laughter has to do with the
social control of frame maintenance. When people are not flexible or
fluid in their ability to adapt to the appropriate social frame, they are
sanctioned by laughter. Laughter, then, is a kind of suture between the
rigid and the flexible, the social and the individual, the mechanical and
the human. The incitation of laughter in the listener and the frame disintegration described above would work to remove anxiety about inter-
acting with a machine, making the phonographic apparatus appear more
"human."[5] The ability of a mechanical recording to break frames helps
it emanate a sense of authentic presence and humanity. Laughing records, then, were important ways of establishing the credibility and authenticity of early recordings, alleviating the anxiety of hearing a disembodied, recorded voice (figure 2).

To stimulate reciprocal laughter from the listener, the laughter on
records such as these is presented as "natural"; that is, it is unrestrained
and unregulated in terms of rhythm and vocal inflection. Those qualities highlight laughter's nature as uncontrollable spasm. In their infectious quality, laughing records have striking similarities to other forms
of what Linda Williams calls "body genres," such as pornography, horror, and melodrama, which produce a direct bodily response in their audience members. In Williams's study of early tendencies in film pornography, she describes presentations of "women in spasm," including
Jean-Martin Charcot's photographs of women "in the grips of convulsive attacks of hysteria" and Eadweard Muybridge's protocinematic
representations, including "a woman's involuntary convulsions" (1989,
48). Williams also mentions other early experiments with film, most
notably the famous *Fred Ott's Sneeze* from the Edison Laboratory in
1893–94, which Williams notes was in fact inspired by a request to see
a "nice looking . . . woman" in the act of sneezing (52). These filmic
presentations of spasm are, in fact, contemporary with the earliest
laughing records.

Figure 2. An advertisement for Okeh Laughing Records released in the early 1920s.

As is true of some early films, the main object of pleasure on laughing records is the traces of a female body in spasm. It is interesting to note as well that while the female body is "voyeuristically" displayed, it is also the vehicle for the derailment of a solemn male performance of high culture. The highbrow framing of these musical performances also suggests how class-based cultural tensions could have been part of the pleasure of the frame breaking. As Goffman notes, flooding out often occurs "when individuals are obliged to enact a role they think is intrinsically not themselves, especially one that is felt to be too formal, and yet no strong sanction is present to inhibit a frame break" (1974, 352). This might well have been the case with the initial concert frame for the typical consumer of popular recordings in the first decades of the recording industry. Indeed, these records' ability to bring the elevated role of the highbrow classical performer down to the level of equal participant in shared bodily spasm might have been experienced as liberating and cathartic.

Consider some parallels between laughing records and a film directed by Edwin S. Porter and released by Edison in 1909 entitled *Laughing Gas*. In the film, an African American woman identified as Mandy goes to the dentist to have a tooth pulled. In great pain, she takes nitrous oxide and is overcome by ecstatic laughter. Her uncontrollable glee is infectious, inducing the dentist and his assistant to succumb to fits of laughter. For the rest of the film, Mandy moves through a series of social encounters and spreads her laughter to everyone she meets.

One such encounter takes place on a streetcar where, through a carefully laid mise-en-scène, Porter manages to depict a world of stark social hierarchies and divisions. We see a row of seated passengers separated into distinct groups by their class and gender. Two bourgeois gentlemen, one wearing a top hat and spats, look over papers and speak to each other. Next to them is a man marked as a country rube by his corncob pipe and somewhat shabby clothes. Three upper-class women sit on either side of the men. A fourth woman enters, whose clothes and stylish hat establish her as bourgeois. The men rise and ostentatiously offer her a seat, but she haughtily moves away to join a similarly dressed woman. Another woman enters the frame, wearing a kerchief that marks her as working class, and perhaps an immigrant. She tries to sit next to the men, but they do not move to offer her a seat, and she is forced to stand. By establishing the scene in this manner, Porter lends Mandy's entrance both a certain pathos and an element of social critique: she matter-of-factly stands and takes a handhold, suggesting that unlike the first and second women, she does not expect to be offered a seat. Porter has carefully framed the scene, using the entrance of three women of various social rank to indicate the pervasiveness of social distinction in even the most mundane everyday public interaction. The movement of the train jostles the two standing women, and Mandy erupts with laughter when she falls between the two bourgeois men. Her laughter radiates to her fellow passengers to both the left and right, first to the bourgeois gentlemen and then to the rube, who raises his hand to slap his leg but accidentally slaps the leg of the bourgeois woman next to him. She reacts in shock at first, but before long she also joins in the laughter (figure 3).

Mandy's laugh in this scene serves a narrative function that is quite similar to that of the laughing records I've been discussing. In an insightful analysis of American films from this era, Jacqueline Stewart describes how black female domestic workers like Mandy were often

Figure 3. Mandy spreads her infectious laughter to everyone she meets in Edison's 1909 film *Laughing Gas*.

depicted breaching social hierarchies and boundaries (2004, 105). Stewart writes that through her laughter, Mandy "brings disorder then harmony" to each of the social situations she encounters (119). Like the eruption of laughter during the highbrow musical performances found on laughing records, Mandy's laughter causes "frame disintegration," transforming a social situation noted by rigid hierarchies into a state of relaxed camaraderie. It is certainly true that through the performance of spasmodic laughter both Mandy and the women heard on laughing records are offered as a kind of bodily spectacle. Compare, for example, the prolonged close-up of Mandy at the end of *Laughing Gas* with a photograph of the comedian Sallie Stembler in a trade journal promoting laughing records in 1918 (figure 4): in both cases we see a woman with eyes closed, mouth open, and head thrown back. But this is only part of the story, since the ecstatic laughter of these women was situated within a narrative context that produced a subtle social critique.

The close-up images of Mandy and Sallie Stembler can also remind us of the fact that the performance of laughter in *Laughing Gas* is seen and not heard. As such, the film illustrates how that expression could be conveyed in silent cinema through a number of broad physical gestures: opening the mouth, slapping the knee, throwing the arms up overhead, rhythmically swaying back and forth, and generally presenting a loose and relaxed posture—note, for example, the dentist as he flops back in his chair. Mary Ann Doane has written that "the absent voice" of silent cinema "reemerges in gestures and the contortions of the face—it is spread over the body of the actor" (1999, 363). We see in *Laughing Gas* that laughter is a vocal expression that is particularly embodied; it is "spread over" the bodies of the actors in a particularly vivid manner, blurring the lines between speech and gesture. Here, then, is another indication of laughter's particular efficacy as an index of embodied presence on phonograph records.

In addition to existing in a gray area between spoken and gestured, the laugh also slides between what Erving Goffman (1959, 18) calls expressions *given* ("a part that is relatively easy for the individual to manipulate at will, being chiefly his verbal assertions") and those that are *given off* ("a part in regard to which he seems to have little concern or control"). Crucially, "truth" is often thought to be found in what is given off: "we often give special attention to features of the performance that cannot be readily manipulated, thus enabling ourselves to judge the reliability of the more misrepresentable cues in the performance" (58). Because it blurs the distinction between given and given off, and between

Figure 4. The "Laughing Girl," Sallie Stembler, pictured
on the cover of a phonograph industry trade journal.
Source: Edison National Historical Site.

spoken expression and gesture, the sincerity of laughter can be difficult
to gauge. The laugh is a vocal expression like speech, but one that involves the entire body, like gesture; it is controllable, and yet it hints at
the "ultimate truth" of spasm.[6] This, in turn, makes the laugh a particularly interesting problem for actors.[7]

One indication of the laugh's problematic nature for acting is evident in its absence from turn-of-the-century acting manuals. Laughter
is notable by its absence in several early acting texts that typify what

Roberta Pearson has called the histrionic code, a style of acting predominant in the second half of the nineteenth century in England and America wherein actors "performed in a self-consciously theatrical fashion, ostentatiously playing a role rather than pretending to be another person" (1992, 21). Edmond Shaftesbury's 1889 *Lessons in the Art of Acting* describes the gestural codes for a multitude of expressions, but laughter is not one of them. He even omits laughter when he lays out a list of "automatic sounds" that includes sighs, gasps, gurgles, whimpers, sobs, sneezes, and death rattles (1889, 277). In Gustave Garcia's *The Actor's Art* (1882), the closest we come to laughter is "Rapturous Joy," but the actor is warned that expression loses its grace "the moment joy becomes noisy and exuberant, and degenerates into such petulance as to cause contortions of the face, and turn the free and graceful movements of the body into the gesticulations of a clown" (1882, 129). Although this evidence is not enough on which to base any definitive statements, it indicates that outright laughter was repressed on the nineteenth-century legitimate stage, perhaps because of the ways in which it could upset the decorum or gentility of performance.[8] It is notable, then, to find uninhibited laughter so frequently on early phonograph records, and that those who often enacted this performance were typically considered to be culturally "other": women, African Americans, and in the case of another genre of early recordings, the country rube.

Along with the laughing records I've been describing, a cycle of records called laughing stories also featured prominent laughter, and they can be seen to anticipate the broadcast laugh track. In the early years of the popular phonograph business, there was a wide variety of popular spoken-word recordings, including political speeches, minstrel show comedy acts, and even reenactments of famous battles. Cal Stewart (1856–1919) was one of the most popular of these spoken-word recording artists during the late 1890s and early 1900s. In his "descriptive specialties," Stewart played the role of a gullible rube named Uncle Josh Weathersby from the fictional town of Pumpkin Center. Uncle Josh films, particularly *Uncle Josh at the Moving Picture Show* (Edison 1902), have received critical attention from scholars, but the phonographic origins of these films are rarely mentioned.[9] Stewart's records described life in rural Pumpkin Center and Uncle Josh's comic encounters with the many facets of modernity in New York City. These performances, as William Howland Kenney writes (1999, 33), could have functioned to demonstrate how and how not to behave in the modern city, and so served as a kind of "cultural survival kit."

Much of what is comic about Uncle Josh recalls Bergson's idea of laughter as social sanction for inflexible behavior. Instead of adapting to the new environment, Uncle Josh stays rigidly in the role of the rube, and so he receives the social corrective of laughter from an audience trying itself to keep up with rapid cultural changes. Uncle Josh's voice is also marked by a certain rigidity, making it prime material for a Bergsonesque social sanction of laughter. Uncle Josh's voice tends to hover in a droning monotone, falling into a very regular pacing and rhythm, often repeating phrases. The vocal flow is punctuated about every twenty to thirty seconds by the most distinctive characteristic of the recordings, Uncle Josh's trademark laugh. This laugh was important to listeners at the time, which is indicated by its inclusion in transcriptions in the original Edison cylinders, its designation as a point of contention for later Uncle Josh imitators, and the creation of textual analogs for it in Pumpkin Center stories released in book form (Feaster 1999a). Much of the pleasure of these recordings derives from the spasmodic release of Uncle Josh's laughter in the flow of his droning speech.

Thus far I have been discussing the laugh as spasm, as a moment of flooding out, but it is important to consider also how the laugh can function as a part of personal interaction. In her study of conversation Gail Jefferson has described (1979, 93) how one technique for inviting laughter is for a speaker to place a laugh "just at completion of an utterance," which is then often mirrored by the recipient's laugh directly after the speaker's laughter. This kind of social laughter serves as a bridge between individuals in a conversation, operating as an invitation to participate in an ongoing interaction. Uncle Josh exploits such laughter to hook the listener and give prerecorded performances a particularly powerful sense of interactivity and presence.

Uncle Josh laughs at his own rigid behavior in the face of modernity, at the same time providing a suture between the listener and the modern apparatus of the phonograph. Uncle Josh recordings, as well as other phonographic laughing stories such as the "Arkansas Traveler," associate the country rube with a performed laugh.[10] As happens in the laughing records genre, where a highbrow classical performance is disrupted, class tensions seem to be projected onto the release of laughter, maybe because of the possibility of social maneuvering when social frames break down. As we shall see, the sound of laughing audiences would serve similar functions for radio and television broadcasting.

THE RAW AND THE CANNED:
THE LAUGHTER OF AUDIENCES

By examining these early phonographic recordings, we can see that the audible laugh as accompaniment to mass-produced comedy was not an invention of broadcast radio. Indeed, Rick Altman has argued that the performance of audible laughter in the context of a comedy show can be traced back even further, to the nineteenth-century minstrel stage: "The minstrel show gave us the banjo and the formulaic straight man/funny man comedy team (the farcical Bones and Tambo always getting the better of the serious Interlocutor), as well as the transfer of laughter from an external audience (as in legitimate theatre, where a joke on stage is met with laughter in the balcony) to an audience located within the spectacle (on stage in the minstrel show, on the laugh track in TV situation comedies). Whenever a Bones or Tambo would get the best of the Interlocutor all others on stage would howl with laughter, thus leading the theatre audience and showing them when to laugh" (1987, 202).

These performance dynamics carried over to the sound media, since minstrel shows were an important genre for the early phonograph industry. For example, George Washington Johnson joined the Imperial Minstrels in 1894 with his fellow recording artist Len Spencer, and he released a series of cylinders duplicating the songs and stories of a minstrel show "first part" (T. Brooks 2005, 37). In the New Jersey Phonograph catalog, Johnson's famous laugh becomes a part of the audience response: "The Interlocutor ventures to ask Bones 'How he finds things?' to which Bones replies, 'I look for 'em.' This strikes the audience as being a witty sally, and they applaud and laugh vociferously, Mr. Geo. W. Johnson's hearty laugh particularly being heard above the din and confusion" (cited in T. Brooks 2004, 38). As with Johnson's *Laughing Song*, racist stereotypes of the "carefree darky" helped to shape conventions of performance that became useful in the context of new mass-produced media.

To explore further the conflation of blackness, authenticity, and the hearable audience, let us briefly return to the 1909 film *Laughing Gas*. The final scene in the film takes place in an African American church, where the movements of Mandy's laughing body are made to resemble the gestures of black religious worship. A similar connection between laughter and expressions of black community can be found in the climactic scene of a Hollywood film made thirty-two years later: Preston Sturges's *Sullivan's Travels* (1941). Sturges's film tells the story of John

L. Sullivan (Joel McCrea), a Hollywood director who has been making comedies and musicals with titles like *Ants in Your Pants* and *Hey, Hey in the Hayloft*. Sullivan is intent on making a "serious" film about poverty to be entitled *O Brother, Where Art Thou?* but the executives at the studio where he works convince him that he knows nothing about the subject. To their dismay, Sullivan decides to learn about "trouble" by traveling the country disguised as a tramp. The resulting film is a parable about the attainment of an authentic artistic voice.

After some false starts, Sullivan gets firsthand experience of the difficulties of poverty: he rides the rails, takes communal showers, sleeps on floors, and walks the streets wearing a degrading sandwich board. Convinced that he has learned all he needs to know about trouble, Sullivan decides to return to Hollywood to make his film—but not before going back to the streets one last time to distribute money discreetly to those who had helped him. Through a series of mishaps, Sullivan finds himself in a brutal Southern work camp. It is at this point, when Sullivan is utterly cut off from his life of Hollywood privilege, that the film asserts that he truly learns about trouble. The work camp sequence functions as a coda in which the emotional tone of the film shifts and Sturges seems to lay his cards on the table. Notably, both race and laughter become signs of authenticity.

Throughout the film, Sullivan's artistic aspirations have been expressed in terms of class, not race: the clip we see of the type of socially conscious film Sullivan wants to make features an allegorical struggle between "capital" and "labor" on the top of a speeding train. And yet Sturges shows us that, when Sullivan moves out into the "real" world, racial differences become crucially significant. For example, when Sullivan and his unnamed girlfriend (Veronica Lake) go to jump a train, we see many African American men waiting along the tracks. Later, in a homeless shelter, a white preacher sternly speaks to a large crowd. A long tracking shot reveals that the joyless audience is composed of white, African American, and Asian faces. These details demonstrate Sturges's awareness of the racial dimensions of poverty in America, but race functions most dramatically in the church scene at the end of the film. After scenes of Sullivan's brutal treatment, culminating in a night spent in the work camp hotbox, there is a transition to a church in a misty Southern swamp, where an all-black congregation listens to a deep-voiced preacher.

It should be noted that "blackness" in this scene is defined largely in terms of the voice. This is not surprising: Alice Maurice has connected the fetishization of the black voice in early sound films such as *Hearts in*

Dixie (1929) and *Hallelujah!* (1929) to assertions from that time that the "Negro voice" was particularly fit for sound recording (2002, 44). Maurice contends that "the hyperpresence of black bodies" served in part to demonstrate the "prowess" of the sound film by foregrounding the "supposedly 'inherent' talents" of black performers (45). The same words might be used to describe George Washington Johnson in relation to the phonograph. Black voices are certainly the main attraction in the church scene in *Sullivan's Travels:* we hear the preacher's rumbling baritone, sounding not unlike Paul Robeson's, the congregation's powerful singing, and, most pertinent to this chapter, their laughter.

As a makeshift movie screen is hung at the front of the church, the congregation twice breaks out into uproarious laughter: the stereotypical depiction of African Americans as being particularly easy with their laughter.[11] Led by the preacher, the congregation sings "Let My People Go" as Sullivan and his fellow inmates—only one of whom is visibly black—file in (figure 5). We see a shot of their chained feet shuffling into the church, which, combined with the congregation's singing, makes the subtext of these images of slavery clear: Sullivan has found authentic trouble because he is living the life of a black man. The lights are dimmed, and as a Walt Disney cartoon is projected on the screen, we are shown close-ups of both the white inmates and the black congregation in fits of hysterical laughter. Sullivan looks around in a daze, and then joins in the laughter himself.

By the logic of the film, it is this communal laugher that makes Sullivan's travels complete. The church setting cues us to the fact that Sullivan takes part in a kind of secular rite in which he is baptized into an authentic sense of group membership. In fact, the audience in the church is remarkably diverse, in terms not just of race, but of age and gender as well, making it a powerful utopian image of communal harmony. The black community, then, becomes a sign of "community" writ large, in stark contrast to the lifeless audience who listened to the white preacher earlier in the film. Richard Peterson has noted that claims of ethnic group membership have traditionally been an important strategy for establishing claims of authenticity in the context of popular music (1997, 218). In Sturges's film, the African American community is the symbolic representation of community, and its laughter becomes the emblematic sign of, and vehicle to, the group bonding that provides Sullivan with the authenticity required to make *O Brother, Where Art Thou?*

Sturges's conflation of black vocal expression with an idealized community is not unique. David Brackett has written that "the slaves'

Figure 5. John L. Sullivan (Joel McCrea) finds authentic trouble in Preston Sturges's *Sullivan's Travels* (1941). Source: BFI.

capacity for communal and spontaneous creation" through vocal tech-niques such as call-and-response often instilled in European listeners a sense of "transgression": "transgression of the boundaries that separated the European's sense of himself or herself from the objects viewed, as the sense of communality and spontaneity threatens to undo the distance be-tween observer and the observed" (1995, 110). White listeners have often interpreted black vocal expression in both essentialized and ro-manticized terms, hearing in it the index of a traditional, "natural" com-munity feared lost in the whirlwind of modernity. Returning to *Sullivan's Travels*, we might well ask whether the African American congregation's singing and laughter is *creating* the sense of their authentic community as much as it is simply reflecting it.

Nevertheless, although race is the key to Sullivan's conversion, that fact is erased in the film's closing montage. Sullivan is rescued from the work camp, and, on a plane flying back to Hollywood, he breaks the news to the studio executives that he is no longer interested in making *O Brother, Where Art Thou?* Instead, he wants to return to making comedies, as he has learned the power of laughter: "There's a lot to be said for making people laugh. Did you know that's all that some people have? It isn't much, but it's better that nothing in this cockeyed caravan. Boy!" We hear a chuckle on the soundtrack, which builds to the laughter of a great multitude and is eventually drowned out by fanfares of orchestral music. On the screen we see a montage of laughing faces: Sullivan's fellow prison inmates, a golden-haired young girl, nurses and patients in a hospital ward, and a group of laughing children. Notably, all the faces shown are white. When this is compared to the African American church scene, one has to say that black expressions of laughter were the vehicle for Sullivan's attainment of authenticity, but only the vehicle: though images of black faces predominate in the church, they are absent from the "family of man" imagery in the final montage.

I don't want to oversimplify Sturges's film, which subtly manages to critique Hollywood for its inability to represent a world of racial difference faithfully. What I want to emphasize is the continuing importance of laughter—in this case the laughter of an audience—as an expression of authentic, embodied presence. It was exactly this sense of presence that broadcast radio would be at pains to replicate for its far-flung audience. In fact, the performance of laughter served an important function on radio broadcasts and established conventions for the hearable audience that were then carried over into television. Paddy Scannell has written of the dilemma facing early broadcasters in the face of the "unprecedented newness of radio as a medium of general social communication" (1996, 4). One of the major issues was to produce programs in such a way that people who turned on a radio or television set would "be able to figure out what was going on pretty quickly" (4). The sound of the laughing audience would play an important role in this endeavor.

Scannell analyzes *Harry Hopeful:* a program broadcast in England's North Region in 1935, and the "first programme that sought to create a sociable occasion as its raison d'etre" (24). The hearable audience constituted what was taking place as a "performed *public* event in the presence of an audience" (28). Scannell shows how the presence of the audience in *Harry Hopeful* was cause for discussion at the time, and also how it provided a sense of the authentic and regional: "The use of a hearable audience as part of the programme aroused considerable curiosity up in London, when heard for the first time. The Director of Talks, Charles Siepman, felt it was the nearest thing to real and typical regional performance that he had heard yet. The whole thing had a great air of spontaneity but he wanted to know if the audience was literally there, whether the laughter and applause were real or recorded, and whether they were genuine characters or actors" (29). A crucial early development in radio broadcasting was thus the establishment in some genres of the hearable audience as "part of a performance produced for absent listeners" (29). The sound of the audience provided a sense of authenticity, spontaneity, and "liveness," as well as formally contextualizing the radio performance.

Some of the reasons for emphasizing that liveness had to do with network politics. Michele Hilmes describes how, as early as 1928, the Federal Radio Commission discouraged stations from playing prerecorded entertainment, and as a result stations broadcasting live entertainment were given "precedence in the allocation of air space because that material presumably remained unavailable in any other form" (1990, 27). Only the big radio networks, with their access to cross-country landlines and local wires, could provide and transmit high-quality live programming, so it behooved them to promote the superiority of the live broadcast (143). The presence of a live audience on radio, then, was determined by economic as well as formal factors.

The sound of a studio audience was not a universal aspect of radio broadcasting. The influential comedy program *Amos 'n Andy*, for example, initially featured the voices of the characters and little else (Ely 1991, 2). Nor was the hearable audience met with unanimous approval. The comedian Fred Allen stated that "the worst thing that ever happened to radio was the studio audience. Somebody like Eddie Cantor brought those hordes of cackling geese in because he couldn't work without imbeciles laughing at his jokes" (Hobson 1966b, 22). Allen's view is important because it shows that the sound of audience laughter was considered by some to be cheap and manipulative. If the laughter of a live studio audience was manipulative, than a prerecorded laugh track was doubly so. With the advent of magnetic tape and multitracking in the 1940s, manipulation of the radio studio audience's response became much easier.[12] On broadcast television the laugh track became both a ubiquitous formal feature and the focus of debate about authenticity and the social experience of mass media.

The same kind of network imperatives that had encouraged live broadcasts on radio also existed for early television. For many of the same economic reasons that made radio networks give priority to live programming, the television networks were initially unreceptive to filmed programming. But as television production began to move from New York to Hollywood and was increasingly shot on film instead of performed live, the recorded laugh track became a fixture of television comedy. The social aspects of laughter made it a potent rhetorical weapon in the battle over filmed TV, a discourse colored by the ideology of presence and immediacy. As television production moved increasingly to film, the laugh track, like the laughter of Uncle Josh, helped to maintain a sense of the "liveness" and presence of the studio audience.

The first television show to use a prerecorded laugh track seems to have been the *Hank McClure Show* in 1950; the practice became much more widespread in the wake of the phenomenal success of the filmed comedy *I Love Lucy* after 1953. Laugh tracks became a crucial component for filmed television comedy, desired by both sponsors and home viewers. Several commentators told the cautionary tales of *My Little Margie* and *Dear Phoebe:* " 'My Little Margie,' a situation comedy first filmed without so much as a titter, raised its rating the week it got a laugh track all its own. 'Dear Phoebe' tried to buck the trend . . . and went on the screens for six weeks with nothing but dialog and soundtrack. The noble experiment came to an end, on the sponsor's orders, and a 'subtle' track replaced the silence" ("Strictly for Laughs" 46).

The laugh track was discussed in the popular press between the years 1954 and 1957, and it reemerged as a topic in the wake of the 1959 quiz show scandal. Under pressure to reform, CBS's president Frank Stanton announced that "canned applause and laughter, 'spontaneous' interview shows that are actually rehearsed, and other deceits common to television are to be weeded out of the schedule of the Columbia Broadcasting System. . . . The practice of dubbing recorded applause or laughter into the sound track of a completed program . . . simply does not accord with [my] belief that a show must be what it purports to be" (J. Gould 1959, 1). Stanton initiated a policy of identifying canned laughter via "announcements of disclosure" after the show. For example, a show might have to display titles reading "audience reaction technically produced," or "audience reaction technically augmented" (J. Gould 1960, 75). Unsurprisingly, TV comics hated this policy, and several prominent performers, including Jack Benny, publicly fought for its removal. Stanton scrapped the policy after only a few months, hoping that the publicity had brought the idea of the laugh track into the open, and he encouraged greater care be employed "to prevent overdoing the use of canned laughter" (75).

The use of the laugh track dovetailed with concerns about the nature of the television audience. Unlike movies and the theater, television played not to a unified mass audience, but instead "to a group of perhaps five or six people at a time" (Boddy 1990, 82). Comics and writers of the time were unsure about, and even suspicious of, this strange new audience: "What the TV audiences lack is a genuine interest in comedy. Most TV viewers drop into place before their sets because they have nothing more diverting to do at the moment. As an audience they cannot be counted upon to be either attentive or receptive because they have been assembled not so much by design as by default. A man who removes himself from a comfortable chair in his home to occupy a less comfortable one in a crowded theatre becomes predisposed to laugh in a way he would never do if he stayed at home" ("Comedy Crisis Worries Comics" 38).

Statements like this reflect the widely held belief in the essentially social nature of laughter. Robert Provine, in his recent scientific investigation of laughter, emphasizes the point: "When we hear laughter we tend to laugh in turn, producing a behavioral chain reaction that sweeps through a group, creating a crescendo of jocularity or ridicule. The contagious laughter response is immediate and involuntary, involving the most direct communication possible between people 'brain to brain' with our intellect just going along for the ride" (2000, 129). For its advocates, the "direct communication" of laughter via the laugh track could help solve the problem of the fragmented television audience. Proponents of the laugh track, such as NBC president Sylvester (Pat) Weaver, stated that laughter was "a community experience and not an individual one": "No one likes to laugh alone, and when you sit in your own living room an honestly made laugh track can project you right into the audience, with the best seat in the house, to enjoy the fun' " ("Strictly for Laughs" 46).

Opposition to the use of prerecorded audience laughter was part of the larger critique of filmed television, what William Boddy calls "the central element in the highly prescriptive critical discourse of television's Golden Age" (1990, 73). For some of the key critics of filmed TV (such as Jack Gould of the New York Times), comedy, laughter, and the laugh track were particularly salient case studies, just as much as the oft-discussed live dramas. In one of Gould's most elaborate polemics against filmed TV (1956, 27), he begins with the example of Jackie Gleason: "The case for natural television against canned television is up for spirited review in industry quarters. [Jackie Gleason] chose to abandon live TV. . . . Jackie doesn't seem so funny anymore; in fact film has made his program distressingly flat."

Many of the opponents of the laugh track rejected the idea that laughter was essentially a social act, emphasizing instead the role of the individual: "I always say nobody has to laugh, canned or live, to let me know

if a show is funny" (Ace 1954, 28). Critiques of the laugh track also emphasized the spontaneous nature of laughter, one of the main tropes in
the attack on filmed television in general: "The very essence of true
laughter is spontaneity. It is unmanageable, unpredictable, impervious to
control" (Shayon 1959, 44). Part of what made the laugh track offensive
was the sense that the viewer was being told when to laugh: "A situation
comedy on film may be quite acceptable until from left field comes a
wave of tinny, doctored and apportioned guffaws. Strips of this pre-
packaged approval are pieced into the film in what some wan director
hopes are the right spots. Usually he guesses wrong. . . . The viewer
loses his sense of being a partner and instead becomes a spectator. It is
the difference between being with somebody and looking at somebody"
(J. Gould 1956, 27). In many critiques of mass culture, the television
viewer is presented as a passive victim of media manipulation. Gilbert
Seldes was one critic who saw the TV laugh track in this light, describing it as a manipulation akin to that of the radio studio audience: "The
canned laughter of filmed comedy carries a step further the deception
that began years ago in the induced laughter of the studio audiences in
radio, the obedient cackles and clappings when the sign was held up"
(1956, 167–68).

The rhetoric against the laugh track sometimes focused on the role of
the television comedy writer. Consider an essay by Max Liebman in the
January 4, 1961, issue of *Variety*. Entitled "Laugh? I Thought I'd Die,"
it is the cautionary tale of an idealistic young comedy writer named
Hank, who learns from an unnamed Big Executive about the laugh machine known to his colleagues as "Mr. McKenzie." Hank's objections to
the laugh machine have to do with its effect on his labor as a writer: " 'I
don't want it,' he said. 'I get paid to write comedy. If my jokes can't score
on their own, they don't belong in the script. . . . I have a craftsman's
pride in my work. I look to the audience to tell me how good I am, or
how good I ain't. I'm valued by the laughs I get. I'm guided by the lines
that conk out. . . . Your Mr. McKenzie is destructive to good comedy
writing. He wrecks a writer's incentive. Who's going to sweat and strain
to get a yock when there's a mechanical pushover handy to deliver it for
you?' " (1961, 86).

Commentators like Liebman saw the laugh track breaking a crucial
circuit that joined writer, performer, and audience. Further, the laugh
track was seen as a threat to established hierarchies in the writing community: "[Hank] had earned his status by struggle and accomplishment.
He had satisfied some of the best comedians on the air. He had won

awards. The tasteless McKenzie could raise any slob of a writer to Hank's plateau by saturating the slob's script with unearned guffaws" (86).[13] One way to understand the comedy writer's anxiety is to recall Provine's description of social laughter as "the most direct communication possible between people 'brain to brain' with our intellect just going along for the ride" (2000, 129). The comedy writer would have a vested interest in asserting that the intellect did indeed play a role, that laughs were produced by clever writing and not some kind of group hysteria. One can see, then, why the comedy writer might have tended to side with those who stressed the individual nature of laughter in the debate over the laugh track.

One of the most vivid attacks on the laugh track can be found in Elia Kazan's 1957 film *A Face In the Crowd,* starring Andy Griffith. Interestingly, Griffith began his career by telling rube stories very much in the tradition of Cal Stewart. Like Uncle Josh, the Griffith rube persona provides naïve, wide-eyed descriptions of modern, typically highbrow events like opera, ballet, and Shakespeare's plays, although his most famous routine was about a football game ("What It Was, Was Football"). After making his television debut playing a rube character in *Make Room for Sergeants,* Griffith starred in the Kazan film, based on a short story by Budd Schulberg called "Your Arkansas Traveler," which tells the story of Lonesome Rhodes, a mysterious drifter who rises to fame on radio and TV telling folksy anecdotes about the fictional town of Riddle, Arkansas. These stories are similar to Cal Stewart's tales of life in Pumpkin Center, and Rhodes is a kind of evil Uncle Josh—a country rube who is not overwhelmed by modernity but, through the use of broadcast media, overwhelms it.

In both Schulberg's story and Kazan's film the rube's body is represented through his laughter. Schulberg writes of Rhodes's "ruddy, laughing face, the haw-haw kind" (1953, 4), which is manifested not only on his face but also his belly: " 'Haw haw haw,' he chuckled from deep in his belly" (7). At another point, "He shook all over when he chuckled" (5). Rhodes's visceral laugh and prodigious sexual appetite make the female narrator uncomfortable: "He had a certain animal charm that made me feel uneasy" (7). In Kazan's film, Griffith's laugh is consistently the subject of invasive close-ups, and it is breathlessly commented upon by his costar, Patricia Neal: "You put everything you've got into that laugh" (figure 6). The narrative bite of Schulberg and Kazan's film comes from the shock of finding Lonesome Rhodes's trademark laugh to be crassly manipulative. As the index of how far Lonesome Rhodes has fallen from country authenticity, we see him crouching in his penthouse

Figure 6. Lonesome Rhodes (Andy Griffith) puts everything he's got into his laugh in Elia Kazan's 1957 film, *A Face in the Crowd*.

apartment, gleefully caressing his new prized possession: a laughing and applauding machine (figure 7).[14]

The rhetorical vehemence and pure outrage of some of the laugh track's opponents show how laughter can stand as an index of the human: "Is this merely another harmless variation of the theatre's advancing technology or is there something profoundly disturbing about the dehumanization, for all concerned, of man's ultimate defense against the gods and himself—laughter?" (Shayon 1959, 44). As it was in the performances of Faber's and Edison's talking machines a century earlier, laughter is seen as a pure indication of individual human presence, an expression that becomes particularly significant and contradictory in the context of mechanical reproduction.

We might better understand the debate over the laugh track by comparing it to another debate concerning sound media production and aesthetics. James Lastra describes how two representational models for the film soundtrack dominated the discussion of sound engineers and technicians in the 1930s. A "phonographic" model imagined the recording apparatus as the surrogate for an invisible auditor; it sought to "unite the spaces of reception and representation—to place the auditor as literally as possible *in* the profilmic space" (2000, 181–82). Engineers working

Figure 7. Lonesome Rhodes (Andy Griffith) and his laughing and applauding machine, from *A Face in the Crowd* (1957).

along these lines would strive to faithfully reproduce the sonic spaces of the profilmic performance by matching sound perspective to visual perspective—for example, long shots of a character would be accompanied by low-volume dialogue. On the other hand, a "telephonic" model emphasized clarity and legibility of dialogue above all else, and so it utilized a clear, dry sound that reproduced well in movie theaters and thus did not faithfully preserve profilmic space. Though the telephonic model became dominant in film practice, Lastra asserts that the phonographic model "ruled the theoretical roost" (139).

The ubiquity of the laugh track is an indication of the lingering influence of a phonographic model in broadcasting. As Sylvester Weaver's comments above indicate, the laugh track was meant to simulate the "best seat in the house," to unite the space of reception in the home with an imagined space of representation in the theater or studio, and so place the "alone together" audience within a simulated social context. The hearable studio audience was one way to simulate a theater atmosphere, but Sarah Kozloff describes how early radio drama programs such as *The First Nighter* also featured the sounds of ushers and curtain calls. Kozloff argues, however, that "the most creative radio playwrights" of the 1930s rejected such a model and shifted their ideal from simulated drama to narration (1988, 27). Orson Welles was a central figure in this shift, and the fact that his influential *Mercury Theater of the Air* was originally entitled *First Person Singular* indicates his refusal to conceptualize radio as simulated theater. Instead of turning the living room into the "best seat in the house," such an approach imagines radio as creating a more intimate, first-person space that is modeled on the subjective experience of literature and sometimes known by the moniker "the theater of the imagination." Recall the way in which Jack Gould framed his critique of laugh track: it turned the viewer from a partner into a spectator and represented the difference between "being with somebody and looking at somebody" (1956, 27). Gould uses spatial metaphors to reject the idea of a simulated theater and instead points to a more intimate, subjective framing for broadcast entertainment.

From this perspective, the sound of any audience reaction, live or taped, could be considered stylistically retrograde. But anti–laugh track rhetoric often made distinctions between the live studio audience and the prerecorded laugh track, holding up the former as the index of authentic presence and communication. But the argument that contrasts the artifice of the laugh track with the authenticity of a live studio audience is problematic because the reactions of the studio audience were rarely free from manipulation. For example, a 1973 television production manual describes how the sound mixer can increase the volume of certain responses in order to "milk the audience": "To produce the right effect the operator must judge precisely the moment when the laugh will come. He has to anticipate the amount of laughter and be able to create realistic swell effect, increasing the natural rise and fall of the volume, without making it obvious that it has been exaggerated" (Alkin 1973, 210). Additionally, a large number of reaction microphones must be used to capture the sounds of the audience laughter, adding another layer of technological intervention. And even though this audience is live in the studio with the performers, it is often prompted by the playback of its own laughter: "Audience reaction can be encouraged by feeding part of the output of the audience reaction microphones back to the audience on the p.a. system. . . . Loudspeakers can be used at the back of the auditorium supplied either with the output of the front reaction microphones or with pre-recorded reaction which acts as a 'trigger' and is not used directly in the studio output" (211). The studio audience is thus being "triggered" and manipulated much as the home viewer is.

Further blurring the line between live and recorded sound, television producers sometimes talked about how the reactions of the live audience were not without their own problems, and they could even seem less real than the laugh track. A 1959 article about Sid Caesar describes how a big part of his decision to use a laugh track had to do with anxiety about the response of the live audience: "The quantity and quality of the local studio audience that would attend was a highly risky factor. If the weather were poor; if the audience were unsophisticated, morose or from Missouri—the degree of laughter on the air might be anywhere from debilitated to disastrous" (Shayon 1959, 44). In a 1966 *TV Guide* interview, Arthur Julian, writer of *F Troop,* stated that "real audiences sound phonier than the laugh track. Sometimes they freeze up and act unnatural" (Hobson 1966b, 21). Similarly, the producer Don McGuire characterized live audiences as "tense and nervous," which made it hard to get "their true reactions" (21). Dick Hobson describes how one of the reasons live audiences "aren't all they're cracked up to be" is that they "can hardly *see* the performers through the swarm of cameras, announcers, lights, sound men, props, musicians, microphone booms, dancers, cameramen, stagehands, and assorted production assistants" (21). Not only that, but sometimes producers complained that live audiences laughed too much or too loudly: "The audiences are so delighted to be there, actually seeing the stars in the flesh . . . that sometimes they laugh too loud and too often. If we played it just as it comes out, nobody would believe it. We have to tone it down to make it sound real" (Levin 1978, 36).

It is clear, then, that in terms of television production, the live studio audience is hardly the bastion of human spontaneity. Similarly, from the standpoint of the home audience, the reactions of live studio audiences as heard on network television do not typically provide a sense of the spontaneous. Take, for example, Norman Lear's *All in the Family,* a show that, in reintroducing a live studio audience, was credited with "bur[ying] the laugh track forever" (G. Jones 1993, 207). But the audience reaction on *All in the Family* clearly reveals the methods of control and manipulation outlined above. While suggesting that we are watching an authentically live event, the laughs and applause of the studio audience are just as seamlessly part of the text as a laugh track.

THE CANNED UNCANNY: LAUGHING MACHINES

We have seen so far how the laugh served as a suture between audience and prerecorded performances. In broadcasting the laugh track was used to locate the isolated viewer in a constructed social context, building on the social nature of laughter, and to give broadcast performances a sense of immediacy. The sounds of the live studio audience were just as much a creation of the processes of media production as was the recorded laugh track. Conversely, the closer one looks at the actual labor involved in creating the laugh track, the less mechanical it begins to seem. Partly because of its uncertain marriage of human and mechanical, reactions to the "laughing machine" apparatus often drifted from the comic to the uncanny, further revealing the nature of laughter and its role in authenticating media texts.

Despite flurries of interest in the popular press, the apparatus and production techniques behind the laugh track were largely kept an industry secret, and they are notable by their absence. Industry magazines like *Broadcasting* and *Television* all but ignored the issue in the 1950s. In a 1953 article in *Variety*, Marc Daniels, the director of *I Married Joan*, noted that "laughs can be dubbed in, using chuckle tracks, laugh tracks, yock tracks or boff tracks in various combinations. . . . Why do there have to be laughs? Well . . . that is a highly controversial subject. Let's skip it" (1953, 37). Similarly, a TV sound engineer in a 1957 *Time* article would discuss the laugh track only anonymously, "so furtive" was "the whole industry" about canned laughter ("Can the Laughter" 40). In 1959 the *Saturday Review* followed the sound engineer Maxwell Russell on his job providing the laugh track for a Sid Caesar special on NBC. The article describes the secretive and isolated nature of this work: "No one in charge gave him any instructions on how to integrate the laugh machine into the program. He followed the rehearsals, marked his script according to his own hunches on where the laughs would or should come. The director did not even acknowledge his presence. It was as if he were not there" (Shayon 1959, 44). The mystique of the laughing machine, or "Laff Box," as it was called in the industry, remained intact well into the 1960s. A 1966 *TV Guide* article described how, "if the Laff Box should start acting strangely, the Laff Boys wheel it into the men's room, locking the door behind so that no one can peek. . . . Everybody and his brother has a theory about what's inside. But mention the name 'Charley Douglas' [inventor of the Laff Box] and it's like 'Cosa Nostra'— everybody starts whispering. It's the most taboo topic in TV" (Hobson 1966a, 4).[15]

Coupled with this aura of secrecy, the laugh track, though introduced to a public familiar with the idea of recorded voices, seems to have been considered eerie and uncanny from the very beginning of its existence. This was the case even with professional TV technicians: "Fellow technicians strolled over to look at the mechanical laughter, shuddered, and said they were glad they weren't operating it" (Shayon 1959, 44). One of the main means by which people expressed their sense of the uncanny nature of the laugh track was by noting that many of the people heard laughing were now dead: "People who once, in a moment of abandon, guffawed at Stoopnagle and Budd can, without knowing it, hear their youthful follies repeated as the background for a TV film. Fred Allen, for one, can never help thinking that much of the merriment is being made by folk long dead" ("Strictly for Laughs" 46). The TV writer Larry Gelbart stated, "It's a standing joke, of course, that most of those people on the laugh track are dead now." He went on to paint a picture of laughing souls trapped in a televisual purgatory: "They laughed those laughs years ago and they'll never be allowed to stop, never" (1984, 17). Something about the recorded laugh seems to have brought these thoughts readily to mind, even to people immersed in over a half century of recorded sound.

Why was the recorded laugh felt to be so powerfully disturbing? For Bergson, laughter is a social sanction against frame rigidity and mechanical behavior. When someone acts like a machine, we laugh. But, following Freud's essay "The 'Uncanny,' " this same ambiguity between human and machine is an important source of our experience of the uncanny. Freud begins his essay by quoting Jentsch on the uncanny's link to "doubts whether an apparently animate being is really alive; or conversely, whether a lifeless object might not be in fact animate," and referring to "the impression made by wax-work figures, ingeniously constructed dolls and automata" (1997, 201). Though Freud went on to find other sources for the uncanny, the laugh machine could similarly blur the lines between living presence and inanimate machine. In articles criticizing the laugh track and filmed television more generally, Jack Gould describes practices like lip-synching that combine live and taped as zombielike: "phony TV with performing half-breeds—half-live and half-dead, the zombies of show business" (1956, 27).

Like Gould's lip-synching zombies, the combination of the taped laugh track and videotaped performers forces the viewer to recognize layers of presence in the broadcast performance. Freud's inclusion of epilepsy as a source of the uncanny also suggests that the spasmlike nature of laughter is prime for the production of such an effect: "These excite in the spectator the impression of automatic, mechanical processes at work, behind the ordinary appearance of mental activity" (1997, 201–2). The uncanniness of the laugh track therefore reveals how the spasmodic nature of the laugh, so often read as an index for the human, can just as easily appear mechanical.

Max Liebman's 1961 essay in *Variety*, which I described above, indicates how the laugh track could confuse the animate and inanimate in unnerving ways. The comedy writer Hank, frustrated by how the Big Executive had forced him to work with the laugh track, revisits the experience of a laugh track dubbing session in a dream. The description of the scene emphasizes the uncanny undercurrents of the laugh track, with its blurring of human and machine: "There was an eeriness about the dubbing studio which Hank hadn't noticed before. The Big Executive had also changed. Seated beside Mr. McKenzie, he seemed to be of the same metallic composition, and the same inscrutability." Note how the machine has a name, but the executive does not. The dream becomes more surreal when Mr. McKenzie refuses to laugh at Hank's show. The Big Executive explains, "He doesn't like your script . . . he doesn't think you're funny." "Hank realized that he was in a realm where madness was the norm. Artistic judgment was entrusted to an arrangement of wires and buttons and tubes, and men born human were accepting robotism as the best means to progress. His frustration was total when he suddenly heard the executive ascribing human emotions to the laugh machine. 'You hurt him when you called him a pushover. He hasn't laughed at anything since' " (1961, 86).

Hank swallows his pride and apologizes to Mr. McKenzie, who then lets out a "bellow of laughter that sounded like thunder coming out of a tunnel": "The sound rose and swelled until it shook the building. Infected by it, the executive added his own maniacal shrieks. Hank was on his feet yelling that that scene wasn't funny. It was destroyed by laughter. But his own voice was soundless in the din, which grew louder, even more cacophonous." Hank wakes up, laughing at the absurdity of the dream, but soon finds himself racing to the next dubbing session, unfed and in a sweat, hoping to influence the process: "After all, Mr. McKenzie was only a machine" (86). This narrative nicely illustrates how troubling the laugh track could be: it made machines seem eerily human and human laughter seem mechanical.

For Freud the uncanny is particularly tied to the involuntary return to the same situation, something of particular pertinence to the experience of the laugh track because of its nature as a tape loop: we hear the same laughs again and again (1997, 213). Indeed, the laugh track apparatus is an unlikely precursor to the tape loop performances in modern avant-garde and popular music, even a kind of proto-sampler: "[the laugh machine is] about the size of a fat suitcase standing up. Behind thin, hardware-drawer panels, small reels of tape revolve in perpetual three- to six-and-one-half-second loops. Each reel is marked to describe the specific kind of laughter it provides. The control panel is a small wood block with ten buttons, five stop and five go. Press the go button and the machine keeps repeating the appropriate laugh cycle ad infinitum. Press stop and the laugh stops at the completion of the brief cycle" (Shayon 1959, 44).

Musical analogies occurred to writers who saw the machine in action, and they repeatedly noted its organlike appearance: "The engineer plays his machine like an organ, rehearses right along with the cast, tailors the laughs snugly to the lines" ("Can the Laughter" 38).[16] Charley Douglas, the man credited with creating the machine, is portrayed as playing "an organlike mechanism with six keys that when played with the left hand, can provide small chuckles, medium chuckles, small laughs, medium laughs, medium heavy laughs, and rollin'-in-the-aisle boffs" ("Strictly for Laughs" 46). The similarity to a musical instrument is heightened in descriptions of the machine that refer to chords and themes: "Using chords, the player can provide some 100 variations on these six basic themes; and his right hand can control the volume. Jess Oppenheimer, producer of 'I Love Lucy,' has another machine, dubbed the Jay-O Laughter, which he claims can produce 100 different kinds of laughs on each of its six keys" ("Strictly for Laughs" 46).

In his 1966 article "The Hollywood Sphinx and His Laff Box," Hobson neatly combines the uncanny and the musical: "Picture if you will Lon Chaney Sr. in 'Phantom of the Opera' flailing at the pipe organ in the darkened cathedral crypt and you have some notion of the Laff Boy at work. Hunched over the keyboard of Charley's box on the darkened dubbing stage, his fingers punching at the keys, his feet manipulating the pedals, he wrings forth his fugues and caprices. He's a veritable virtuoso of titters and snorts" (1966a, 4).

These musical comparisons underscore the fact that laying down the laugh track was a performance that relied on skill, timing, and taste: "When the lights come up, the Laff Boy is frequently drenched in sweat. . . . The trick of the Laff Boy's trade is timing. . . . To manufacture a natural-sounding laugh, the Laff Boy must let a few 'people' in his box anticipate a joke. This is called 'giving it a little tickle.' Then he might punch in a 'sharpie' just before the main laugh. . . . Gags frequently build, each capping the last, so the Laff Boy must likewise build and hold his biggest laugh for the pay-off" (6). Compare this intricate and subtle performance with the degree of manipulation of the live studio audience discussed above, and it becomes even harder to declare one more authentic than the other.

The keyboard design of the Laff Box reveals a morphological resemblance that helps to place it in a historic lineage with Joseph Faber's laughing Turk. Moving forward in time, we can place it with other, more modern machines that used tape loops, such as the Chamberlin and the Mellotron. The keys of these instruments triggered recorded loops of instruments playing the notes of the scale. The Mellotron was state-of-the-art studio technology in the 1960s; the haunting sound of its flute setting can be heard on Beatles' recordings such as "Strawberry Fields Forever." Indeed, the Beatles' recording of "Tomorrow Never Knows," which has been heralded for its use of swirling psychedelic tape loops, pays an unconscious tribute to the laughing machine: the loop, vaguely reminiscent of the sound of seagulls, is a speeded-up recording of Paul McCartney laughing.[17]

The debate over the laugh track didn't end in the 1960s, as the comments and career of Larry Gelbart illustrate. A vehement opponent of the laugh track, Gelbart rearticulated the belief in the individual nature of laughter: "Laughter is a very personal act. It has to start with the individual, although it can end up a group experience. But first, it has to work for you; then you can work in a crowd" (1998, 184). Gelbart reluctantly agreed to allow the laugh track on his series *M*A*S*H,* but after the success of that show, Gelbart had the clout to produce his new program *United States* without it: "[We] did away with the laugh track, rejecting outright the suggestion to the viewer that there were three hundred people living in the same house as our couple, going from room to room with them and laughing their heads off at their intimate and/or hilarious exchanges" (94). His rejection of the laugh track went hand in hand with his insistence that this new series was more personal and autobiographical than anything else he'd ever done. As has often been the case with television comedy, artistic aspiration is indexed by the absence of the laugh track, making it an important index of genre and authorship.[18]

The Laff Box and the laugh track can be placed in the context of the practices and discourses surrounding the recorded laugh that I've traced through various media of the past century. The flooding out of performed laughter is one example of a modern vocal style that was forged in the context of these new sound media technologies. The use of the laugh track to simulate social experience and so suture the audience to the prerecorded text, the uncanny experience of the Laff Box, and the assertion that laughter is a quintessentially individual expression all illustrate how laughter has been regarded as a powerful index for authentic human presence in the production and reception of mass media. Returning to the scene in Steven Spielberg's *A.I.* described at the beginning of this chapter, we can see that the laugh continues to be used to test the boundaries between the human and the mechanical. The android David's laugh works much like the media texts I have analyzed above, slipping from the human to the mechanical, from the social to the individual, from the comic to the uncanny.

Laughter has consistently been mobilized as a barometer of the authentically human, a choice that is not without consequences. Holding up laugher as the definition of the self-motivated individual is problematic in light of the inherently social and spasmodic nature of the laugh. If laughter is so connected to instinct, spasm, and the social, then its identification as a citadel of the individual self is already compromised: the raw, living laugh and the cooked recording become harder to disentangle. The anxiety about the laugh track demonstrates the potentially disturbing nature of blurring these boundaries and the difficulty of defining both the human and the mechanical, the can and the canned, in the context of modern mass media.

CHAPTER 2

Erotic Performance on Record

In Edward Bellamy's 1898 short story "With the Eyes Shut," a traveler falls asleep on a train and dreams about a world of the future where the technology of sound recording is put to a variety of uses. The dream begins on a train, where the man encounters "phonographed" books, magazines, guidebooks, and train announcers. At the end of his journey, the man stops in a hotel. In the middle of the night he finds himself sitting up in bed "with half a dozen extraordinary sensations contending for right of way" along his backbone: "What had startled me was the voice of a young woman, who could not have been standing more than ten feet from my bed. If the tones of her voice were any guide, she was not only a young woman, but a very charming one. 'My dear sir,' she had said, 'you may possibly be interested in knowing that it now wants just a quarter of three'" (1898, 339). The man is startled, describing this female voice as "so thrilling and lifelike in effect" that he did not have "the nerve to light the gas to investigate" until he had put on his "more essential garments" (339). Once the light is on, he discovers that the voice came from "a phonographic device for announcing the hour": "I found no lady in the room, but only a clock." Despite this discovery, the recorded voice retained its powerful effects: "I had never before been impressed with any particular interest attaching to the hour of three in the morning, but as I heard it announced in those low, rich, thrilling contralto tones, it appeared fairly to coruscate with previously latent suggestions of romance and poetry, which, if somewhat vague, were very pleasing. Turning out the gas that I might the more easily imagine the bewitching presence which the voice suggested, I went back to bed, and lay awake there until morning, enjoying the society of my bodiless companion and the delicious shock of her quarter-hourly remarks" (340–41). This narrative indicates how, at the dawn of recorded sound, the very fact of a disembodied, recorded voice could carry with it erotic undercurrents. The presence of the voice in all its "low, rich, thrilling contralto tones" could powerfully suggest the presence of a body, and so serve as a form of erotic entertainment. It is notable that in this story the erotic dimension of the voice could overtake the phonograph's intended purpose of announcing the time.

In this chapter I will investigate the nature of erotic vocal performance through an analysis of phonograph records that, unlike Bellamy's clock, were specifically made as titillating entertainment. More specifically, this chapter is a study of a little-known genre of phonographic recordings called "blue discs" or "party records" made between the 1930s and 1950s. Sold under the counter, and often made anonymously or by tiny, independent labels, these records are not commercially available, although collectors of vintage 78-rpm records have frequently obtained them.[1] It is my contention that mapping out the range of performance styles found on these records can illuminate dimensions of performance in the media and help define a modern vocal style. This chapter will, like the last one, be concerned with the development of styles of vocal performance that are closely connected to the way in which sound media technologies such as the phonograph separated performers from their audiences in time and space. In the case of erotic performances, this separation is of particular importance because of the way in which it changes the dynamics of risk in performance. As we saw in the last chapter, a performance characterized as flooding out can be seen as part of a modern style of performance, one that provides a sense of human bodily presence.

Blue discs can help to bridge the historical and technological gap between an oral tradition of erotic performance and the cinema, as well as adding context to the discussion of dynamics and tensions found in film pornography. In addition, blue discs offer a case study in the use of woman's voice in the sound media, a topic that has stimulated a diverse body of research. These overlooked recordings provide another stage for testing theories about gender, performance, and sound media. The role of sound and verbal performance in the presentation of the erotic has not received enough critical attention, and blue discs provide a useful case study in that area.

In her essay "Crackers and Whackers: The White Trashing of Porn," Constance Penley suggests that if the "breakthrough" of Linda Williams's study of film pornography, *Hard Core*, was "to get us to think of pornography as film," then "the next logical step" would be "to consider pornographic film as popular culture." As a way of determining the traits that pornographic film shares with "the production and consumption of a whole range of popular forms," Penley points to a tradition of bawdy songs and dirty jokes that she sees as having a connection to the use of humor in pre–World War II American stag films (1997, 95–96). This is a productive connection to make, but one that omits a body of mass media erotica that can be particularly illuminating for the study of film pornography: I refer to recorded erotic performances on phonographic records. Following Penley's suggestion to address a "range of popular forms," I'll contextualize these recordings in terms of performances in several adjacent media: the burlesque stage, radio, film, and oral forms of riddling. First, I must place the genre of blue discs in a larger legislative history of "obscene" phonograph records, roughly between the 1890s and 1950s. This historical overview will explain my focus on the media culture of the 1930s.

If Bellamy's encounter with the talking clock shows the inherent erotic potential of the disembodied voice, it will perhaps come as no surprise that the use of the phonograph to make "obscene" records seems to have coincided with the birth of the recording industry. The existence of records of this kind is revealed through accounts of actions taken by Anthony Comstock in the 1890s. The leader of the New York Society for the Suppression of Vice, Comstock is best known for his crusades against "obscene" printed materials and birth control information, but he also pursued the makers of phonograph records.[2] Consider this article from the June 26, 1896, *New York Times,* which describes Comstock's arrest of the early recording artist Russell Hunting:

> The arrests are the result, Comstock says, of a hunt for over two years. During all that time Comstock and [Detective] Oram have been arresting various people for exhibiting phonographs that had cylinders containing vile songs and stories, but they had never been able to catch the person from whom these cylinders were purchased. They noticed that all the cylinders gave forth exactly the same voice, and finally they learned, it is alleged, that it was the voice of an actor traveling with Frohman's "Shenandoah" company. They were told that this actor's name was Hunting, and that he was on the road with the show. Several weeks ago Oram learned that Hunt-

ing was in the city, and, accompanied by witnesses, he called at his home Wednesday. Hunting would not at first admit that he made the cylinders, but Oram played the part of a customer with such success that Hunting took him in the "laboratory" and showed him how the cylinders worked. Oram bought three cylinders for $1.50 apiece. ("Comstock Arrests an Actor" 3)

This event reveals Comstock's dedicated pursuit of obscene phonograph recordings, and it also provides information about their production and reception. In terms of the latter, evidence suggests that these cylinder recordings were often heard in taverns. The twenty-third annual report of the New York Society for the Suppression of Vice, presented on January 19, 1897, states that "prior to July, many complaints were received of most obscene and filthy matters sung and spoken in phonographs which were exhibited in saloons" (Comstock and Sumner 1897, 6). I will have more to say about the importance of the saloon context later in the chapter, but for now it should be noted that these records were associated with a public, male-dominated setting.

Several small collections of risqué cylinders from this era have recently been found, some of which may feature performances by the notorious Russell Hunting.[3] A wax cylinder dated June 3, 1892, is a part of a collection of early phonograph "smut" kept at the Edison National Historic Site in West Orange, New Jersey.[4] The cylinder contains a number of risqué jokes and conundrums, but it is mostly taken up with a monologue about President Grover Cleveland and his mistress Frances Folsom. The performance begins with statements that frame it as "a special dispatch" from the "War Department" in Washington, D.C.:

> Last evening, as the pretty little clipper *Frances Folsom* was cruising about, she was observed by the government ram, *Grover Cleveland*, which immediately hove down upon her with the intention of boarding her. The *Frances*, seeing there was no way of avoiding the encounter, pluckily lay to, threw her stern into position, and barred poles for action. The *Grover* managed to strike the *Frances* with two balls between wind and water, intending thereby to impede the action of her pump. As he bore down upon her, the *Grover*'s polished ram struck the *Frances* at the waterline, penetrating her interior to a considerable depth.

Two aspects of this performance should be noted. First, the metaphorical structure of the monologue means that the erotic content is always suggested, never presented outright. Second, the speaker recites the words in a full-voiced, droning, stentorian tone. His tone is partly motivated by the fact that it is framed as a special dispatch from the War Department, but it is also typical of spoken performances during this acoustic era in recording history, when the voice had to be projected into the horn of the phonograph with enough volume to make a suitable etching into the wax. Besides giving the erotic content of the performance a particularly strange flavor for the modern listener, this mode of erotic performance is particularly well suited to face-to-face contexts, where the risks of telling a risqué story make it important to be able to deny any obscene intentions. These are dynamics of performance to which I will return in a more systematic manner.

The account of Russell Hunting's arrest also reveals some aspects of the production of this type of recording. Specifically, the newspaper account reveals that the "vile songs and stories" found on these wax cylinders were made on request. The wax cylinder records prevalent in the 1890s were difficult to duplicate by means of a master molding, and so recordings were made in repeated small batches. This meant that one of the job requirements for early recording artists was sheer vocal endurance: they could be called on to deliver up to fifty performances in a day. In such a context, the production of large numbers of risqué recordings would have been time-consuming and dangerously conspicuous, which would have helped foster the kind of small-scale, on-demand mode of production described above. Improved techniques for massproducing a single master recording were introduced for both cylinder and disc formats after 1903.[5] By the mid-1910s cylinders had been largely replaced in phonograph production by discs, which were easier to press from a master and so made easier the making of copies from a single performance. For this reason, the 1920s can be considered the earliest time that mass-produced blue discs would have been in circulation. Indeed, most sources place the records that I will analyze below in the 1930s and 1940s. There seems to have been a legislative and cultural sea change in regard to obscene records in the mid- to late 1940s. At this time there was an increase in the coverage of obscene records in the national press, which led to federal legislation in 1950.

Evidence from the popular press reveals how obscene phonograph records increasingly became the target of law enforcement throughout the 1940s. Accounts of arrests and changes in legislation can also demonstrate how the obscene record industry of this time differed from that of the 1890s. The November 1, 1942, *New York Times* reported that in Newark, New Jersey, a "campaign against dealers in indecent phonograph recordings" was ordered by Judge Ernest F. Masini after "four owners of radio and music shops" were charged with possessing obscene records. Unlike the Hunting case, in which a performer-distributor was arrested, here the focus of prosecution was on retail distribution—specifically on music shop owners. The fact that the judge also ordered a warrant for the arrest of an "undisclosed distributor alleged to have 10,000 objectionable records in stock" reveals the extent of mass-production and distribution in such an operation ("Fights Obscene Recordings" 49). Prosecution of those involved with the production and sale of obscene records seems to have increased toward the end of the decade, the market expanded perhaps by returning servicemen.[6] On October 1, 1948, the *Nebraska State Journal* reported that the FBI "arrested a Kansas man on a charge of illegally transporting obscene phonograph records between states." An FBI special agent stated that this was "the first case of its kind handled by the bureau, although there have been several prosecutions for interstate transportation of obscene literature." The arrested man was James Leroy Davidson, thirty-six, the operator of the Kansas City Music and Sales Company, and the phonograph records were said to be sold to "select customers on an under-the-counter basis" ("Obscene Records Cause of Arrest" 13). As in other cases during the 1940s, law enforcement frequently targeted music shops that sold these records to an exclusive clientele.

A similar case that year led to a Supreme Court decision and a change in federal obscenity law. Alexander L. Alpers, a San Francisco record shop operator, was fined two hundred dollars by a district court in December 1948 for sending packages of allegedly indecent records out of state (" 'Indecent' Records Eligible for Mails" 19). This conviction was overturned by the Ninth Federal Circuit Court in June 1949, which stated that the law forbidding the shipment of obscene "matters" did not apply to phonograph records ("Obscene Record Ruling" 42). That ruling was overturned by the Supreme Court on February 7, 1950. In *United States v. Alpers* (338 U.S. 680 [1950]), the Court, in a split decision, held that shipment of obscene phonograph records could be prohibited by the U.S. Code. In the wake of this Supreme Court decision, President Harry Truman updated the law that Anthony Comstock had helped write in 1873 to include "obscene phonograph recordings and electrical transcriptions" in the federal ban on the interstate shipment of obscenity ("Bill on Obscene Records Signed" 46). An article in the May 3, 1950, issue of *Variety* illustrates how arrests continued after this legislation: "Albert L. Miller, owner of Palda Records" was indicted by a federal grand jury "on charges of shipping pornographic recordings." The case was called "the first of its kind" in Philadelphia, and it was described as being "the result of a recent U.S. Supreme Court decision" ("3 Indicted in Shipment of Pornographic Disks" 41).[7]

These two eruptions of press coverage and legislation on obscene phonograph records—one in the 1890s the other in the 1950s—can help define historical brackets for the erotic recordings that are my main focus: blue discs made between the 1920s and 1950s. If before the 1920s wax-cylinder recording technology made mass-production of risqué recordings difficult and antiobscenity zealots like Anthony Comstock made it dangerous, legislation made distribution of these records a federal crime after 1950. The 1930s and 1940s were therefore a window of opportunity for an obscure but culturally resonant form of media entertainment. I have begun this chapter by describing this phenomenon in the larger context of the phonograph industry, and I now want to consider it in the broader media context of the 1930s, looking at adjacent forms of media such as the burlesque stage, radio, film, and oral forms of riddling.

BIFURCATED BURLESQUE

The blue discs I examine were being made at the historical moment when the tradition of the American burlesque stage was coming to an end, one marked symbolically by New York Mayor Fiorello La Guardia's refusal to renew licenses for the Minsky burlesque theaters in 1937 (Minsky and Machlin 1986, 278). In his historical study of that tradition, Robert Allen describes how nineteenth-century burlesque had featured the "transgressive power of the union of charismatic female sexuality and inversive subordination," embodied respectively by a visual and a verbal performance. Over the course of the century, women on the burlesque stage became increasingly mute, visual spectacles, as their performances moved from intricate punning on high art conventions to graphic sexual displays like the striptease, which "did not become a standard feature of burlesque until the mid-1920s" (1991, 282).

Allen's historical overview presents a trajectory in which "the appeals of burlesque became increasingly bifurcated: verbal humor provided usually by male comedians and sexual display provided by female performers." The female burlesque performer morphed into either the mute, unthreatening "doll-like, decorative sexuality" of the Ziegfeld girl, or the "unruly" female performance of Mae West, Sophie Tucker, or Bessie Smith: figures whose transgressive power "was channeled and defused through their construction as grotesque figures" (243). In the later embodiment of burlesque, the verbal work of salacious, double entendre humor was performed almost entirely by men, especially by the male "top banana" (238). In fact, it became so customary for women to be "the mute objects of sexual humor in burlesque sketches" that a special term was invented to designate one who actually spoke: the "talking woman" (240). Seen in this context, the blue disc (which features male and female speaking performers, and a solely verbal performance), both captures and goes against the grain of the fading burlesque stage tradition.

THE BREATH OF THE NATION

While the mid-1930s were the twilight of the American burlesque stage, the same period is considered by many to be the dawn of the "Golden Age" of network radio broadcasting. Blue discs reflect the influence of radio both in relation to production and in form. In terms of form, some of these recordings directly parody radio conventions. Consider a recording called *The Pioneer*, which begins: "Good evening, ladies and gentlemen of our radio audience. This is station G-I-N, the breath of the nation, operating on a clear-channel frequency of 300 crap-o-cycles by order of the Federal Bullshit Commission. Now, my dear friends, we've had so many letters complaining about the goddamn lies that you've been hearing on this station that to satisfy all you cocky bastards we are going to present something very, very serious." Another record called *Kentucky Trail* features the parody of a radio advertisement for Flan-o-san Manure: "From the results of a nationwide survey, more gardeners use Flan-o-san Manure than any other manure. Because Flan-o-san is nothing but shit taken only from bulls, which make it pure bullshit."

The parodying of radio conventions illustrates that the makers of these records were, to use Ed Cray's term, "educated authors." In his book *The Erotic Muse*, Cray notes that bawdy songs and limericks were almost exclusively the work of authors who were extremely literate in the forms and conventions of their time, a fact that is reflected most clearly in "the great number of parodies" these forms present (1999, xxx). Similarly, many of the creators of blue discs seem to have been literate in the field of radio. In a personal interview, David Diehl, a blue disc collector and discographer, describes how these discs seem to have been frequently created by radio professionals: "Broadcast folks really loved to make dubs of party records for their advertising clients." Diehl states that one recording called *The Crepitation Contest*, an elaborate radio parody, "was performed by CBC people at RCA Canadian studios."[8] This record seems to have been made by media-savvy professionals, in a fashion similar to that of the stag films described by Linda Williams, which are thought to have been created by professional filmmakers during their off-hours. Blue discs began to be widely heard at a time when broadcast radio was culturally important, and these audio performances refer to radio in terms both of form and of mode of production.

Unlike radio, the phonograph industry was particularly hard hit by the Depression, and record sales plummeted. Fewer people could afford records for home use, so public listening became more widespread. This public listening was centered on the jukebox: "Recorded sound weathered the Depression of the 1930s with the help of coin-slot players in public places." In fact, "by 1936 over half of all record production in the United States was destined for [jukeboxes]." Jukeboxes at the time were often found in bars and taverns: "the repeal of prohibition in 1933 brought about a dramatic change in social life as Americans flooded back to bars and clubs. No self-respecting drinking establishment was without [a jukebox]" (Millard 1995,168–69).

The social context of listening in a neighborhood tavern was particularly conducive to a certain kind of talk. Anna McCarthy's study of early television's tavern audience describes how the neighborhood tavern of post-Prohibition America was characterized by its frequent exclusion of women, its atmosphere of male "egalitarianism," and, notably, its function as a kind of "working-class public sphere." People came to "talk, exchange ideas," and discuss problems, as well as to drink and listen to the jukebox (2000, 455). Anthony Comstock's pursuit of obscene phonograph recordings in the 1890s had centered on saloons. Similarly, blue discs made between the 1920s and 1950s seem to have been made largely for a tavern jukebox audience. David Diehl describes how blue discs often have "an old sentimental sing-along tune on one side and a risqué number on the other," so as to more easily hide the obscene material on jukeboxes. Diehl also notes that the advertising for one blue disc manufacturer, Larry Vincent's risqué Pearl Records, carried the slogan "Rockin' the boxes."

The narrative of a blue disc entitled *Beer Joint* takes a male tavern culture as its topic, and so it merits a close consideration. As the disc begins, we hear the sound of a door opening, and a male voice states, "Well, come right in, Mrs. Jones, you're my very next patient." Sobbing, the woman replies, "Thank you, Doctor. I had to come and see you. I don't want a divorce, but that looks like the only way out." The doctor's response encourages the listener to conjure up the woman as an erotic spectacle, an indication that this recording might be keyed to a primarily male audience: "Now, now, now, my dear, you're such a lovely young girl, all those tears! Now tell me, what are your troubles?" Mrs. Jones's troubles turn out to hinge on the tavern and its connection to sexual dissatisfaction: "It's my husband's drinking . . . we've been married six months and yet we've hardly had a honeymoon!" When asked to describe her husband's drinking, the woman explains, "He is a habitual drinker. Every afternoon when he leaves his father's bank, he stops off with friends to drink beer." She continues to describe how, when her husband finally gets home after dark, they end up arguing instead of consummating their marriage.

It should be noted that, at this point in the narrative, we have heard a frank female perspective on male sexual inadequacy and its connection to a male culture of tavern going. The doctor's suggestion, however, seems aimed more toward allaying male anxieties than toward responding to Mrs. Jones's complaints: "Now just a minute, my dear, calm yourself. Have you stopped to think that the trouble might be in your own mind? Perhaps your husband isn't the habitual drinker that you picture. Perhaps the absence of—ahem—sex in your life is your fault. Let's try this. Tonight, when your husband comes home, forget those silly quarrels. Be sweet to him for a change. Play up to him. Turn on your own natural charm. You have sex appeal—display it. Try this just once, and then we'll know if he really can pass up those beer joints."

She agrees to try the doctor's suggestion, and the next sounds we hear are those of the husband arriving home that night. The listener is then presented with the same story of marital dissatisfaction, but this time from the husband's point of view: "Well, here I am, home again. Ready for the usual battle with the wife, I guess. Hmm, I wonder where she is? She usually meets me at the door with a big mouthful of argument about my beer drinking. Well, I know she's here somewhere. I'll probably find that lazy old bag flat on her back in bed."

When the husband finds his wife in bed, he thinks aloud to the listening audience: "Brother! What a picture. My beautiful wife in bed with no clothes on. All powdered and perfumed." As happened with the doctor's comments, this is a moment when the speaker seems to collude with a male audience, encouraging it to picture the wife as an erotic spectacle. What follows seems to demonstrate that the doctor's prescription for Mrs. Jones was a success, since Mr. Jones has regained his sexual interest in his wife: "What a beautiful pair of knockers you've got there, honey! And to think that I'd almost forgotten about them! Well, that's what twin beds will do for a young married couple. Baby, I'm going to give you the sweetest kiss you ever got." We hear exaggerated kissing noises, while Mrs. Jones coos, "Ooh, darling, how wonderful." Mr. Jones continues, telling his wife that he's going to give "those pretty little knockers" the "working over they deserve." Mrs. Jones continues to encourage him as he moves down to kiss her "soft little tummy." Breathlessly, Mrs. Jones says, "Don't stop now, move on down and do it some more." Suddenly, Mrs. Jones's tone of voice signals a shift from sensual abandon to frustration, and she scolds, "Oh, fine, now you're kissing me on the knee. If it was a beer joint you wouldn't pass it up!" The record thus ends with a complicated and ambiguous relationship to the anxieties of male listeners. Taking the doctor's advice as a narrative frame points to its function as male wish fulfillment: keyed to a male audience, it addresses sexual anxieties only to put the responsibility on the woman and, in the end, laugh them off. Yet, while suggesting that the Joneses' marital trouble is primarily the responsibility of the woman, this record still presents a husband unable to sexually satisfy his wife. The punch line works by punning "beer joints" with the female genitals, further underscoring cultural associations and antagonisms between tavern culture and women. The narrative of *Beer Joint* addresses gendered tensions surrounding the tavern, which might very well have been the setting in which it was heard. This textual evidence can be added to other indications that the reception of these records involved a predominantly male audience, and a place (the tavern) associated with joking and discussion.

THE EMBARRASSMENT OF SILENCE

Although blue discs were heard in taverns, there is evidence to suggest other important sites of their reception. Consider the opening monologue found on a blue disc called *Uncle Tom's Cabin:* "This is not really a story, it's more of a routine, and it's best told when everyone is sitting around during the evening, had a few drinks. Uh, in mixed company, you know. So somebody's dared to tell a little bit of a risqué story, and you finally say, 'Well, I know a [laughs] story, but it's ah . . .' 'Well, go ahead and tell it,' everybody says. 'Oh, no [laughs].' 'Well, go ahead: you know

Frank, you know Marn, you know everybody.' Well, finally you say, 'Well, all right,' and you start out. You pull your handkerchief out, and you say, 'Well, once upon a time, there was a poor old broken-down whore.' Everybody looks at you, and looks at everybody else, they look at the floor. You don't pay any attention, you go right on talking. You say, 'This poor old whore was sitting in the parlor . . . ' " Here is a fascinating glimpse into what might have been a typical scene in which blue discs were heard: mixed-gender gatherings featuring sessions of risqué storytelling.[9]

Moreover, the fact that blue discs are also referred to as party records points to their use both in social gatherings such as the one described in *Uncle Tom's Cabin,* and in all-male parties like the stag smoker.[10] Linda Williams describes the stag audience in terms that suggest similarities to the tavern audience: they were a "group of horny, vocal, curious, misogynist boys and men," in a "stag party in the home, fraternal hall, or brothel" (1989, 295). In fact, these dynamics of reception are one of many similarities between blue discs and stag films. Besides this similarity, both blue discs and stag films were made between the 1930s and 1950s, both were sold under the counter, and both were made by fly-by-night media-savvy production outfits. The stag film and the blue disc are polar opposites in one regard, however: the stag film was a purely visual experience, and the blue disc a purely auditory one. Stag films remained silent long after Hollywood had switched to sound, and Williams postulates a viewing context for stag films that was marked by an "embarrassment of silence," filled with "verbal jokes and embarrassed laughter" (295). An analysis of blue discs might add an audio track to those contexts of reception, suggesting the kinds of verbal jokes that might have filled the embarrassment of silence. The stag film is the last aspect of the media landscape of the 1930s that I offer in order to place the blue disc in context. The stag film can also provide an interpretive framework for the vocal performances found on blue discs in several ways, the first having to do with the female voice.

In addition to contributing to the understanding of the stag film, blue discs offer a productive and overlooked case study in the analysis of the woman's voice in sound media. As scholars such as Kaja Silverman, Amy Lawrence, and Michele Hilmes have shown, discourses surrounding the sound media have frequently presented women's voices as a "problem": "A theme that resurfaces time and again in phonography, radio, and sound film is the persistent 'problem' of recording, transmitting, or reproducing women's voices" (Lawrence 1991, 29). As Amy Lawrence notes, the "problem" of the woman's voice is "always a tangle of technological and economic exigencies, each suffused with ideological assumptions about woman's 'place' " (32). As I will show, blue discs feature the female voice in ways that overlap with radio and the sound film, but which are also peculiar to their cultural and technological contexts.

I begin my examination of the verbal techniques found on blue discs by borrowing a theoretical framework from Linda Williams, who describes two poles of visual pleasure in stag films: one inherited from the striptease and featuring the bodies of women on display to a collective male group, and the other consisting of a more fully developed narrative and identification with a male protagonist (1989, 80). I argue that similar dynamics exist on blue discs, which contain techniques of speech play such as the pretended-obscene riddle, as well as forms of erotic performance more specific to recording that seek to embody a "breakthrough out of performance" via the verbal traces of authentic arousal.

DIRTY WORDS, DIRTY MINDS

The most frequent generic form found on blue discs is similar to the oral genre of the pretended-obscene riddle. The pretended-obscene riddle has two specific parts, the question and the answer, with "the obscene situation" presented in only one of the two parts: "In almost all cases the obscenity is non-existent, no obscenity is voiced at all, but rather so implied as to force the listener to imagine an obscene situation that is never evidenced in the answer" (W. Brown 1973, 90). For example, "What is it that's hard, long, and leaks?" The answer: "A fountain pen."

An important factor in this form is the way that it mobilizes the participation of listeners by forcing them to imagine the obscene situation. In this way the listener actually becomes the author of the obscene dimension of the joke. Also, the obscenity of the riddle is a breach of social decorum, but one that is "group-approved" (Hullum 1972–73, 54). That is, the riddle cannot be performed in just any social context; it tends to be enacted in "small group interactions" among a "relatively homogeneous group" (W. Brown 1973, 90).

This homogeneous group was sometimes exclusively male, much like the tavern setting of the blue disc and typical exhibition sites of the stag film. Brunvand provides the example of a male society for whom off-color performance is an important part of group identity: the Turtle Club, described as "an American riddling mock organization that is popular in the military services," where "the whole routine of asking the riddles, issuing the [membership] cards, and quizzing others for their membership is often performed in bars" (1986, 95). This form of male group interaction recalls both the tavern context of the blue disc and typical exhibition sites of the stag film: brothels and American smokers hosted by exclusive male clubs (Williams 1989, 74).

Blue discs utilize forms of speech play much like pretended-obscene riddles, often in a situation involving a dialogue between a man and a woman that results in mishearing and misframing.[11] That is, the performers are in what Erving Goffman calls different "information states": "the knowledge an individual has of why events have happened as they have, what the current forces are, what the properties and intents of the relevant persons are, and what the outcome is likely to be" (1974, 133–34). One way to create a typology of these performances is to gauge the information states of the participants—to note which of the characters are aware of the sexual or obscene connotations of the joke, which character is "in" the erotic frame, and which is "out." What follows is a typology of the records I have encountered.

Woman Is Out

In my experience, the most frequent type of blue disc presents a woman who is seemingly unaware of the erotic nature of the dialogue in which she is involved. Consider *Bull Fight, Part 1*. On this record, a man and a woman discuss a bullfight. As the woman describes the proceedings, the man reframes her words in sexual terms. For example, the woman tells the man that when he is "fighting the bull," he will have to pull out his "bandolero," to which he replies, "You mean right in front of all those people?" "Certainly," she says, "that's what they came to see." "Well," he replies, "they'll have to look goddamn close!" Her discourse is straight, while his rekeys her words to an erotic frame.[12]

One thing that is notable about this joke is the way it frankly addresses male anxiety, and, in fact, penis size is a recurring topic on blue discs. Indeed, some blue discs present a masculine image similar to the one Eric Schaefer finds in burlesque films of the 1940s and 1950s, in which men were presented as "depleted, flaccid, and weak, the antithesis of the contemporary masculine ideal of the strong, active provider" (1999, 320). Consider a record called *Newlyweds*, on which we hear a newly married couple eagerly checking in to the Sock-it-in Hotel. "How do you like our room, honey?" the man asks. "Just fine, Daddy," his wife replies. Feeling bashful, she goes to the bathroom to undress, while he disrobes in the bedroom. She emerges dressed in a robe, and asks, "How do I look?" "O sweetheart," he exclaims, "you look beautiful!" In his excitement, the husband asks if she would open up her robe and give him "a little peak." She complies, and he gushes: "Oh, mama . . . you're so cute. If I had a camera I'd take your picture. . . . I'd take it down to my office, put it on my desk and look at it all day long." The wife suggests that he return the favor, and give her a peak. "Well, here you are," he says boldly, "Take a look!" A loud gasp is heard. "What's the matter?" the husband asks. "Did I scare ya?" "No," replies the woman, regaining her composure, "you surprised me." "You know, Daddy, I wish I had a camera too," the woman says with a somewhat resigned tone of voice. "What would you do with it?" the husband asks expectantly. "I'd take your picture," she answers. "And then what would you do with it?" he asks. "I'd have it enlarged!"

On other blue discs this type of male anxiety is expressed negatively, in terms of female anatomy. When the woman in *Bull Fight, Part 1* describes how the king, the queen, and her ladies-in-waiting "all walk over and sit in the queen's box," the man replies, "I've heard of putting your foot in it, but I'll be damned if I ever heard of anyone sitting in it." "Well that's nothing," she continues, "she has four or five guards standing in it." "Four or five guards standing in it?" he asks, dumbfounded. "Now you're stretching things too damn far." Jokes directed toward the female genitals are found on many blue discs. Gershon Legman notes that this is a common trait of obscene jokes more generally, and he offers an explanation for their resonance with the male audience. For Legman, jokes representing the female genitals as "too big" represent a "direct expression of the anxiety" that the penis is too small: "Rather than admit that the penis is 'too small,' as is fearfully believed, it is far simpler to state that the vagina is 'too big' " (1982, 377). On recordings such as *Bull Fight,* a male audience colludes with a male performer in projecting male anxieties onto the female body.

Another example in which the woman is out of the erotic frame can be heard on *Just Another Mount* (Hi-Lite Records). As on several other records, the situation is framed by the introductory reading of a letter. A man's voice intones: "How do you find things in Los Angeles? While you're there, you might look up the girl I told you about, the one I met at Santa Anita racetrack. Boy, she's a honey. And she's got the cutest sister you ever saw. They're both crazy about the races, so tell them you're a jockey and you're all set." This letter ensures that the (male) audience and the male protagonist will be in on the erotic frame of the situation.

The following dialogue between the man and the girl from the Santa Anita racetrack reveals her obliviousness to its erotic dimensions, since she thinks he's talking about her racehorse, which happens to be named My Sister. "I'm looking for a good man to ride My Sister," she says. "How's her form?" the man asks. "Great!" she replies. "And she's the trimmest thing you ever saw. Long, tapering legs, and hips like a model." "Well," he says, "sounds all right to me." "Now, how will you mount her?" the woman asks. "Well," he replies, "I'll just throw one leg over first and kind of sneak the other one over." "That's the stuff," she answers. Unlike *Bull Fight*, in which the woman is never let in on the joke, this record ends with the woman catching on to the man's real intentions and scolding him.[13]

Several conclusions can be drawn about the "Woman Is Out" dynamic, in my experience the most common type of blue disc. Framing the dialogue this way encourages the presumably male audience to identify and collude with the male protagonist. The woman participates in the obscene dialogue and situation, but without taking responsibility for the erotic dimension of the proceedings. She is allowed to stay "pure," uninvolved in the sexual insinuations. Despite the fact that she is speaking, the woman also becomes a kind of passive verbal spectacle: she is saying things without understanding them, functioning as a straight man.

Compare this dynamic to Freud's suggestion that the "smutty joke" is "directed toward a certain person who excites one sexually, and who becomes cognizant of the speaker's excitement by listening to the smutty joke, and thereby in turn becomes sexually excited." For Freud, the smutty joke was "like the denudation of a person of the opposite sex toward whom the joke is directed," in that "through the utterance of obscene words the person attacked is forced to picture the parts of the body in question, or the sexual act, and is shown that the aggressor pictures the same thing" (1916, 139–41).

The introduction to the *Uncle Tom's Cabin* record suggests a mixed-gender context in which listening to blue discs might have served to "denude" female listeners. But one might—following Freud—expect the female character in the narrative world of blue discs to be more clearly aroused, angered, or embarrassed, and so provide a pleasure akin to "denudation." In contrast to this, the woman in this prevalent type of blue disc is typically not aroused or ashamed, but instead is kept oblivious and out of the loop. Returning to Robert Allen's descriptions of the later burlesque tradition, recall that the women onstage had become mute visual spectacles and objects of the verbal joking of male burlesque comics. A similar dynamic exists on these types of blue discs. There are no "unruly women" in the tradition of Mae West, and the female performer's involvement is titillating without being threatening. The prevalence of this dynamic may reflect a context of homosocial listening by a Depression-era male community, the masculinity of whose members was particularly threatened.[14]

Man Is Out

Constance Penley has noted that, in terms of the humor found in American stag films like *On the Beach* (a.k.a. *Getting His Goat*), "the joke is usually on the man" (1977, 95). I have found only a few instances of blue discs featuring a man who is out of the erotic frame. *Candid Camera* (Party Record) begins with the reading of a letter: "Hmm. Looks like a government letter. Dear madam, as you perhaps know, the government, under code number 6842 for the propagation of the race, has made it mandatory for all married couples to produce children before the termination of their fifth married year. Our Mr. Socket will call on you, and explain our method, and render such assistance as you may need in complying with the code." This institutional key depersonalizes the situation that follows, and it also takes the woman off the hook to a certain degree—though she might have erotic thoughts, they are brought about by her obediently following (male) government orders.

Still, despite the way the letter reduces the agency of the female performer, she is still operating in the erotic frame while the man is out of it. "Good morning, Mrs. Haywire," says a man at the door. "I see by the paper that you've just celebrated your fifth wedding anniversary. Any children?" "I'm afraid you've come to the right house," she answers, "and I'm ready to listen and act according to your instructions." "Very well," he says, "we might as well get busy. You see, we have the thing reduced to a veritable science. I should recommend at least two in the bathtub, one or two on the couch, and a couple on the floor." "Good heavens!" she answers. "Well," he replies, "you want your child natural don't you?"

One aspect of Mrs. Haywire's performance that is notable by its absence is vocal inflection. As we shall see in part 2, vocal inflection became an important part of modern vocal styles, particularly after the introduction of radio microphones that could capture subtleties of vocal tone. By contrast, Mrs. Haywire, like many of the female performers on these discs, recites her lines in a rather rote and monotonic way. A comparison can be made to another erotically charged female performer of the time: Mae West. Matthew Murray describes the outcry over West's 1937 appearance on the *Chase and Sanborn Hour*. During the final rehearsal for the show, West recited her lines straight, but during the broadcast she added her own prosodic insinuations, which, according to some, "added plenty." After West's guest spot on the *Chase and Sanborn Hour*, NBC issued numerous public statements that, like this one, reveal the difficulty of policing inflection: "It is a well-known fact that it is well-nigh impossible to detect in a written script, words or phrases, which written innocently enough, may be subject by innuendo and intonation to interpretation other than meanings which the words were intended to convey" (Murray 1997, 117–18).

West's vocal inflections on innocuous lines provoked outcry and controversy, which demonstrates the importance of vocal inflection to key the erotic frame. West came from a stage tradition in which banal words could, via vocal inflection and gestural cues, be made suggestive.[15] This is certainly part of West's film performances as well. Take, for example, a scene from *She Done Him Wrong* (1933). When Lady Lou (West) is introduced to Serge Stanieff (Gilbert Roland), she purrs, "And you, mister . . ." while lasciviously looking him up and down. She climbs the stairs to her room, looks down at him from the balcony, and drawls a sensuous "mmm" while rolling her eyes. As was true of her radio appearance, it is her suggestive play with vocal inflection even more than wordplay that packs a wallop. Though West was known for her many suggestive quips and double entendres ("when women go wrong, men go right after them"), it's notable that in verbal encounters like the one just described, she essentially inverts the late burlesque stage model of speaking man and mute woman. Although the men with whom she flirts are clearly in on the erotic framing of her insinuations, they say very little.

Elaborate inflection and extraverbal display like West's rolled eyes and suggestive saunter are important ways in which the erotic can be keyed, neither of which is present on these discs. While the phonographic performance obviously eliminates gestures, it lends itself to the capturing and reproduction of the subtleties of inflection. It is notable, then, that this dimension of performance is minimized on blue discs. This kind of female display allows the performer a level of transgressive power, as can be seen in the case of West, who Pamela Robertson Wojcik argues was both a "sex object and a sexual subject," capable both of provoking desire and of transgressing "the bounds of that desire" (2004, 34). The absence of such a style on blue discs suggests that it might have been too threatening to the predominantly male audience. On the blue disc *Candid Camera,* the "official key" of the letter helps to justify the reduction of adventurousness in terms of vocal inflection. Female desire is presented, but it is blunted by the frame of the letter: she's just following orders.

Ramona Curry points out that Mae West's performances of innuendo-laden song lyrics in the "dirty blues" tradition associated her with performers such as Ma Rainey and Bessie Smith, and so with "the unrestrained sexual behavior that racist U.S. society attributes to lower-class African Americans" (1996, 2, 12). Blue discs perpetuated the association between unabashed female desire and race since they feature female African American characters who are aware of the erotic dimensions of the proceedings. Consider *What a Kitty,* in which a man begs a woman to let him "look at it." "I ain't showing my pussy to every man what comes along," she replies in a caricatured African American dialect. "Maybe you ain't, but, honey, half the boys in Harlem have seen it," he answers. When it becomes clear that the man is asking to see a cat, the woman becomes enraged and sends him away: "If you're so dumb you thought I was talking about cats, then you ain't the man I want in my bedroom. Go on, get outta here!" A similar dynamic can be heard on a record called *Dandy Dan.* "Now come on, honey," says a man in an exaggerated black dialect, "sit down beside me here on this sofa. That's it, that's it. Now, we sittin' here like this, honey. You reaches over and takes a good hold of the joystick." A woman replies, "I've gotta take hold of that thing!" "Yes, honey," says the man, "After you get the feel of it, then we'll start the upside down business." "Upside down!" the woman replies. "Man, you is different." The man eventually reveals that he has been talking about airplane lessons, to which the woman responds, "And all the time I thought you were talkin' about something else!"

Such representations of lascivious African American women are, of course, the product of centuries of institutionalized racism. Eugene Genovese has argued that the African slaves brought to America did not share "guilt-stricken white sexual attitudes," a fact that whites often perceived as "proof of the immorality of the slaves, especially the slave women" (1976, 459, 461). What is more, Genvoese asserts that white men denigrated black women in large part to "excuse their own impudent trifling with them" (462). Winthrop Jordan agrees that the trope of the hypersexual black woman functioned as "the best possible justification" for white men's own desires: "Not only did the Negro woman's warmth constitute a logical explanation for the white man's infidelity, but, much more important, it helped shift responsibility from himself to her. If she was *that* lascivious—well, a man could scarcely be blamed for succumbing against overwhelming odds" (1968, 151). Robert Staples connects the sexual exploitation of black women by white men to the "double standard" that allowed "premarital and extramarital expression for men and denied it to women." Thus, Staples argues that "the sexual subjugation" of black women by white men functioned to maintain the sexual "purity" of white women (1967, 8). Blue discs depict that tradition of racist exploitation by overplaying the sexual desires of African American women while mitigating or concealing those of white women. The black women depicted on blue discs are thus paradoxically allowed a certain circumscribed agency that their white counterparts are denied, albeit an agency that reinforces troubling stereotypes.

Man and Woman Are Both In

On the record *He Put the Dix in Dixie* (Party Platters), the male and female interactants exchange one-liners and obscene riddles, and they are both clearly in on the erotic frame. A very rudimentary narrative quickly dissolves into back and forth double entendre–laden dialogue. Noting the relative equality of their position vis-à-vis the erotic frame, it is interesting that this performance leads to conflict between the two and to the foregrounding of gender issues. "Didn't your father and mother get along?" she asks. "No," he answers, "they fought all the time." "By the way," she proceeds, "who was your father?" "That's what they fought about," he says. "So that makes you a woman hater, huh?" she asks. "Well," he says, "you can't get along with 'em." "You can't get along without 'em, you mean," she replies. She continues, "Say, if it wasn't for we women, where would you men be?" He answers, "In the Garden of Eden, playing Ping-Pong with a female monkey." "Oh, yeah," she says, "well if it wasn't for we women, who'd sew the buttons on your pants?" "If it wasn't for you women," he says, "us men wouldn't need any pants." "Is that so?" she asks. "Suppose there wasn't a woman on this Earth, then what would you men do?" The record ends with his response, which is to sing, "Oh, the sheep's in the meadow, the cow's in the corn," as he walks away from the mike.

Although the man gets the last word and the woman is still essentially acting as a straight man, the eruption of conflict points to the risk of giving the woman an equal footing in the erotic frame, where she might become unruly or threatening. Recall Allen's description of the later years of the burlesque stage, which featured the mute female visual spectacle, addressed by a talking man. In contrast, here we find a dynamic in which both man and woman speak and are in the same information state. The woman is allowed to be in the erotic key without becoming a spectacle. The potential power of the speaking female figure is enacted here in the record's denouement: the man retreats offstage, his joke reflecting defeat as much as sarcasm.

Compare this dynamic with the double entendre–laden dialogue found in some film noirs of the 1940s. Take, for example, the horse-racing banter between Lauren Bacall and Humphrey Bogart, portraying Vivian Sternwood and Philip Marlowe, in the 1946 film *The Big Sleep*. The exchange is reminiscent of the record *Just Another Mount,* described above.

> *Vivian Sternwood:* Well, speaking of horses, I like to play them myself, but I like to see them work out a little first, see if they're front-runners or come-from-behind, find out what their whole kind is, what makes them run.
>
> *Philip Marlowe:* Find out mine?
>
> *Sternwood:* I think so.
>
> *Marlowe:* Go ahead.
>
> *Sternwood:* I'd say you don't like to be rated, you like to get out in front, open up a lead, take a little breather in the back stretch and then come home free.
>
> *Marlowe:* You don't like to be rated yourself.
>
> *Sternwood:* I haven't met anyone yet who can do it. Any suggestions?
>
> *Marlowe:* Well, I can't tell until I've seen you over a distance of ground. You've got a touch of class, but I'm not sure how far you can go.
>
> *Sternwood:* A lot depends on who's in the saddle.

While Bacall's deep, husky voice helps make her a spectacle, it is notable that she is clearly in the erotic frame with the male noir protagonist.[16] On *He Put the Dix in Dixie,* this frame equality led to tensions between the male and female participants and the eventual retreat of the man. Many writers have noted how the "sexual woman," or femme fatale of film noir, has a certain power that is typically presented as a danger to the male character (Place 1998, 43). Though the power and danger of the femme fatale have often been described in terms of the visual image of the woman, or her effect on the narrative, when these performances are seen in the context of those heard on blue discs, part of the threat of the femme fatale can be seen to be her equal engagement with men in these verbal erotic performances.

Man and Woman Are Both Out

On some recordings, the man and woman are *both* out of the erotic frame. Here there is no specific sense of audience collusion with a particular character. On *The First Night* (Off the Record), we hear a situation that is not clearly keyed for the audience, which forces us to infer the situation. A man's voice says, "Aw, come on, let's try it once more." "No," replies a woman, "I'm tired, and besides it's too big, you'll never get it in." "But we've got to get it in," the man says. "You want to enjoy your honeymoon, don't ya?" "Say," she says, "maybe if I sit on it, it'd be easier." Excited, the man answers, "Hey, let's try it that way, it might work swell!" Like the hearer of the pretended-obscene riddle, the audience infers an obscene situation: that the couple is engaged in sexual intercourse. It is only in the last few seconds of the recording that we are let in on the real situation: "Boy, we've got enough in that steamer trunk to fill a moving van." This gag relies on the sound-only nature of the record, and so it is one of the most "phonographic" of blue discs. While it borrows jokes and riddles that easily could have been performed on the burlesque stage, it is particularly well suited to the phonograph recording.

Some recordings of dialogues of this sort include a third party in the narrative who eavesdrops on the scene. For example, a record called *The Bell Boy* presents the same conversation heard in *The First Night*, but it is framed as being overheard by a hotel bellboy. The record begins with the bellboy's direct address to the listener: "You know, being a bellboy in a hotel is a mighty interesting job sometimes. Last night, for instance, I was walking down the hall on the sixth floor when I heard a man and a woman talking in one of the rooms. The transom was open so, well, naturally, I stopped to listen for a minute. Of course I didn't know it at the time, but they were just starting to pack a suitcase. Here's what I heard . . ." The bellboy addresses the listener again at the end of the record, when he can no longer contain his curiosity and exclaims, "This, I've gotta see!" Also consider another blue disc called *The Lower Berth*, which opens with a newlywed couple discussing the fact that they must share their train berth with the wife's Pekinese dog. The husband complains that they'll have to keep the dog out of sight, and when they see the porter coming, they quickly jump in their berth and close the curtains. "Boy, oh, boy," says the porter in an African American stage dialect, "that couple was sure in a powerful hurry to get into that berth. Oh, well, they look like honeymooners so I can't blame 'em. Think I'll tiptoe up and listen to 'em." For the rest of the record the couple talk about the wife's dog, which the porter misinterprets to be a discussion of her genitals. "It wants to play when it looks up at you and wiggles like that," says the wife. "Hot damn!" the porter exclaims. "Reminds me of my own honeymoon!" Like *The Bell Boy,* the record ends when the porter becomes so aroused and curious that he is compelled to get a look at the scene on which he has been eavesdropping: "Hot damn, this I got to see!"

The inclusion of the third party eavesdropper makes these records resemble the Freudian primal scene, wherein a child first encounters his parents' lovemaking. Elisabeth Weis notes that though Freud initially described the primal scene in visual terms, he came to emphasize the importance of children's *overhearing* their parents make love: a "violent-sounding business" onto which they "projected their own fantasies" (1999, 82). Blue discs on which the man and the woman are both out of the sexual frame recast that primal experience of eavesdropping in comic terms: a listener overhears a heterosexual couple and imagines the "worst," only to discover a mundane, nonsexual explanation. On *The First Night,* which lacks a third character in the narrative, the listener has a direct experience of the confusion and titillation of misunderstanding the couple's exchange. The presence of the third party on *The Bell Boy* and *The Lower Berth* serves to blunt the raw sense of eavesdropping by framing the suggestive dialogue as part of a larger narrative scene. Instead of engaging in a reenactment of primal eavesdropping, we are cued to laugh at the bellboy or porter for foolishly misconstruing the dialogue we have been told is innocent. Thus, the eavesdroppers function as scapegoats, and so it is not surprising that they are socially marginal figures: an adolescent, working-class bellboy and a black porter.[17] Note, however, how the white bellboy colludes directly with the audience ("You know, being a bellboy in a hotel is a mighty interesting job sometimes . . ."). By contrast, the black porter's words are not clearly directed to the audience, and what is more, the record begins with the couple's perspective. As a result, it is harder for the listener to identify with the eavesdropping porter, and thus he becomes a more laughable figure.

Weis asserts that the presence of "intermediary diegetic eavesdroppers" in some film narratives serves to mitigate guilt about listening in on private activity (1999, 94). Similarly, the presence of the bellboy or porter allows listeners to distance themselves from their participation in the erotic proceedings. In fact, issues of risk in the performance of erotic material emerge as an important factor in shaping the content of blue discs. We have seen that blue discs typically use a verbal technique akin to the pretended-obscene riddle to present erotic ideas and situations. Those verbal forms were originally performed in the face-to-face contexts of the burlesque stage and riddle telling, where risk in performance is high. Kwesi Yankah writes that "the simultaneity of performance and evaluation" in such co-present forms makes them "a voluntary exercise in risk-taking" (1985, 135). The consideration of dynamics of risk in performance can help explain some aspects of their form. There is heightened risk involved in the performance of erotic or obscene material. The performer could potentially offend the audience, or even, as in the case of the burlesque stage, be held criminally responsible. Hence, humor plays an important function, in that it minimizes the risks in performance. The risk-reducing function of humor was addressed by Freud: "The obscenity . . . is tolerated only if it is witty" (1916, 145–46). Waln Brown writes that the pretended-obscene riddle "has an inherent cleverness that differentiates it from blatantly obscene folklore forms" (1973, 91). Also, the dual level of the pretended-obscene joke means that the obscenity is always inferred by the listener, and so it can potentially be denied by the performer. The author of the obscenity is arguably the audience, not the performer.

In the context of modern sound media like phonograph recordings, the performer is separated from the audience in time and place, often anonymous and so unaccountable, which makes an erotic performance less risky. Verbal forms like the riddling described above offer a level of safety unneeded in the new context of the anonymous phonograph performance. But these are more than just residual oral forms, and they work in interesting ways in the recorded context. Because they invite a high level of audience participation, they make the experience of the recording more immediate, creating a dynamic similar to the function of laughter described in chapter 1. Similarly, Hullum (1972–73, 56) describes how the pretended-obscene riddle "may be interpreted as a threat to face" and so can lead to what Goffman calls "interchange": a sequence of acts set in motion "by an acknowledged threat to face and terminating in the re-establishment of ritual equilibrium." This makes a prerecorded performance take on aspects of the face-to-face: it seems more interactive, ritualized, participatory, and, not coincidentally, erotic.

HARD-CORE SOUND

If aspects of the pretended-obscene riddle are more apt in face-to-face or stage contexts, there is another kind of performance found on blue discs that takes fuller advantage of the phonographic context. This can be compared to Williams's mode of visual pleasure in film pornography that is distinguished by identification with a "surrogate male" and a further organization of screen elements into narrative events. This mode, which Williams associates with the hard-core feature film, seeks to prove that not only penetration, but also satisfaction, has taken place.

Sound plays an important role in this project by seeming to authenticate the pleasure of the female performers: female voices serve as "aural fetishes of the female pleasure we cannot see" (Williams 1989, 123). This is a type of verbal performance that Rich Cante and Angelo Restivo call porno-performativity (2001, 221). The apparent spontaneity of the female performer's moans and sighs is particularly important in the pornographic quest to represent the female desires and pleasures that come from "deep inside." Using the terminology of Dell Hymes, porno-performativity seeks to present a "breakthrough out of performance." For Hymes, performance is an "emergent," "unfolding or arising" mode of communication that occurs within a specific context. He examines moments in anthropological fieldwork when modes like the "report" break through into full-fledged performance (1975, 13, 24). I want to read this dynamic the other way around and see porno-performativity as a mode that attempts to enact a breakthrough *out* of performance, thereby offering a tantalizing suggestion of the uncontrolled, authentic, and spontaneous "real" expression, via traces of the body in spasm.[18] Though becoming the central component of the sound in porn films, this kind of dynamic can be found on only a few of the blue discs I've heard, one of which is called *Silent George*.[19]

The record begins by being keyed as a public performance: the listener is addressed as one of a group. "Hey, folks, gather around. Here's a pip of a story about a man known to his many girlfriends as Silent George. Now, the time is midnight, and Mary Jones, a beautiful young girl, is in her bedroom asleep."[20] The speaker's vocal inflection makes this keying somewhat ambiguous, since he delivers the lines in a half whisper that suggests an intimate conversational aside and so goes against the grain of his group address ("Hey, folks"). There is a knock on the door. Mary whispers, "Oh, my goodness, a burglar. But it might be, gosh, I hope it isn't who I think it is." More knocks, and then the door opens. "George,

what on earth!" Mary exclaims. "What are you doing out here? You
know how Daddy feels about us keeping late hours. No, George, you
cannot come in this time of night."

For the rest of the record, we are encouraged to identify with George,
who lives up to his moniker, remaining utterly silent throughout the proceedings. George's actions are revealed through Mary's half-whispered
statements: he comes in, takes off his coat, sits on the bed, takes off his
shoes, and gets under the covers. Throughout all of this, Mary has been
protesting and threatening to call her "Daddy" ("Daddy might come
in!"). George becomes more aggressive, kissing her breast, fondling her
("no, please don't put your hand down there on me"), and Mary's
protests become more desperate: "George, you're forcing me, why do
you have to be so rough?" As the record builds to its climax, Mary cries
out. These cries ("Daddy, Daddy, oh, Daddy") become moans of ecstasy,
and the record ends with a throwaway punch line ("George, I'll give you
just four hours to take that big thing out of me").

This record, with its talking woman and mute man, presents a strange
inversion of the late burlesque stage. On *He Put the Dix in Dixie,* on
which both man and woman had been in on the erotic key, the woman
spoke but avoided becoming a spectacle. On *Silent George,* only the
woman speaks, and her performance becomes a kind of striptease, a verbal spectacle. Vocal inflection is limited by the whispered nature of
Mary's speech, but in the porno-performativity at the end of the record,
inflection takes center stage, suggesting a tantalizing breakthrough out
of performance to the spontaneous expression of sexual pleasure. This
is not the leering prosodic play of Mae West, though, and on the level of
narrative, Mary is certainly not in control of the situation.

The duration and intensity of Mary's performance overwhelm the
punch line she throws away at the end of the record. Humor is mobilized
to legitimate this performance, but it works much differently from the
way it does on other blue discs. Humor is clearly not the main object of
pleasure here; it is Mary's breathless moans and the listener's voyeuristic identification with George. The lack of humor on this record recalls
the distinction made by Penley between the stag film and the hard-core
feature film: "As porn films 'progressed' as film, technically and narra-
tively, and began to focus on the woman and her subjectivity, they became more socially conservative as they lost the bawdy populist humor
whose subject matter was so often the follies and foibles of masculinity"
(1997, 101). Additionally, the empty, silent space of identification with
George becomes unsettling and vaguely sinister, and it doesn't quite

work: the opening key to the group audience ("Hey, folks, gather around") is in tension with the rest of the record, where Mary addresses the listener as an individual.

Silent George suggests a modern mode of verbal performance of the erotic similar to the hard-core feature, in which narrative and identification with a "surrogate male" figure are key elements. It suggests this mode of performance without fully embodying it: it vacillates between addressing a group and an individual, and it employs both humor and porno-performativity without much success on either front. This record's use of porno-performativity makes it arguably more phonographic than other blue discs, since that mode takes advantage of the anonymity and the resulting reduction of risk inherent in a prerecorded performance.[21] The fact that it is a female performance that dominates this record suggests that it is important to consider it in terms of scholarly writings on gender and the voice.

Kaja Silverman has argued that the female voice "functions as a fetish within dominant cinema." The male voice in film tends to be situated "in a position of apparent proximity to the cinematic apparatus" via nondiegetic narration and reveals a certain aspiration "to invisibility and anonymity." By contrast, the female voice is isolated from "all productivity," becoming identified with "spectacle and the body": "At its most crudely dichotomous, Hollywood pits the disembodied male voice against the synchronized female voice" (1988, 38). Lawrence analyzes specific performances by Ingrid Bergman and Rita Hayworth in which the woman's voice becomes an "audio-fetish": "Rather than the woman *using* her voice to communicate, the voice communicates the body as *object*, bypassing any attempts at female subjectivity or female control of signification" (1991, 149).

Silent George certainly embodies some of these dynamics: the mute male who becomes associated with the recording apparatus, and the spectacle of the woman's voice communicating her objectified body. But at the same time, Mary is the narrator—the sole disembodied speaker on the record, who literally constructs the narrative world. She is using her voice in a particularly structuring way at the same time that her voice becomes an audio-fetish. This record, then, and the medium of the recorded blue disc more generally, seems to fall outside some of the ways that woman's voice has been categorized in film theory, since it embodies both narrative pleasure and spectacle, and it is both disembodied and objectified. As such, blue discs underscore Constance Penley's call to study film pornography as popular culture.

As we have seen, female voices are central to many of the performances heard on blue discs, representing varying degrees of agency and objectification. These records seem to restate what Allen's history of the burlesque stage has shown: that there is transgressive power in a female performance that combines the verbal and the erotic, a power that, for the sake of the male audience, is actively policed. On the level of performance, *Silent George* indicates the emerging importance of the female voice flooding out in media representations of erotic material. Of course, the capture and dissemination of all of the subtleties of the ecstatic voice required technologies such as the microphone, a topic to which I will turn in the following two chapters.

A Finer Grain of the Voice

CHAPTER 3

The Nearness of You;
or, The Voice of Melodrama

In David Lynch's 2001 film *Mulholland Dr.*, we are shown the same lines of dialogue performed twice. The first time, Betty Elms (Naomi Watts) rehearses lines for a film audition with the amnesiac Rita (Laura Elena Harring), who has mysteriously appeared in her apartment. Betty speaks the lines loudly, with furious emotion. We are signaled that this is to be taken as a hack job, since she herself cracks up in self-deprecating laughter, joking about how she must say the lines "I hate you, I hate us both" with "big emotion." Later, at the actual audition, Betty gives a much different performance. As Betty whispers her lines in her costar's ear, her voice quavers with a complex emotional subtext: she seems to be sexually aroused and filled with guilt and self-loathing, all at the same time. She says, "I hate you," but her tone suggests otherwise. Again, Lynch telegraphs the way in which this performance should be read: the audience in the film applauds open-mouthed, clearly impressed with Betty's approach.

The point behind these contrasting performances seems clear: the first time through we're seeing a relatively ostensive, one-dimensional style, whereas the second time we see a low-key style with an undercurrent of conflicting emotions. Before the scene begins, Betty's costar, a lecherous older man, tells her to play the scene "nice and close, just like in the movies." But when we try to describe the differences between these two contrasting performances, the familiar dichotomy between "film acting" and "stage acting" seems too restrictive. During her re-

81

hearsal, Betty is framed in medium shot and the dialog is rendered with shot / reverse shot editing. The audition is a long take framed in close-up. But the major difference between the two scenes has more to do with the microphone than with the camera. While gesture is certainly a factor, the most important issue is the quality of Betty's voice: we move from a loud, ostentatious performance to a hushed, more emotionally ambiguous one.

Just as twentieth-century acting has been discussed in relation to the cinematic camera and the development of the close-up, we should consider acting in relation to the closely held microphone, which had an influence on acting just as it did on styles of popular singing and public speaking. In this chapter I investigate styles of vocal acting that developed in tandem with sound media technologies such as radio microphones. The use of the microphone and the formal particularities of radio drama are resonant areas of inquiry because the voice and techniques of vocal training have consistently been pivotal issues in moments of stylistic change in acting. Of course, neither the techniques of filmmaking nor the microphone existed in isolation, and my discussion of vocal style will be framed by considering historical shifts in acting that began before the influence of radio or the cinema.

This chapter continues my overarching concern with mapping out the development of modern styles of vocal performance. Where the two chapters in part 1 are concerned primarily with how modes of performance adapted to the ways in which recording separated performers from audiences in space and time, both this and the next chapter deal with the ability of sound technologies to capture and reproduce nuances of vocal performance that would not have been audible to a theater audience. The microphone's ability to faithfully capture and disperse subtleties of vocal timbre and inflection opened up the possibility of new forms of performance that exploited the increased semantic significance of those aspects of the voice. The term *timbre* refers to the specific quality or resonance of a sound, as determined by its pattern of harmonic overtones. Timbre is that aspect of a sound which tends to be described by what Roland Barthes has called the "poorest linguistic category: the adjective" (1985, 267). Thus, the aspect of the voice that Barthes so famously characterized as its "grain" is often described with words like "raspy," "clear," or "reedy." I use the term *inflection* to refer to the pitch and loudness of the voice.[1]

I do not want to argue that the microphone had a monolithic effect, or that there is a single mode of vocal performance that can be identified as being the "microphonic" style. The microphone, like any technology, did not dictate any single style. But though it is important to recognize that many cultural factors shape how a technology will be used, it is clear that new media technologies intervene in existing social structures and so can alter, at least temporarily, some of the hierarchies of a given cultural field. In other words, I am taking what Ruth Finnegan calls the "weak view" of the influence of communication technologies: one that considers such technology to be "merely an enabling factor creating certain opportunities, or merely one cause among several," as opposed to a "strong view" that understands communication technology as "the single determining cause of a social development" (1988, 38). Finnegan argues that the weak view accords better with empirical evidence and benefits from the assumption that technology itself does not "give rise to social consequences," since it must be "used by people and developed through social institutions" (41). In terms of performance, my analysis will illustrate how microphone technology provided an outlet for certain styles that might not have been able to gain access to the cultural stage. Other factors such as genre conventions and ideologies of gender were equally important in determining the ways in which those styles were understood by performers and audiences. I begin with brief discussions of popular singing and political oratory—two forms about which there has been the most discussion of the effect of the microphone on performance style.

WHISPERING

Historical studies of the singing styles of the twentieth century have paid considerable attention to the transition from acoustic to electric recording that occurred in the 1920s. The use of the microphone provides what seems to be a clear instance of a new technology's influence on performance style. The prevailing wisdom is well summed up by Michael Jarrett and Simon Frith:

> In the mid-1920s, advances in electronic amplification transformed singing in a manner analogous to cinema's earlier transformation of acting. Just as the movie camera (and, specifically, the discovery of the close-up) eliminated the need for the broad gestures of stage performance, microphones and loudspeakers eliminated the need to project the voice as in classical singing. A wink could be seen on screen, a whisper could be heard on radio, by millions of people. (Jarrett 1998, 207)

> The microphone made it possible for singers to make musical sounds—soft
> sounds, close sounds—that had not really been heard before in terms of
> public performance (just as the film close-up allowed one to see the bodies
> and faces of strangers in ways one would normally only see loved ones).
> The microphone allowed us to hear people in ways that normally implied
> intimacy—the whisper, the caress, the murmur. (Frith 1996, 187)

During the era of acoustic recording, performers in the studio had to
sing into a horn and etch their voices into wax with the sheer force of
volume. Once the recording studio was electrified, a closely held microphone could capture more frequencies and quiet subtleties of performance, what Steven Connor calls the "individuating accidents of intonation and timbre": "The microphone makes audible and expressive a
whole range of organic vocal sounds which are edited out in ordinary listening; the liquidity of the saliva, the hissings and tiny shudders of the
breath, the clicking of the tongue and teeth, and popping of the lips"
(2000, 38). Where before there were Al Jolson and Enrico Caruso, belt-
ing it out to the back rows of full concert or vaudeville halls, now there
were crooners like "Whispering" Jack Smith and Rudy Vallee, with their
hushed, emotional intensity.

Allison McCracken has described how Vallee in particular came to define the crooner image and made "the term *crooning* a household word
in 1929" (2001, 105). Not coincidentally, he was also the first "singing
heartthrob," and like Rudolph Valentino, Vallee had female fans who
were credited with rocketing him to stardom (105). McCracken argues
that crooning's appeal to the female audience in particular was due
largely to the sense of intimacy and vulnerability presented by the singer:
"What is most sexually suggestive and characteristic of crooning songs
is that the crooner can't quite reach the higher notes; the effort is almost
too much for them and they seem constantly on the verge of expiring"
(114). While male crooners were wildly popular, especially with female
audiences, they were also a cause of concern for some, since they did not
perform in a traditionally masculine manner. Male singing at that time
tended to be framed as a form of exercise, a fact illustrated by John Philip
Sousa's famous jeremiad against the "menace of mechanical music":
"Singing will no longer be a fine accomplishment; vocal exercises, so important a factor in the curriculum of physical culture, will be out of
vogue! Then what of the national throat? Will it not weaken? What of
the national chest? Will it not shrink?" (1906, 281). Crooners such as
Vallee were Sousa's worst nightmare: male singers whose voices relied on
media technology rather than strength and technical mastery. "At a time

when a white man's masculinity was defined by his physical vigor and muscularity, radio offered a disturbingly disembodied, artificially amplified male presence, one that competed with traditional patriarchal authority for the attention of the family" (McCracken 2001, 107). McCracken argues that anxieties about crooners were "contained" by the traditionally masculine star persona of Bing Crosby, whose vocal style differed from previous radio singers in that it was more jazz-inflected, lower in pitch, less emotionally intense, and seemingly required a greater degree of effort (119–20).

The sense of an intimate connection between crooner and listener was aided by developments on the decoding as well as the encoding end of the electronic media circuit. Although the microphone could capture and amplify vocal nuance, performances were broadcast to a radically new kind of listening audience: one at home, often alone or in small groups, and often close to the speaker, where the quiet style of the crooners could feel particularly direct. We have seen that the laugh track functioned in such a context of reception to simulate the social spaces of performance. Crooning addressed the problem of the broadcast audience by suggesting another type of space: the proximity of face-to-face interaction. In fact, Connor offers "the voice of seduction" as an example of a "vocalic space," a term for the "ways in which the voice is held both to operate in, and itself to articulate, different conceptions of space" (2000, 12). For Connor the crooning voice produces a seductive effect because "it appears to be at our ear, standing forward and apart from the orchestral background with which it is nevertheless integrated" (38). Both the hearable audience and the crooning voice, then, create a sense of immediacy in broadcast entertainment: the former achieves this by framing the listener's living room as a concert hall, and the latter takes the performer out of the concert hall and into the living room.

Another way to explain this distinction is by reference to Patrick Feaster's notion of a "descriptive" or "substitutive" mode in early phonograph records. Feaster argues that the descriptive mode is concerned with depicting "an event as it might be passively overheard," and the substitutive seeks to "replace an event as its functional equivalent, inviting an identical response from its listeners" (2006a, 369). For example, after making a painstaking survey of dance records released during the early decades of the phonograph industry, Feaster observes an "industry-wide shift in representational strategy" from the descriptive to the substitutive mode. That is, the earliest dance records depict the scene of a social dance, complete with comic interaction between fictional dancers, whereas records made after the turn of the century—when phonographs could be played back at higher volumes—were often intended to accompany the actual dancing of home listeners. Using Feaster's terms, we can consider the hearable audience as a technique for keying the descriptive mode, while the crooning voice keys the substitutive. What is certain is that the crooning style of Vallee and others like him was well matched to the technological and cultural contexts of radio.

CHATTING

The intimacy made possible by radio has also been discussed in terms of radio announcing and political speaking. A December 6, 1942, *New York Times* article by John Hutchens, "The Secret of a Good Radio Voice," describes how radio overturned received wisdom about public speaking:

> Many good radio voices are not agreeable. Many agreeable speaking voices are ineffective on the air. . . . Brassy, hoarse voices that would cause their owners summary ejection from schools of speech are balm to a sports fan, replete as they are with excitement and drama. Liquid tones that would melt the collective heart of a matinee audience have been known to sound merely empty and monotonous after being poured into the sensitive microphone. And voices which were "wrong" in every respect—pitch, tone, diction, emphasis—have been powerfully stirring on the air, given the proper circumstances. (1942b, SM26)

These comments reveal how radio was thought to be shaping a new paradigm where the old rules of oratory no longer held sway. According to Hutchens, what mattered most on radio was not "old-time pyrotechnics," but conveying a "conversational approach" and exuding subtle qualities like spontaneity, naturalness, and, above all, "personality": "Rough or smooth, high or low, a good radio voice must have personality, with all the intangibles and seeming contradictions the word implies." The good radio voice was achieved not by following standardized rules but through cultivating a highly idiosyncratic and individual style: "At its best, [the radio voice] is really distinctive to the point where you would recognize it if you had not heard it for months or even years" (SM26).

In his 1939 book on radio advertising, Warren Dygert describes the findings of the Radio Voice Technique Committee, which was formed in 1925 at the request of RCA and New York University to determine the characteristics of the perfect radio announcer. The committee came to a number of conclusions about such questions as rate of speech, breathing, the use of dialect, and vocal pitch. The issue that was found to be most important of all, however, was "voice personality," what Dygert called "that telepathic power of thought transference which assures the announcer's immediate acceptance by the listening audience. The 'voice with a smile' the telephone company calls it. And it is voice personality today that makes the successful announcer, radio artist, or news commentator" (1939, 56). Dygert made the connection between radio "personality" and the spaces of radio reception explicit: "The forensic presentation of the lecture platform is ludicrous in the front parlor. Adopt the conversational tone of the personal interview. It can be dignified, chatty, even whimsical, but it must be keyed to a 12- by 20-ft. room, to the family in the intimacy of its own home. . . . One cannot successfully use the sweating brow, red-of-face dynamic presentation of a great evangelist shouting before an audience of 2,000 people" (124–25). These sentiments are echoed in radio "how-to" books of this era, where the same words recur: naturalness, spontaneity, sincerity, and personality.[2]

In many of these texts, Franklin D. Roosevelt is held up as the model of the modern radio speaker. Hutchens writes that President Roosevelt is "the accepted master" of radio speaking. "Mr. Roosevelt long ago mastered . . . the problems peculiar to radio speaking. For, while radio is a mass medium, it is also intensely personal, and he developed his radio style accordingly, notably in the Fireside chat" (1942b, SM26). Orrin E. Dunlap, in his 1936 instructional guide, *Talking on the Radio,* quotes a "Washington announcer" who stated that FDR "does not make a speech; he just visits with the people." Roosevelt's vocal cords are described as "more sensitive, more susceptible to the influence of the man's emotions than the strings of a violin to the master's touch of the bow" (1936, 39). The radio microphone was perceived as encouraging a vocal performance that was, like crooning, distinguished by an idiosyncratic, intimate, conversational style.

The emphasis on "personality" in radio speaking can be seen in relation to larger cultural shifts that were taking place during the early twentieth century. The rise of the notion of the individual has frequently been associated with the era of modernity. In his summation of the scholarly work on the social consequences of modernity, Ben Singer points to a range of "ideological currents" that "converged to form a new conception of the centrality of the individual" (2001, 30–32). Singer writes that in the modern era, the subjectivity of individuals was no longer "predetermined by birth into a particular status, religion, or community, or by feudal obligations and ties to a particular parcel of land, by vocational ties to a family trade passed from generation to generation, by kinship customs or similar bonds seemingly preordained by divine will and immutable tradition" (30). The weakening of such ties and the increased mobility of the modern era stimulated an interest in vivid and unique individual subjectivities and histories.

Warren Susman has described this shift as a change from a culture of "character" to a culture of "personality." Where the culture of character had been noted by a concern with moral imperatives like citizenship, duty, democracy, and work, the culture of personality was concerned with strategies for distinguishing the individual in the modern crowd by making oneself fascinating, stunning, attractive, and magnetic (1984, 274–77). In his 1931 study of the radio voice, T. H. Pear made use of the same distinction between personality and character. Pear wrote that personality was "the effect upon others of a living being's appearance, behaviour, etc.; so far as they are interpreted as distinctive signs of that being," whereas character was "the comparatively stable structure of the mind, wrought by habits, sentiments, and by their integration into a relative unity" (1931, 37–39). The distinction is principally a temporal one; personality is considered a more fleeting presentation of self, one that was increasingly malleable owing to the growing influence of consumer culture. "In these days," Pear wrote, "deliberate, extensive alteration of the visible aspects of personality is not only allowed, but expected" (38). As modern fashions and cosmetics were allowing consumers to visibly express their individual personalities, Pear argued that modern media, such as the sound film and radio, were encouraging the cultivation of voice personality. Susman points to the role of cinema in the emergence of this culture of personality, referring to the importance of the close-up and stars such as Douglas Fairbanks. The intimate vocal performance style heard on the radio can also be understood as a crucial ingredient in this process because of the way in which it encouraged an idiosyncratic and individualized presentation of self.[3]

The crooning of Rudy Vallee and FDR's quiet, intimate Fireside Chats are well-known paradigms of the radio era. Both illustrate how a modern vocal performance was shaped by the contexts of radio production and reception. One way to describe this modern style and its connection to the sound media is to note that both crooning and the Fireside Chat are less formally marked off from everyday speech than their more boisterous predecessors. Richard Bauman defines performance as "a mode of spoken verbal communication" that consists "in the assumption of responsibility to an audience for a display of communicative competence" (1986, 11). Bauman describes how the performance frame must be keyed, a process by which the communicative situation is marked and defined (15). Performance is typically keyed by a variety of means, including specially coded language ("Once upon a time" keys an audience that a fairy tale will follow), repetition or rhyming structures, or "paralinguistic features" of the voice such as ritualized inflections or timbres (16–20). Spoken performances on the radio are already so clearly set off from the audience by the spatial and temporal dislocations of broadcasting that there would be less need to frame them from everyday speech. The development of these styles, then, is due not only to the reduced need for vocal projection in the radio studio, but also to how the dislocations of the sound media changed the parameters for establishing a performance frame.

If the radio microphone played an important role in shaping styles of popular singing and political speaking, what influence did it have on acting? Before considering performances found on radio broadcasts and sound films, I want first to address changes that were taking place in acting style on the nineteenth-century stage.

ACTING

Acting on the English and American stage before the late nineteenth century has frequently been described as featuring a "presentational" style of performance. Roberta Pearson refers to this tradition as the histrionic code of acting: "Until the second half of the nineteenth century, most English and American actors in most theatres performed in a self-consciously theatrical fashion, ostentatiously playing a role rather than pretending to be another person. Disdaining to mask technique in the modern fashion, actors proudly displayed their skills" (1992, 21). James Naremore has described how this pantomimic school of acting was popularized by teachers like François Delsarte, who described formulaic poses and gestures and their connection to specific expressive meanings (1988, 52). The pleasure of "good" acting in this tradition came less from "participating in an illusion" than from "witnessing a virtuoso performance" (Pearson 1992, 21).

As the actor's body was ostentatiously displayed in codified expressions, so too was the voice. Edmund Shaftesbury, one of Delsarte's American imitators, wrote the training manual *Lessons in Voice Culture* in 1891, which can serve as an example of voice training at this time. Much of the book is made up of practical exercises meant to strengthen the voice for speaking on the stage. To get a sense of the importance of vocal volume, consider that Shaftesbury offers nine principles of the voice in his introductory chapter and all but one of these have to do with the power of vocal delivery. Volume is described in terms such as intensity, richness, sustainability, force, strength, and growth. One of the exercises is for "Placing the Voice" and involves the following: "Go into a larger room, hall, church, theatre or field, and select objects at various distances away. Aim the voice at one of them, and mentally push each syllable toward the object. Then change the direction, and so continue until the voice has been sent to every object in the place" (1891, 119–20). As was true of singing and political oratory in the era before electronic amplification, the strength and projection of the voice were essential requirements for acting on the stage.

In his book *Lessons in the Art of Acting* (1889), Shaftesbury codified gesture and posture. Similarly, in *Lessons in Voice Culture* he charts out connections between specific attributes of the voice and their meanings on the stage. For example, Shaftesbury describes the nine "Degrees of Pitch" available to the voice, from "Extremely Low" to "Extremely High." For each he provides a corresponding "expressional meaning" and a quotation to be used to practice matching vocal pitch to that meaning. "Extremely Low" is matched with the meaning "Profound," and one should rehearse it by performing the line "Eternity! Thou pleasing, dreadful thought!" (1891, 60–61). Connections between voice and meaning are also made in terms of timbre. In a chart called "Timbres and their meanings," we are told that a "Bright" tone of voice relates to "Cheerfulness or Vitality," a "Pure" voice to "Beauty," and a "Gutteral" voice to "Hatred" (107–8).

Performances found on some phonograph recordings from the turn of the twentieth century provide examples of how a voice trained in this manner might have sounded. The use of codes of vocal performance such as those outlined by Shaftesbury can be heard on two recordings featuring Len Spencer, one of the most prolific phonograph artists in the 1890s and early1900s. A remarkably versatile performer, Spencer recorded comic skits and songs, as well as famous speeches and dramatic scenes (Tim Gracyk 2002, 314–19; William Howland Kenney 1999, 34). An example of that last category can be heard on a cylinder released in 1905 called *Transformation Scene from "Dr. Jekyll and Mr. Hyde"* (Columbia).[4] This recording illustrates how codified vocal timbre might have functioned in histrionic acting. Indeed, one suspects that this scene might have been chosen for recording because of the way in which it allows a performer to demonstrate a mastery of the "gutteral" and the "pure" vocal timbres.

The record begins with Spencer as Dr. Jekyll, his voice a deep, pure baritone, speaking the lines with a lilting, musical cadence: "I have ransacked London in vain, for the drug which has been the cause of all my misery. Soon I shall be transformed into the terrible creature that is within me. This, then, is the last time that Henry Jekyll can see his own face, or think his own thoughts." The crucial moment of this performance is the transformation into Hyde: "Ah, the fiend is coming, Hyde is here!" Spencer emits several short gasps and is vocally transformed into Hyde, whose voice is throaty and rough, higher in pitch, and more rapid in delivery than Jekyll's: "They come for me. They're going to take me to the gallows, but I don't die on the gallows! Holla! Holla Holla!" Spencer's performance suggests how vocal acting skill at this time was often equated with the virtuosic enactment of codified timbres and intonations that represented the essential moral qualities of a character.

A similar dynamic can be found on Spencer's *Flogging Scene from "Uncle Tom's Cabin"* (Edison 1904), which also features a stark contrast between a "pure" and "gutteral" vocal style. The record begins with Tom's low, rich voice slowly intoning, "I've come at last to the veil of shadows. My heart sinks and the tears roll from my poor old eyes." Spencer then quickly shifts to a high-pitched, raspy sneer for the cruel overseer, who tells Tom, "Quit that howlin'. So you've made up your mind to run away, huh?" For the rest of the record, Spencer alternates between these two characters and their starkly defined vocal styles. In both this and the scene from *Dr. Jekyll and Mr. Hyde,* the vocal performance of each character is steady and consistent: the patterns of the voice do not so much adapt themselves to the meaning of particular lines as represent the unwavering moral nature of the characters. One might even say that in some regards, the lines become superfluous, or, as Simon Frith has stated in regard to popular singing, the words function primarily as the "signs of a voice" (1981, 35). These dynamics of vocal performance have particularly important implications for the genre of melodrama, which I will address below. For now, these records can demonstrate the functional utility of vocal training courses like Shaftesbury's.

The histrionic code of acting as embodied here can seem stilted and mechanical when compared to modern notions of acting. Using a metaphor of "surface" and "depth" often mobilized in discussions of acting, the presentational style appears to be acting only on the "surface" or "outside." But in his 1891 book, Shaftesbury makes some striking comments about the voice that can reveal what was thought to be at stake in vocal training. Note, for example, how closely he describes the connection between the voice and identity:

> The true character or inner life of a person shows itself in the timbre that prevails in that person's voice. He who leads a gloomy, solemn life, will fall into the unconscious habit of using the dark form, and generally a low pitch. If this gloom is mingled with sorrow or suffering, the pitch is higher and there is a mixture of the laryngeal timbre in the voice. . . . A man or woman, whose life has more of happiness than of sorrow in it, will fall into an unconscious habit of using the bright form. . . . A person whose life has been devoted to an admiration of the beautiful in nature, in art, in life or in religion, will fall into an unconscious habit of using a peculiarly pleasant and agreeable tone. (1891, 108)

Here a direct connection is made between the psychological state of the character and the timbre of the voice. Shaftesbury goes further, arguing that the reverse is true as well. Offering a doctrine that "all timbres of the voice are reactive," he explains that "as the mode of life we lead develops in us a natural use of one or more timbres, so the development of a timbre, by an inverse process will create in us a feeling of the same nature as that which would have created the timbre. Thus a person who loves the beautiful will possess the pure timbre; and a person who establishes by artificial means a pure timbre will learn to love the beautiful things of life" (109). According to Shaftesbury, "This is an important principle. Its truth will do more to advance and develop the geniuses of the world than any other" (109). In more cynical terms, we might say that voice training of Shaftesbury's sort is equivalent to a kind of behavioral training intended to inculcate middle-class values. Nonetheless, these comments reveal some of the theoretical complexity of the "presentational" model of stage acting often disparaged as being a superficial approach to performance.

That actors of the presentational style of acting typified by Shaftesbury were closely identified with a display of their voices can be gauged by an acting manual published twenty-seven years after *Lessons in Voice Culture*: Louis Calvert's 1918 *Problems of the Actor*. Calvert describes a recent past when, "on the street, or in the club, or in the shop the finished thespian . . . was always the actor with the trained voice, he could not be mistaken" (1918, 47). Calvert refers to this type of acting to argue that it was in the process of being eclipsed by a more modern style. Vocal training was one of the primary ways in which a shift in the acting styles of the late nineteenth century was understood.

Janet Staiger notes a change from the presentational style to a "representational" one between the years 1865 and 1890. For Naremore, this was "a shift from semiotic to a psychological conception of performance" that occurred in the period between 1880 and 1920 (1988, 52). The new representational style of acting featured a "reserved force, few gestures," and "no posturing or raised voices" (Staiger 1985, 16).[5] Christine Gledhill concisely lays out some of the key factors in this transition:

> By the late nineteenth century . . . the rise of New Drama, with its more literary, analytical and naturalist bent and the influential rise of psychology and related disciplines, all of which catered to the tastes of a growing middle-class audience, define a shift in character construction and performance mode. Characters referred less to pre-existing types; their particularity strove for the illusion of random individuality. A new set of techniques based on psychology and observation from life, valued restraint, underplaying and subtlety and sought to displace what seemed now the limitations of pantomimic ritual and rhetorical dialogue in order to convey the inner life and private personality of the characters. (1991, 219)

The figurehead of this school of acting came to be Konstantin Stanislavsky, whose approaches to acting had significant influence in the 1920s.

The kind of vocal training outlined by Shaftesbury would have been inappropriate for the psychological drawing room dramas coming into vogue at this time. It is in light of these changes on the theatrical stage that Calvert points back to the unmistakably trained voice of the actor and suggests that "it is for us of the present to go further than they thought necessary. It is for us to learn all they knew of voice production, and correct intonation and inflection, but learn also how to make it all seem perfectly effortless and natural" (1918, 47). While continuing to advocate vocal training, Calvert's book contains numerous warnings about it: "We should not lose sight of the danger which frightens so many young actors away from the study of voice cultivation altogether: the danger of falling in love with our voice. Henry Irving once said, 'What a wonderful actor Wenman would be if he didn't know he'd got a voice'" (58). In conclusion, Calvert says that "if, when the audience is leaving the theater, the comments are mostly in praise of the star's voice, there has been something wrong with his performance" (59).[6]

Another record featuring Len Spencer can illustrate that the conventions of the stage voice were becoming outmoded by the early teens.

Some of Spencer's most famous work was done in conjunction with Ada Jones, one of the first female recording stars. In *The Crushed Tragedian* (Edison 1911) Spencer plays a pompous actor named Richard Chatterton who encounters a street-smart city girl played by Jones:

> *Spencer:* Alas, to all me greatness! [dramatic sigh]
>   *Jones:* Ah, don't cry, mister.
> *Spencer:* Stand aside, gal, and let me pass!
>   *Jones:* Say, are you a for-real actor on the stage or just in the moving pictures?
> *Spencer:* Do I look like a reel of moving picture film?
>   *Jones:* Well, you look pale and thin, but maybe you're a little out of focus.
> *Spencer:* Crushed again!
>   *Jones:* Why don't you go out in the country and work on a farm?
> *Spencer:* I had enough of the farm in *The Old Homestead* and *Way Down East.*
>   *Jones:* Down east? Did you ever play in Boston?
> *Spencer:* Why, yes, on the outskirts.
>   *Jones:* Without skirts? Ooo!

The girl's distinction between acting on the stage and in films nicely demonstrates Richard deCordova's assertion that the status of motion picture performers at this time was unclear: "Acting was a profession associated with the legitimate stage, and the contention that people acted in films was neither immediately apparent nor altogether unproblematic" (2001, 31–32). But Chatterton becomes a laughable figure to the extent that he has, in Calvert's terms, fallen in love with his own voice, as can be heard by his extravagantly rolled R's and grandiose tones. Those affectations are thrown into stark relief by Jones's comparatively natural Bowery dialect. As had Calvert's acting manual, this record suggests that the vocal conventions of the histrionic stage were becoming all too audible as conventions to many listeners.

What we find in this shift from the histrionic to the realist stage is a change in the role of the voice and, by extension, the role of vocal training. Not surprisingly, the subject of the voice and vocal training was an issue of debate when the Method was taught by Lee Strasberg at New York's Actors Studio. Strasberg downplayed vocal training as a purely "mechanical skill": "any training that stresses the verbal is a return to the old-fashioned form of declamation" (quoted in Hull 1985, 236).[7] To its critics, the Actors Studio was training actors who could not speak clearly enough to be heard onstage.[8] On the presentational stage, the effective actor was trained in matching vocal timbre and intonation to the moral lives of characters, and the voice was a virtuosic attraction of its own. I will return to the subject of the Method at the end of the chapter, but for now it suffices to note that modern drama as embodied in influential schools of acting, such as the Method, favored a style wherein the actor "is encouraged to behave more or less normally, letting gesture or facial expression rise 'naturally' out of deeply felt emotion" (Naremore 1988, 51). Thus, the actor on the realist stage would strive for a more low-key, conversational vocal style. Returning to the work of Richard Bauman, one could say that, like crooning and the Fireside Chat, this "modern" style of acting was less overtly framed as a performance.[9]

From this brief historical overview, one can see that vocal performance on the English and American stage was taking a turn toward a subdued, "natural" style at the same time as the rise of modern sound media—the phonograph, radio, and sound film. Histories of acting have tended to pick up the story of the emergence of a representational style in Hollywood and the development of the cinematic close-up. But given the importance of the voice and vocal training and the instances of stylistic upheaval found in popular singing and public speaking described above, radio and the microphone need to be considered as equally important factors in the development of modern acting styles.

Radio performance has largely been ignored in media studies, and it is not hard to find reasons why. The neglect of radio performance has been triply determined: first, by the tendency in writing about film to neglect sound in relation to the image; second, by the difficulty of analyzing performance in general; and third, by the relative dearth of historical research on radio until recent years. Recent scholarship has demonstrated the cultural prominence of radio in the decades that also saw the emergence of the classical Hollywood sound film. Matthew Solomon refers to a national survey in 1946, "the year that American movie attendance reached an all-time high," which gave respondents a choice of either giving up movies or giving up radio: "84% chose to forgo movies, 11% to give up radio, and 5% were unable to decide" (1997, 23). Evidence such as this suggests that the neglect of radio performance style in relation to film is perhaps out of sync with the cultural significance of those forms of media during the time of their greatest influence.

Thus far in this chapter I have been describing several rather broad stylistic shifts: from stage forms of singing and public speaking to those that developed in tandem with radio and the microphone; and from the presentational to the representation acting style. But all stylistic changes of this sort are retroactively defined by critics; they never occur evenly over time or across media forms and genres. One genre in particular can serve as a nexus for these stylistic developments: radio melodrama, a form in which the unprecedented intimacy of radio acting was perhaps explored most fully.

OVERACTING

To begin to consider some of the issues involved in melodramatic radio acting, let me return to the scene from *Mulholland Dr.* that began this chapter. As we've seen, one way to describe the difference between Betty's two performances is to note that the first time through, the inflection and timbre of Betty's voice reflect the literal meaning of her words: she says, "I hate you," and delivers the line with an aggressive and angry voice. The second time, however, the meaning of the words and their vocal delivery are in tension: she says, "I hate you," in a breathy whisper that suggests she might actually feel the opposite.[10] Plugging in the film's judgment about these two performances, we deduce another lesson in acting—that timbre and inflection of the voice trump words as the site of authentic or truthful expression.

In chapter 1, I referred to what Erving Goffman calls expressions given ("a part that is relatively easy for the individual to manipulate at will, being chiefly his verbal assertions") and given off ("a part in regard to which he seems to have little concern or control") (1959, 18). Goffman writes that "truth" is typically believed to be found in what is "given off": "We often give special attention to features of the performance that cannot be readily manipulated, thus enabling ourselves to judge the reliability of the more misrepresentable cues in the performance" (66). In terms of the voice, the "given" can relate to words, and the "given off" to qualities of the voice like timbre and intonation. This distinction demonstrates the semiotic complexity of the voice, since tone and timbre are often unconscious, "given-off" bodily expressions that work much like posture and gesture. The voice works as word and gesture simultaneously. Lines in a drama that are delivered in such a way as to create tension between these two levels of expression provide a showcase for a particularly virtuosic performance, but they also emphasize the polysemous nature of the voice. They reflect a distinction between gesture and language that has historically been an important aspect of melodramatic performance.

Peter Brooks has described how melodramatic performance on the nineteenth-century stage made frequent use of the grandiose gesture and diction typical of the histrionic code (1985, 41). Brooks argues that the use of codified gestures à la Delsarte and Shaftesbury in melodrama served to express fully the emotional dimensions of a dramatic situation: "Emotions are given a full acting-out, a full representation before our eyes. . . . Nothing is *under*stood, all is *over*stated" (41). Crucially, while it was thought that emotion could be made external and legible in the melodramatic tradition, gesture was seen to be superior to the spoken word as the site of emotional representation: "Words, however unrepressed and pure, however transparent as vehicles for the expression of basic relations and verities, appear to be not wholly adequate to the representation of meanings, and the melodramatic message must be formulated through other registers of the sign" (56). Similarly, Gledhill refers to "eighteenth-century theories of expressivity which saw in the spontaneities of movement, gesture, facial expression and inarticulate vocal sounds a 'natural,' and therefore more authentic language which could bypass the constraints of socio-linguistic convention. Gestures reveal what words conceal" (1991, 210).

As an example of the primacy of gesture in melodramatic performance, Brooks points to the tableau, the "single device of dramaturgy" in which one can "grasp melodrama's primordial concern to make its signs clear, unambiguous, and impressive" (1985, 48). The tableau was the moment when characters on the stage would freeze, arranging themselves in a composition meant to highlight the emotional and moral dimensions of the action, in the process creating a "visual summary of the emotional situation" and a "resolution of meaning" (48). The prevalence of the tableau illustrates how gesture was thought to be better than the spoken word at conveying emotional and moral truths on the melodramatic stage.

Performances found on turn-of-the-century phonograph parodies of stage melodrama can serve to illustrate how some of these issues in melodrama related to vocal performance. Consider *Drama in One Act*, performed by George Graham for Berliner on May 15, 1896. Like Len Spencer in the performances described above, Graham plays two roles on this record: a female in a falsetto register and a male in his chest voice. The record begins with the female voice saying, "I have just received a note signed H.D. stating, 'I will call upon you tonight at eight o'clock on important business.' I wonder who this H.D. can be?" There is a knock on the door. "Ah, good evening, Gertrude," says a man's voice. The woman replies, "How dare you enter this house! Leave at once or I shall summon the police. I know you perfectly well: you are Harley [Dalen], escaped convict from California." The plot unfolds in such a way as to parody melodramatic clichés about the revelation of a hidden past: the man replies, "Come, girl, I wish no nonsense. And remember one thing, that I am acquainted with the secret of your life." "Good heavens," says the woman, "can it be possible? The secret I have kept . . . for the past twenty years has at last been discovered! And now the whole world will know that my mother's husband was my father!"

As the dialogue continues, the villain demands to have the papers that will give him "unlimited control over your father's beautiful country estate on the Bowery." She refuses: "Villain, my answer shall be to you as it has always been in the past: never, never, never! I would die first, I would die first." He threatens to throw her over "yonder precipice," where her body "will be dashed to pieces on the rocks nine hundred ninety-nine feet and seventy-two inches below." She still refuses ("Never! Never! Never!") and is thrown over the precipice amid much loud protesting: "Help! Help! Murder!" The record ends with a punch line that parodies the repetitions of the melodramatic stage: "She's dead, she's dead, and I'm going home. That's the hundred and ninety-eighth consecutive murder I've committed today."

My second example of a phonograph parody of stage melodrama features Len Spencer and Ada Jones, the stars of *The Crushed Tragedian*, described above. Jones and Spencer are teamed up on *Hand of Fate: A Burlesque Melodrama*, released by Zonophone circa 1906. This recording has many similarities to *Drama in One Act*. Spencer plays the villain, Cavanaugh, who is in love with Gladys (Jones), who in turn is in love with a train engineer named Jack Manly. The record repeats the joke about the fateful discovery of a character's secret past: Gladys reveals that she has learned that Cavanaugh's father was his "mother's husband." Like those on the cylinders described above, this performance allows Spencer to use both a low, "profound" style of delivery as he muses, "How it thunders. How it thunders!" and the "gutteral" timbre when he learns of Gladys's devotion to Manly: "Ach, curses on him, I'll get him! Give me those papers!" In another similarity to Graham's *Drama in One Act*, the record's climax features the female character screaming in mortal danger: Gladys cries for help, tied to the train tracks as Manly's engine approaches.

Several points can be made about the depiction of melodramatic vocal performance found on these recorded parodies. The vocal intonation of each character hovers around a few pitches in a steady singsong pattern. This gives each voice the kind of regular, monotone musical quality I described with regard to Spencer's performances in scenes from *Dr. Jekyll* and *Uncle Tom*. The voice is locked into certain conventional tones and timbres that remain constant throughout, working not so much as a conveyer of lines, but as a conveyer of the essential moral qualities of the characters. Returning to Brooks's comments on conventions of the melodramatic stage, this might be thought of as the vocal equivalent of the freezing of gesture in the melodramatic tableau. As theorists such as Walter Ong have pointed out, it is difficult if not impossible to freeze sound and still perceive it in the same manner as one can arrest an image. The goal of the tableau, to make inner moral and character essentials evident in a particularly vivid manner, is achieved on these records through freezing the voice in terms of tone and timbre. Finally, these records reveal how the climax of the melodramatic stage was often the loud, full-voiced emotional excess of a female character in distress. Evidence from these records suggests that the vocal performances heard on stage melodramas at this time were characterized by loud, declamatory voices that hovered in a rather monotonous pattern of delivery, punctuated by loud, impassioned shouts.

SOBBING

As histories of acting have tended to move from stage to film without much consideration of radio or the microphone, so histories of melodrama have often focused either on nineteenth-century stage traditions or on the Hollywood family melodramas and television soap operas of the 1950s. Recent work on early cinema, such as Ben Singer's study of the serial queens, has provided important new perspectives on modern melodrama, and writers such as Robert C. Allen and Michele Hilmes have demonstrated the importance of the melodramatic radio serial, both in the landscape of broadcasting in the 1930s and 1940s and as the predecessor to television soap opera. The study of radio has much to offer this scholarly discourse. In light of the tension I've been describing between word and gesture in the melodramatic form, melodramatic performance on the radio comes to be a particularly salient topic.

My discussion of crooning and political speaking has demonstrated the development of vocal styles that exploited the way in which close miking could capture a conversational style. This can be illustrated in radio melodrama by reference to Carlton Morse's *One Man's Family,* a popular radio melodrama that ran from 1932 to 1959, one that reveals the "radio roots of the middle-class, suburban family sitcom" (Hayes 2004).[11] Morse's show provides a good example of how close miking allowed for an intimate, everyday, conversational acting style that was perceived at the time as an innovation of radio. In his foreword to a collector's edition book on *One Man's Family*, Dave McElhatton writes that "Carlton and his cast invented radio acting":

> Oh, there were actors on radio before "One Man's Family," but they were stage actors who still projected to the top balcony as they stood in front of the microphone. The effect was ludicrous, but it was the accepted style. Carlton would have none of it. He wanted his actors to talk the way his listeners talked in real life. After the first few shows were broadcast transcontinentally out of San Francisco, New York issued the following order to its upstart producer: "Have your actors speak louder. Talk up!" Carlton's feisty reply: "This is normal voice quality, and that is what people in this situation would do. Your engineers are simply going to have to live with it." Since The Family was such a success by that time, New York allowed the talented tail to wag the executive dog. Within a year, there were half-a-dozen dramatic shows on the air in which the dialogue was performed with a sense of naturalness, not stage techniques. (Morse 1988, n.p.)

Morse's show created a sense of intimacy with the Barbour family, in part because of the fact that it did not seek to simulate the public context of theater through a hearable studio audience: "To preserve their complete naturalness, he rightly excludes audiences from their broadcasts" ("Life on 'One Man's Family' Will Continue" 33). The quiet, conversational mode of dialogue featured on *One Man's Family* illustrates how radio encouraged the development of melodramatic performance styles other than the histrionic acting of the nineteenth-century stage.

Morse's show was a relatively highbrow example of the radio serial: it was broadcast in the evening and was strongly associated with its male author. Daytime radio soap operas offer the best example of how a new form of melodramatic vocal excess was emerging that differed from the stage melodrama of the turn of the century. For example, consider a scene from *The Romance of Helen Trent* (1933–60), in which we find Helen with her abiding love interest, Gil Whitney. As the two speak to each other, their voices waver and gasp with quiet intensity.[12] The announcer sets the stage: "We find Helen in her own lovely home; at this moment she's in the sunroom, holding up a beautiful white evening gown. She drops it suddenly as she sees Gil Whitney standing at the open French door, the sun on his fine, handsome head." We hear Gil's distinctive bass voice, "May I step in?" Coyly, Helen replies, "You are in, aren't you darling?" Overcome with emotion, Gil says, "Oh, Helen, Helen, when you use that tone . . ." Helen breathlessly replies, "Oh, you're crushing my gown!" "Never mind your gown," Gil answers. "I'd like to crush the very breath out of you Helen, with kisses." Helen lets out a breathy gasp, whispering, "Oh, Gil, Gil, darling, let me go, you . . . you make me quite dizzy."

This scene provides a sense of intimate, passionate interaction. More typically, however, daytime soaps were associated with a vocal expression of anguish. In fact, the radio melodramas of the 1940s were referred to in the popular press as "washboard weepers."[13] John Hutchens wrote in a March 28, 1943, article in the *New York Times* that "the prevailing sound effect" on daytime radio melodramas was "the barely repressed sob" (1943, SM19). This "sob in the throat" is not the kind of hysterical shrieking or "protracted oratorial posturing" that would have been part of the stage melodramas parodied on the phonograph cylinders described above; it represented a new mode of performing emotional excess geared to the possibilities of the radio microphone (Singer 2001, 190).[14] In effect, radio both "naturalized" the vocal tropes of the melodramatic stage and preserved the melodramatic concern with emotional excess. Melodramas on the radio would have been particularly compelled toward this kind of excessive vocal performance because of formal aspects of the radio medium. To demonstrate this, I offer a comparison of two versions of the much-discussed melodramatic narrative *Stella Dallas*. The first text I will consider is the 1937 film directed by King Vidor and starring Barbara Stanwyck. The second is the October 11, 1937, radio broadcast of *Lux Radio Theater* that promoted the film and featured almost the same cast.

Comparing the film and radio broadcast makes clear the marked reliance of film acting on reaction shots. Naremore has argued that the cinema camera's mobility, "tight framing of faces," and ability to focus on different players from moment to moment has meant that "films tend to favor *reactions*": "As a result, some of the most memorable Hollywood performances have consisted largely of players isolated in close-up, responding nonverbally to offscreen events" (1988, 40). This is particularly pronounced in film melodramas, whose central image has tended to be "the full close-up of a woman suffering for love" (112).[15] Examples abound in the film version of *Stella Dallas*. For example, take the scene where Stephen Dallas (John Boles) has arrived at his estranged wife's apartment to see if their daughter, Laurel (Anne

Figure 8. Expressive reaction shots of Stella Dallas (Barbara Stanwyck) from King Vidor's 1937 film, *Stella Dallas.*

Shirley), can spend Christmas with him. After talking with Stella (Stanwyck), Stephen suggests that they take a later train so that they can spend some time together, perhaps signaling a thaw in their relations. Unfortunately, the ever-bumbling Ed Munn (Alan Hale) makes an appearance, and Stephen's interest in patching things up with Stella quickly fades. "What did you find out about the train?" Stella asks eagerly, while the camera frames her in a medium shot. As the camera stays on Stella, we hear Stephen's offscreen reply: "I'm afraid it would be too late, Stella. I'm sorry." His words register on her face, and she looks down (figure 8). The scene ends with Stephen and Laurel leaving, Stella silently arching her head and shoulders while the screen fades to black.

The kind of reaction shot found here merits closer consideration. Theorists of film sound such as Michel Chion and Kaja Silverman have placed great importance on those moments in film when a character's voice is disengaged from the image of his or her body. A case in point is Chion's category of the *acousmetre:* the character in a narrative whose voice we hear but whose body we do not see. As examples of this useful category, Chion points to Hal in Kubrick's *2001* (1968), Norman Bates's mother in *Psycho* (1960), and the child killer in *M* (1931). These examples show how the dislocations of voice and image can produce an uncanny effect. But it should be noted that a similar disconnect exists in the reaction shot, a technique that is at the very heart of film language. Using another of Chion's terms, one might say that the voice of one character is "magnetized" to the face of the other: the words spoken by an unseen actor are performed by the gestural nuances of another's face. The prevalence of this technique, which opts to show the gestures of the hearer rather than the speaker, can stand as an illustration of the continued precedence of gesture over language in the expressive language of melodrama.

Notably, the reaction shot is impossible on radio: "While one character is speaking it is not possible to show the listener any reactions she might produce in the other characters, to counterpoint what is heard with what is seen" (Crisell 1994, 144). The expressive languages of film and radio are quite distinct in this regard, despite the fact that both use close miking. In film the reaction shot allows us to hear one actor's voice and watch the way those words are registered on the face of another. On radio it is as if each line of dialogue were a close-up on the speaker. Noting the importance melodrama has traditionally placed on gesture, and the prevalence of the reaction shot in film language, one can imagine that the enacting of melodrama on radio would present a formal challenge. The expressive power of gesture and the reaction shot would need to be rendered in another way.

With that in mind, consider the scene I've described from Vidor's *Stella Dallas* as performed on the *Lux* radio broadcast. Stella again asks, "What did you find out about the train?" We then hear Stephen's reply, "I'm afraid it would be too late," but without seeing Stanwyck's face the line's emotional importance is less clear. As if to compensate, Stanwyck adds a pained, "Uhh, oh, I see." Similarly, at the end of the scene, the expressive lighting and lonely silhouette of the film are replaced by Stanwyck's chocked sobs, "Lolly, oh, Lolly." Vocal expressions of emotion are mobilized to replace not only gesture but also reaction shot and expressive mise-en-scène.

Perhaps the most dramatic contrast between film and radio *Stella Dal-las* can be found in the film's famous climactic scene. James Naremore has written at length about Stanwyck's performance outside the window of her daughter's wedding. That performance features another important aspect of film acting, the use of an expressive object, in this case a white handkerchief (1988, 87). It goes without saying that this is also an aspect of acting that is difficult if not impossible to achieve on the radio. On the *Lux* broadcast, instead of biting on a handkerchief and express-ing emotions through facial expressions, Stanwyck has recourse only to her voice. We hear a policeman tell her to move along, and she sobs, "Just let me see her face when he kisses her, please." After a long pause, Stanwyck emits a brief, wordless vocalization. Somewhere between a sigh and a moan, it comes across as profoundly ambiguous: it could index sadness, or relief, or just as easily discomfort or sexual arousal. Where the film ends with a long tracking shot revealing Stella's smile, perhaps signaling her final sense of triumph, the radio broadcast must in-terject another line of dialogue with the policeman to try to register some of this emotional nuance. "All right," the policeman says, "now you've seen it, are you happy?" Stanwyck moans again, "Ugh, yes, thank you," her voice choked with emotion. What we're left with is at once a more vocally excessive ending and a more ambiguous one.

A comparison of the film and radio version of this scene demonstrates how traditionally crucial sites of meaning in melodramatic performance must be presented on the radio by wordless vocal expressions. The trans-ference in radio drama of visible forms of stage business into a verbal form is what Crisell calls transcodification: instead of trying a key in a locked door, for the action to be discernable to a listener a character on the radio must say, "I'll just try this key in the door" (1994, 149). The need for transcodification would be particularly great in the melodra-matic genre, where gesture has traditionally taken on heightened impor-tance as the conveyer of the moral dimension of situations and the vehi-cle of overstated emotional expression. Radio melodrama, then, is predisposed to the "sob in the throat," to the quiet, wordless expression of emotional excess.[16]

That style of emotional excess became the target of critical invective in some of the same ways that the crooners had. Much has been written about the critical disparagement of the daytime soaps, but it should be emphasized that, in their rhetoric, critics often referred to vocal perfor-mance style and excessive emotion. Sometimes critics discussed the ex-cess of emotion in terms of a lack of good dialogue, suggesting that radio melodrama not only had bad writing, but had, essentially "no words." Take an article in the *Washington Post* of January 18, 1951, in which the writer sarcastically recalls a "fragment of soap opera I once caught in a cab and which left an indelible mark on my soul":

He: . . . and so I thought we'd take the apartment and move here.
She: Here?
He: Yes, here.
She: You mean here? To New York?
He: Yes, here to New York.
She: You don't mean to New York?
He: Yes, what did you think I meant? (Stein 1951, B13)

A similar jab at radio melodrama's emotionally excessive vocal style can be found on a parody released by Stan Freberg in 1951. *John and Marsha* is a send-up of daytime radio soaps that features a male and a female performer who interact for three minutes, each saying only the name of the other. The gag of this recording is that the performers, while limited to one word, create a kaleidoscopic range of emotional meanings through vocal inflection. The words *John* and *Marsha* are made to convey passion, sorrow, suspicion, and hysterical joy. The overt message of the record, like that of the article in the *Washington Post,* was to denigrate the soaps for lack of substance. But in the context of my argument about modern styles of performance, *John and Marsha* can be seen as quite an apt illustration of a new regime of emotionally subtle acting made possible by the microphone. Indeed, one might gauge the changing modes of melodramatic style by comparing George Graham's 1896 *Drama in One Act* (with its hysterical shouts of "Help! Murder!") and Freberg's minimalist, unintentional tribute to the stylistic possibilities of close miking.

I offer a final film example to demonstrate how a type of vocal delivery made possible by the microphone became a model for melodramatic performance. The 1937 film *Stage Door,* based on the play by Edna Ferber and George S. Kaufman, offers two versions of a single acted scene. The two performances work much like those I've described in *Mulholland Dr.* The film revolves around the hard-luck lives of the residents of the "Footlights Club," a New York boardinghouse for aspiring female stage performers. Terry Randall (Katharine Hepburn), the daughter of a wealthy businessman, is slumming at the Footlights Club, hoping to embark on a theater career. When her wealthy father pulls some strings, Terry gets a starring role in a new play. During a rehearsal, we see Terry

Figure 9. The audience reacts to a performance by Terry Randall (Katharine Hepburn) in *Stage Door* (1937).

exhibiting bad acting by mechanically reciting the lines in an emotion-less monotone. What's more, she is seen to be thinking too much about the literal meaning of the lines: she stops in mid-sentence to argue about the lines with the play's writer. The director coaches her, urging her to play the scene in terms of the tension between expressions "given" and those "given off": "there's a smile on your face and you're crying in your heart." Terry doesn't understand this: "Well, I don't see how you can do two things at the same time."

On opening night, Terry discovers that her friend Kaye Hamilton (Andrea Leeds) had desperately wanted her role, and in despair she has committed suicide. Crushed by the news, Terry steels herself to take the stage and gives a performance that is in stark contrast to the one we saw in rehearsal. One should note the visual style of the scene. Although we hear Terry's voice, during most of her performance we are shown reaction shots of audience members listening to her (figure 9). This stylistic decision serves to underscore the centrality of the "given off" as expressed through subtle nuance of the voice and the reaction shot as the crucial components of modern acting.

But, as is true of *Mulholland Dr.*, the central difference in the two performances in *Stage Door* is in terms of the voice. Overcome with pain over Kaye's death, Terry delivers the lines in a slow, hushed tone, her voice choked by suppressed sobs much like the "sob in the throat" so characteristic of daytime radio soaps. Indeed, this second performance is nearly unthinkable without the microphone: Hepburn speaks with such quiet intensity that it is hard to imagine some of the other players onstage hearing her, let alone the audience members in the back of the large auditorium where the play is being staged. Here a realistic depiction of stage acting is rejected in favor of the emotional expressiveness made possible by close miking. What's more, that style is presented as the epitome of quality melodramatic acting. This scene reflects how an intimate, emotional style of performance made possible by the microphone had come to represent modern acting.

READING

I have been arguing that a style of acting found on radio melodrama was modern in the same way as crooning: it exploited the microphone's ability to capture nuances of emotional vocal performance. But vocal excess on the radio could go only so far. Speech on the radio is always working on multiple fronts, not only to convey ideas and emotions, but also to present the character in the manner that costume and makeup do on the stage. Further, Andrew Crisell argues that without a visual dimension to fill out prolonged silences, sounds on the radio have to maintain a fairly unbroken flow in order to hold the listener's attention (1994, 145). This means that radio performance must maintain a certain forward propulsion to prevent the entire narrative world from fading away: radio actors must, above all, keep talking. In daytime radio melodrama, this led to a certain stylistic tension, reflected in the form's association with the "sob in the throat": melodramatic situations keep characters perpetually on the verge of sobs, but dialogue must be kept in motion.

Another prevalent and influential style of radio acting utilized a casual, conversational tone delivered with a steady momentum, but in contrast to the soaps, it conveyed hardly any emotion at all. I refer to a type of male narration often found on nighttime crime thrillers. The stylistic developments of radio melodrama are best seen in relation to this contrasting style. Shows such as *Suspense* and *The Adventures of Philip Marlowe* often featured a male narrator characterized by a casual, monotonous, and world-weary delivery.[17] If a steady, de-theatricalized voice is a hallmark of radio style, then the hard-boiled, emotionless male narrator stands as a particularly ideal example of it.

Hard-boiled narration has provided one of the few areas in which scholars have addressed radio's influence on other media forms. Sarah Kozloff points to the influence of radio style in "the rich abundance" of voice-over narration in the Hollywood cinema of the 1940s (1988, 34). In an insightful article on radio adaptation, Matthew Solomon notes Frederic Jameson's comments on the role of voice-over narration in the film noirs of the 1940s, which he suggests index "the omnipresence of radio culture as it resonates out into other genres and media" (1997, 37). Hard-boiled narration is an important and influential mode of vocal performance that became synonymous with radio style and that reveals radio's influence on Hollywood films of this period.

Though his greatest radio success came at the very end of the 1940s, Jack Webb can stand as a paradigmatic figure of this style of performance. Webb, producer and star of the radio hit *Dragnet* (figure 10), provides an interesting case study in the context of this chapter because of his distinctive vocal style and the way in which that style was framed by a discourse of "authenticity" in the popular press. Webb began working in radio after he got out of the army, getting his first break on a network production in 1946 as the star of *Pat Novak for Hire*, a show about

Figure 10. The hard-boiled noir narrator taken to its most deadpan extreme: the anti-crooner Jack Webb. Courtesy of Photofest.

a hard-boiled private eye fighting waterfront crime in San Francisco. Webb's trademark low-key delivery developed when that show's writer, Dick Breen, suggested that Webb depart from "his normal aggressive delivery" and underplay the role of Novak (Moyer and Alvarez 2001, 45). An important turning point in Webb's career came when he took a role in the film *He Walked by Night* (1948), which was based on an actual Los Angeles crime case. Influenced by that film's approach, Webb became involved in developing the radio series *Dragnet*, which was also based on real LAPD crime cases. The radio version of *Dragnet* went on the air on June 3, 1949 (60).

Dragnet was a stylistic departure from contemporary radio shows in several ways: it was based on real crimes; dialogue on the show was heavy with police jargon; and Webb used sound effects tape-recorded on location rather than tapes from the stock sound effects libraries (Hewes 1951, 103). Indeed, the show's use of sound effects is one of its most striking features, and sizable stretches of the broadcast were turned over to showcasing feet walking down long corridors, jail cell doors opening, and the sounds of everyday business in an office. Elements such as these led to the show's remarkable success with critics, who often referred to its "authenticity":

> Authenticity has paid off for the producers of the police action mystery se-ries "Dragnet" with the awarding to the show of an Edgar by the Mystery Writers of America. . . . Webb and his crew have left no stones unturned to ensure bringing authentic reproductions of work by the Los Angeles Police Department to the air. (Ames 1951, 28)

> Authenticity is the keynote Webb insists upon in "Dragnet," and it's paid off handsomely. According to ecstatic press agents, Webb and his show have garnered more awards than any program of its type in broadcasting history. (Kovitz 1952, 26)

> Because their interpretations are patterned on actuality rather than fiction they are infinitely more credible. (J. Gould 1951, 48)

Most important for this chapter is the way in which the vocal deliv-ery of Webb and his cast was described in terms of authenticity. As op-posed to the kind of emotional nuance I've described in crooning and daytime soaps, Webb specialized in a detached, emotionless vocal deliv-ery: the hard-boiled noir narrator taken to his most deadpan extreme. Notably, this style was greeted by accolades from radio critics at the time. The influential *New York Times* critic Jack Gould praised Webb for the way his show avoided "speech-making," and "emotional histrion-ics," instead containing only "the cryptic and pertinent observations of the officials as they raced against the clock" (48). A 1952 article in the *Los Angeles Times* explained that Webb and "all the actors he casts" are "never permitted to go off on dramatic wing-dings—just the opposite. They underplay their roles" (Kovitz 1952, 26). In a statement that nicely encapsulates the distinction between close-miked emotional excess and his show, Webb said that "we do a lot of our recording at some distance away from the microphone. It sounds more authentic to us" (Hewes

1951, 103). In fact, the show frequently allowed ambient room tone to become a part of the sonic picture and give a sense of the space in which the action was occurring.

The fact that Webb's robotic underplaying produced an effect of authenticity for critics at the time is an exception that illustrates the rule of radio performance. Webb's style seemed refreshing to listeners in a radio context where overacting resulted from the way in which voices were typically called on to convey so many different kinds of information. Further, following Michele Hilmes's important description of the ways in which the broadcast day was gendered, it is impossible to overlook the critics' disdain for the emotional excesses of the daytime soaps and respect for Webb's stoic and traditionally masculine vocal performance. Hilmes has argued that, under pressure to present itself as a public service in the 1930s, the radio industry differentiated between daytime and nighttime programming, presenting daytime as "the venue for a debased kind of commercialized, feminized mass culture" and nighttime as a "more sophisticated, respectable, and masculine-characterized arena" (1997, 154). The contrasting critical responses to daytime soaps and *Dragnet* suggest that this distinction was also registered in terms of styles of performance. Here decisions about style are clearly linked to cultural conceptions of gender.

Besides resisting the microphone's ability to capture and project emotional nuance, Webb also went against radio practice by openly addressing one of the most defining yet seldom discussed aspects of radio acting: the fact that, unlike stage or film actors, radio performers were almost always reading their lines from a script. Erving Goffman has described an important stylistic imperative of radio announcers to transcend the fact that they were reading, in order to "produce an effect of spontaneous, fluent speech" (1981, 237). But Webb, in his quest to avoid all "pointed-up, stilted" dialogue, proudly asserted that he and his cast read their lines: "We just read" (Hewes 1951, 103).[18] Webb's commitment to reading carried over to television when *Dragnet* went on television in 1951. Christopher Anderson has described how Webb had his actors "read directly from TelePrompTers placed beneath the camera lens, rather than waste valuable time memorizing lines" (1994, 67).[19]

Dragnet also brought a style of editing to television that can serve as a counterpoint to the reaction shot described above. The film editor and sound designer Walter Murch has described an editing style that ignores the rhythms of actors. Murch calls this the *Dragnet* system: "The policy of the show seemed to be to keep every word of dialog on screen. When someone had finished speaking, there was a brief pause and then a cut to the next person, who was now about to talk, and when he in turn finished speaking there was a cut back to the first person who nodded his head or said something, and then when *that* person was finished, they cut back again, etc." (1995, 66). Much notes that at the time that the show debuted, "this technique created a sensation for its apparently hard-boiled, police-blotter realism" (66). But Much decries the *Dragnet* system as simple and shallow and, most damning of all, unrealistic: "[The *Dragnet* system] doesn't reflect the grammar of complex exchanges that go on all the time in even the most ordinary conversations" (67). What should be noted is that this editing style is a visual analog to the experience of radio, where there are no reaction shots.

Both the radio and television versions of *Dragnet* reveal an aesthetic that is in contrast to the melodramatic forms I've discussed. Melodrama on the radio is noted for its high degree of "transcodification," rendering emotional excess in the "sob in the throat" style of performance made possible by the microphone. In film, melodrama's traditional reliance on gesture and expressions "given off" encouraged the use of the reaction shot. *Dragnet* illustrates how the same sound technology could be used for distinctly different ends: an emotionless, read performance and, on television, a visual style that practically eliminated the reaction shot.

Some differences in these regimes of vocal performance come into focus on recordings of Jack Webb trying his hand at crooning. On *You're My Girl: Romantic Reflections by Jack Webb* (Warner Bros. 1958)—a record that has since become a camp classic—Webb brought his deadpan delivery to recitations of popular songs such as "Try a Little Tenderness." If Bing Crosby made the gender-bending aspects of crooning more safely masculine, Webb's lifeless performances bled that style of any hint of sexuality at all, and in the process demonstrated that a closely held microphone is no guarantee of intimacy. Indeed, Webb's stultifying stiffness in this context corroborates—through their very absence—the central role played by the nuances of timbre and inflection in the vocal performances of the past century.

Another performer who, unlike Webb, was able to combine these different modes of microphonic performance successfully was Frank Sinatra. Beginning his career as an adolescent crooner along the lines of Rudy Vallee, Sinatra remade himself in the image of the film noir antihero Humphrey Bogart: note, for example, Sinatra's mid-1950s album art on which he wears a fedora and overcoat. We might say that both Sinatra and Webb present versions of the world-weary, hard-boiled hero as read through Bogart. Although Sinatra does not recite his lyrics the way Webb does, he was known as being a particularly "actorly" singer: Pleasants quotes Sinatra as stating that he "talk[s] words expressively to a background of music" (1974, 192). More specifically, Robert Ray has pointed out that as a singer, Sinatra "worked like a method actor, conveying a tortured interiority whose role was outlined by his songs' often anguished lyrics" (2001, 106). Perhaps that approach had something to do with Sinatra's success, and it is with a brief return to the Method that I will conclude this chapter.

RADIO AND THE METHOD

Although radio had a large influence on the culture of the 1930s and 1940s, one might argue that radio acting's biggest legacy was to establish norms against which Method acting defined itself. Method acting, as taught by Lee Strasberg at the Actors Studio in New York, became increasingly prevalent and influential in television and film throughout the 1950s. The Method might be best understood when considered in relation to the practices of radio acting. Where radio acting prized performers who were versatile and could read copy with little or no rehearsal, Method actors turned rehearsal into a quasi-spiritual and essential ritual of embodying a role; where radio required a smooth, unbroken flow, Method acting is known for its abrupt shifts in tone and sudden outbursts; where the radio actor reads, the Method actor improvises— Strasberg paraphrased Stanislavsky's famous quote when he said, "An actor never reads lines, he speaks them" (Hull 1985, 154). Casting directors for early live television drama preferred theater actors who understood rehearsal and building a character over actors trained in radio.

As I noted above, critics of the Actors Studio claimed that Strasberg was training actors who could not speak clearly enough to be heard onstage. Of course, those aspects of vocal style that created problems on the stage ended up being tailor-made for film. Virginia Wright Wexman writes that Stanislavsky's theories were "readily adaptable to film performance" since Method actors were trained to ignore the audience, and their presentation of inner emotional conflict could be documented by close-ups and long takes (1993, 162–63). As we have seen, it is important to add that their often inarticulate vocal style could be captured by microphones. Wexman understands Method performance in relation to certain social contradictions in male roles during the 1950s, and she notes that male Method actors indulged in "the kind of emotional out-pouring traditionally associated with female behavior" (170).[20]

Indeed, the two most famous Method actors of the 1950s, Marlon Brando and James Dean, are often described in terms reminiscent of the daytime radio melodrama "sob in the throat." "The inarticulate style they made famous, whether feigned or real, was a signal that words were inadequate to convey the tangle of inner feelings. Their war with words—the failed struggle toward verbal expression that became an emblem of a generation—told us, in effect, that they had emotions that went deeper than language" (Hirsch 1984, 295). Naremore writes that Brando tended to display "an uneasiness with official language and no words for his love or rage," creating an "inarticulateness" that becomes what Frederic Jameson called "the highest form of expressiveness" (Naremore 1988, 201).

When seen in the context of this chapter, these male Method actors might be viewed both as a stylistic rejection of the hard-boiled, emotionless style of Jack Webb, and as firmly embedded in the melodramatic tendency to favor gesture over words that has run through the stage and daytime soap performances I've been examining. The fact that this excessively emotional male performance style did not create the same moral panic about masculinity as did the crooners of the 1930s points, perhaps, to the fact that the culture at large had become used to an intimate, close-miked style of performance. Method actors also made visible the labor of acting through their eruptions of energy and discourses of preparation and improvisation, all of which made their "feminine" emotional excesses conform to traditional ideologies of masculinity and work. Krin Gabbard has claimed, however, that some important aspects of Brando's style involve a subtle appropriation of the codes of African American masculinity, even suggesting that he represented a new kind of "blackface" performance in American popular culture emerging at a time when literal blacking up was disappearing. It is to these issues of race and performance that I turn in the next chapter.

CHAPTER 4

Rough Mix

In his book *The Recording Angel,* Evan Eisenberg identifies Louis Armstrong and Enrico Caruso as "icons of phonography." For Eisenberg, this term refers to a person "with a personality so powerful," and who is "so in command of his art" that he can turn the disadvantages of a new medium into advantages, and so reveal its expressive potential (1987, 147). Eisenberg argues that if Chaplin was the "great icon of film," it was Caruso and Armstrong who demonstrated that the phonograph was not a "toy" and so became iconic figures for early recorded sound. "It is no accident," Eisenberg writes, "that when one thinks of a stack of old 78's one thinks first, depending on one's predilections, either of Armstrong or of Caruso" (147–48). Historians of recorded sound have made it clear that the phonograph industry was an important cultural force by the 1890s, suggesting that people no longer considered the phonograph to be a toy well before the careers of Caruso and Armstrong. But Eisenberg evokes a convenient image for the purposes of this chapter: an iconic representation of recorded male vocal performance as a Januslike figure, with one voice characterized by Armstrong's throaty rasp and the other by Caruso's operatic round tone. This chapter is an analysis not of the careers of these two influential performers, but of two styles of singing for which they can stand.

The difference between these styles is best described in terms of vocal timbre, an aspect of the voice that was captured in a new way on the records of the past century. Styles of singing were preserved on sound recordings in all of their textural specificity and then disseminated far beyond their particular social contexts and cultural associations. That process allowed vocal techniques such as the rasp to compete with the more culturally dominant tradition of bel canto. The pairing of Caruso and Armstrong makes clear that the history of these vocal timbres in American popular singing is also the history of the performance of race. I do not mean to imply that bel canto and the rasp were the only important vocal styles heard on early recordings, or that either African American or European American vocal expression has been monolithic or one-dimensional. Nevertheless, despite being only one style utilized by African American performers, a raspy tone took on heightened meaning as an index of blackness in relation to the bel canto tradition of vocal training.

This chapter is concerned, then, with the role of vocal timbre in what Eric Lott refers to as the "social relations of 'racial' production": the structural and emotional pressures that produce "blackness" as a cultural commodity. Recorded vocal performances of the past century were certainly one of the most resonant locations of what Lott calls racial "interaction rituals" (1993, 39). Records by black singers such as George Washington Johnson, Bert Williams, and Louis Armstrong demonstrate the importance of vocal timbre in the creation of black performance styles that were both well suited to the recording studio and able to circulate in a racist society. To paraphrase Richard Dyer, these artists reveal the type of black singing stars permitted by the early phonograph industry, and their recordings allow us to hear the kinds of black voices that were tolerated by white society at this time (1986, 69).

That white singers have co-opted what they considered to be "black" styles of performance is not news to anyone, but records by turn-of-the-century blackface minstrel singers reveal the complexity of that process. Minstrel show recordings are an understudied source of information about that troubling but undeniably influential form of American mass entertainment. Lott writes that the study of the minstrel show has inclined toward relying on "the printed record (songsters, playlets, and so on)," a fact that he argues has tended to downplay how the minstrel show was "a negotiated and rowdy spectacle of performer and audience" (1993, 9). Reliance on print evidence also leaves many aspects of performance out of the equation; recordings from the turn of the century are thus all the more valuable as sources. If minstrel recordings have suffered from underexposure, the same is certainly not true of the subject of the last section of this chapter: the records of John Lennon of the Beatles. That said, there has been a surprisingly small amount of academic analysis of either the Beatles as performers or the phenomenon of "Beatlemania."[1] I will argue that Lennon represents a pivotal point in the cultural understanding of the rasp, owing in part to his association with an influential therapeutic movement during the early 1970s.

We shall see that the rasp became increasingly freighted with cultural meaning for male singers over the course of the century; it indicated blackness, class conflict, masculinity, and catharsis. That so much meaning could be carried by the rough edge of a singer's voice demonstrates the importance of sound technology's ability to preserve specific timbres, as well as the power of the voice as a conveyer of cultural meaning and identity. As so much of this chapter hinges on the meanings conveyed by the grain of the voice, it will be necessary to begin with a discussion of timbre as a quality of sound. What will become clear is that the experience of timbre is surprisingly complex, and that it has special importance in terms both of a consideration of the human voice and of sound recording.

IT'S THE SINGER, NOT THE SONG

The term *timbre* refers to the specific quality of a sound as determined by the combination of its fundamental resonating tone and pattern of harmonic overtones. We distinguish different instruments largely by timbre: a saxophone and trumpet could make a sound of the same pitch and loudness, but we discern them by their respective "reedy" or "brassy" timbres. Roland Barthes's complaints about the difficulty of describing timbre are echoed by writers who point out that it is an aspect of music that has received comparatively little attention in Western cultures. Cornelia Fales describes "a perceptual proclivity on the part of Western listeners, including ethnomusicologists, to focus on melody," even in music in which "the dominant parameter is timbre," a tendency she refers to as "pitch-centrism" or "timbre deafness" (2002, 56). Fales writes that in the West, pitch has tended to be "governed by law while timbre is governed by taste," and musical performance is "judged correct or incorrect according to variations in pitch, while variations in other parameters of music are judged pleasing or displeasing" (56). For most listeners, timbre is considered to be "what a sound is," not "what a sound does," which makes it relatively difficult to perceive as a discrete aspect of sound (58).

There is evidence that our difficulty with timbre might go beyond cultural conditioning. Theodore Gracyk refers to research that suggests that the human perception of timbre is quite limited in regard to memory: "Auditory memories seem to be restricted to species of timbre. We can hear minute differences between similar timbres while listening, but these nuances begin to be forgotten about a second after the sounds cease. It just seems to be a brute fact that human perception and memory of timbre are parallel to those for both musical pitch and visual color. As with memories of pitch and color, memories of timbre 'fade' after a moment, becoming more imprecise with the passage of time" (1996, 59–60). Gracyk suggests that melody and form are easier to store in memory than timbre. For example, though one can quickly bring to mind the rhythm, melody, and the overall structure of a favorite song, it's more difficult to recall the particular timbre of the instruments that performed it. This argument can be overstated, and Fales cautions that though we might have "a peculiar amnesia in regard to timbre," we're not deaf to it: "We hear it, we use it—no one has much trouble telling instruments apart" (2002, 57). It seems to be the case, however, that in many cultures most people are not used to listening for timbre, and though we perceive it on an unconscious level, we typically have little language to describe it.

Despite these cultural and perhaps even biological limitations, timbre still plays an important role in what several authors describe as the key function of listening: location and identification. Barthes claims that mammals mark their territory by reference to odors and sounds, and he compares this to the human domestic space, "a space of familiar, recognized noises" (1985, 246). Listening, for Barthes, has to do with "intercepting whatever might disturb the territorial system," and it thus serves a double function that is both defensive and predatory, since it is a mode of defense against surprise as well as a way to locate prey (247). Fales also claims that auditory perception is "precisely geared to source identification" (2002, 61). Timbre plays a central role in that process since "listeners generally seem to base their knowledge of a source and especially of its location, largely on qualities of timbre" (59). This is due to the fact that timbre carries a great deal of information about a sound's source and location as well as about the environment through which a sound has traveled.

To explain this sonic representation of space, it is important to note that timbre is actually a complex bundle of information. Fales describes how the auditory cortex in the brain groups "an immense collection of individual acoustic elements" into perceptual units. Pitch and loudness can be determined relatively easily by the information received in the inner ear, but timbre is the result of a "process of perceptual fusion" whereby numerous signals are grouped by the auditory cortex into the "unitary sensation of tone quality." Since the perceived timbre of a sound is determined by a range of frequencies, there is no single acoustic event that corresponds to the experience of timbre, a fact that leads Fales to state that "perceived timbre exists in a very real sense only in the mind of the listener, not in the objective world" (61–62). Consider, for example, a sound that is "wet" with reverberation. That "wetness" is actually a perceptual image of the source of the sound combined with the influence of the large reverberant space through which the sound has traveled. Notably, many audio recording systems identify the strength of a reverb effect by referring to a hypothetical space that surrounds the source of the sound. For example, the digital audio program Cool Edit Pro has reverb settings with names such as "basement," "empty parking garage," "long hallway," and "water closet." These titles indicate how the perception of timbre, in this case degrees of reverb, represents a fusion of the sound source and its surrounding space. Timbre is thus a complex perceptual amalgam of sonic information, one that calibrates sound and space and, in so doing, inherently indicates the subjective nature of all perception. The fact that this sonic information is perceived to a large degree unconsciously perhaps only adds to timbre's potential for emotional expressiveness.

If timbre is a particularly dense aspect of sound, the human voice is a particularly flexible instrument of timbre.[2] This is due in large part to the fact that the timbre of the voice can be altered separately from its source of production: using Wayne Slawson's terminology, the source and filter of the sound can function independently. Slawson explains that a sound is produced "when an object is struck, or excited, by some kind of mechanical energy and the object in turn changes the excitation in some manner" (1987, 23). Slawson calls the excited object the "source" and the resonating object the "filter" (23). For many musical instruments, the source and the filter are "strongly coupled," that is, a change in the filter or resonator will also change the source pitch. Slawson provides the example of a clarinet: "The clarinet source is not independent; it is driven by the filter. In the clarinet and most other musical instruments, the filter affects the source frequency. In fact, the usual method of changing the pitch of a musical instrument is to alter, not its source characteristics, but the effective length of the horn or the string—in other words, the filter" (28). By contrast, in the case of the human voice, the source (air blowing through the vocal cords) and filter (the resonant cavities of the throat, head, and mouth) are weakly coupled. For example, consider how the timbre of the voice changes as one forms a tone into different vowel sounds. By changing the shape of the resonant chambers of the throat and mouth, one is able to change the pattern of the sound's overtones and so shape distinct timbres while keeping the pitch of the tone constant: "In vowel production the filter changes the amplitudes of the source components but does little else to the source; source and filter are weakly coupled" (24). The fact that timbre can be manipulated independently from pitch is part of what makes the human voice such a wonderfully expressive instrument.

The voice is an instrument of timbre par excellence, and sound recording allowed that dimension of vocal performance to be preserved and considered in a radically new way. Indeed, the neglect of timbre in the West can be partly explained by reference to the fact that the tradition of Western classical music has taken as its central work the written score. Compared to pitch, rhythm, and loudness, timbre is difficult to notate and so has played a relatively less important role in the consideration of Western music. As Robert B. Ray has pointed out, recording allowed for a shift in the ontological status of music, most dramatically in genres such as rock and roll, which made the record, not the written score or live performance, the central work: "What distinguishes rock & roll from all the music that precedes it—especially classical, Tin Pan Alley, and jazz—is its elevation of the record to primary status. While classical and jazz recordings for the most part aimed only at approximating live performances, regarded as the significant event, many of rock's most important musicians, beginning with Elvis, made records before ever appearing in public" (2001, 72). Along these same lines, Theodore Gracyk bases his aesthetics of rock and roll on the perception of timbre. Unlike Western art music, which placed a premium on form and structural complexity, "rock is a music of very specific sound qualities and their textural combination. Specific sounds are as central to the music as are specific colors in painting" (1996, 61). Instead of compositional complexity, the pleasure of much modern recorded music depends on the experience of timbre, a fact that, coupled with his arguments about timbre and memory, Gracyk posits as an explanation for the desire to listen to the same records again and again: "Where the tone color of a recorded guitar contributes to the expressive character of the music, one can only experience the contribution of that tone by actually hearing it again in its total musical context" (61).

Though these authors argue that musical genres of the 1950s reflected a shift to a primary concern with timbre, recorded sound has always had an effect on the experience of timbre. With recording one is able to experience, revisit, and analyze nuances of particular sounds and voices, so that improvised genres of music such as jazz can be heard and discussed in the same manner as a written score. Recording thus encouraged a paradigm shift from an emphasis on the composer and the written score—and by extension the relative unimportance of timbre—to an emphasis on performers and the experience of timbre, a distinction neatly summed up by the title of the Rolling Stones song "It's the Singer, Not the Song." In light of the voice's great expressivity as an instrument of timbre, and the ability of recorded sound to make timbre a more tangible part of musical experience, it makes sense to take that aspect of performance seriously and so consider specific timbral styles as carriers of cultural meaning. In that regard, I return to Eisenberg's two-headed icon of phonography in order to consider first the vocal timbre represented by Enrico Caruso: operatic bel canto.

THE SOUND OF CHIAROSCURO

The phrase "bel canto" literally translates as "beautiful singing," but the tradition of operatic singing to which it applies can be difficult to define, since innumerable and varied pedagogical techniques have claimed to be bel canto. Despite the inherent difficulty in pinning the term down, there is wide agreement about the origins and general qualities of bel canto singing. *The New Grove Dictionary of Music and Musicians* states that bel canto refers to "the Italian vocal style of the 18th and early 19th centuries, the qualities of which include perfect legato production throughout the range, the use of a light tone in the higher registers and agile and flexible delivery" (Sadie and Tyrrell 2001, 161). James Stark, in his history of bel canto pedagogy, connects bel canto's origins to the rise of virtuoso solo singing for the operatic stage dating back to the late sixteenth and early seventeenth centuries (1999, xvii). Stark describes the sound of bel canto as the "classically" trained voice of opera and concert singers, featuring "special qualities of timbre, evenness of scale and register, breath control, flexibility, tremulousness, and expressiveness" (xx–xxi). Henry Pleasants defines bel canto as "a mellifluous kind of singing aimed at an agreeable, well-rounded tone . . . and a disciplined avoidance of shouting, nasality, harsh or open sounds" (1981, 20).

The "well-rounded" tone of bel canto has sometimes been described by the word *chiaroscuro*. The ideal quality for the classically trained voice was a chiaroscuro or, "bright-dark" tone, each sung note having a "bright edge as well as a dark or round quality in a complex texture of vocal resonances" (Stark 1999, 33). The double nature of chiaroscuro nicely illustrates the above-mentioned flexibility of the human voice, since it exploits the ability to shape timbre in two ways: with the glottis, or lips of the vocal cords, and with the resonating chambers of the throat and head. According to Stark, the "bright" element of chiaroscuro is achieved through "firm glottal closure," which produces a tone that is "rich in high-frequency components" (38). Once sound is produced by air moving through the glottis, it can be shaped by the vocal tract between the glottis and the mouth and nose by lowering the larynx, or voice box, raising the soft palate, or changing the position of the tongue, lips, or jaw. To create the "dark" or "round" tone of chiaroscuro, the larynx is lowered and the chambers of the throat and head are expanded (38). Stark compares this coupling of tones to "the vivid contrast of silvery white and deep red on each petal of a 'fire-and-ice' rose, or the taste of something sweet-and-sour" (34).

An important motivation for the development of the chiaroscuro tone was that it helped to project a solo voice over an orchestra and into a large auditorium. The bright quality of chiaroscuro is also referred to as "the singer's formant."[3] Formants are broad bands or clusters of high-intensity harmonics or overtones that play an important role in creating vocal timbre (Fales 2002, 72; Stark 1999, 46). The singer's formant, which exists at frequencies around 3000 Hz, was needed for projecting the voice in large opera halls. Johan Sundberg, in his book *The Science of the Singing Voice*, describes how "the loudest partials of the orchestral sound tend to appear in the neighborhood of 450 Hz," and so a singer whose voice is rich in frequencies around the singer's formant would encounter "only moderate competition from sound components of the orchestra accompaniment" (1987, 123). Further, Sundberg notes that though the lower frequencies of the voice "scatter almost equally well in all directions," the bright, high frequencies of the singer's formant are more directional, radiating "more directly to the audience, provided that the singer is facing toward it" (123).

The function of the singer's formant illustrates how the performance spaces of the operatic stage shaped the bel canto style. James Lastra makes a similar point when he claims that musical performances before the technology of sound recording were already subject to "technological" transformations. The technology to which Lastra refers is the architecture of concert halls, designed as they were to shape the sound of musical performances: "Before the appearance of the microphone, the symphony is *already* the product of an advanced sound technology—architecture—and therefore not innocent of technological mediation in its primary form" (2000, 133). Though Lastra's insight reminds us not to assume an unmediated original performance that existed before sound recording, the introduction of sound media technologies and electronic amplification could certainly stimulate competing definitions of "beautiful" singing. Before turning to sound recording and the ways in which it interacted with bel canto, however, we must first consider another pre-phonographic technology that, like architecture, had an influence on the tradition of concert singing.

SEEING VOICES

A *New York Times* article from March 18, 1905, described the celebration of the one hundredth birthday of Manuel García II, a professor of singing at the University of London. King Edward of England received García at Buckingham Palace and "bestowed on him the Commandership of the Victorian Order" ("García a Centenarian" 7). Later he was presented with the Royal Order of Alfonso XII by King Alfonso of Spain. From Emperor William of Germany came the Gold Medal for Science. García also received a portrait of himself painted by John Singer Sargent and "congratulatory addresses" from the New York Academy of Medicine, McGill University of Montreal, the Royal Society of London, the Prussian Academy of Sciences, and the University of Königsberg, which had in 1862 conferred on him the honorary degree of Doctor of Medicine (7; Mackinlay 1908, 304–5). Why was this vocal instructor considered prominent enough to be celebrated by three kings? And why would a man who trained opera singers be feted by the international medical community?

In an introduction to his translation of García's written works, Donald V. Paschke attributed García's influence to the way in which he linked bel canto traditions with "scientific research" (García 1975, ii). Similarly, Stark writes that García represented a "point in music history when the tradition and science of singing met" (3). For the purposes of this chapter, what is important about García's legacy is the way in which it marks a modern conceptualization of the voice as well as a modern approach to vocal pedagogy in the bel canto tradition. García should also be considered as part of a tradition of nineteenth-century investigation into the senses that played an important role in the development of sound media technologies such as the phonograph and telephone.

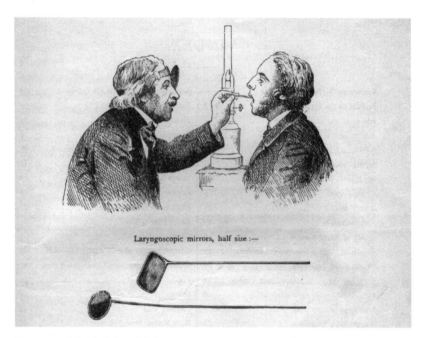

Figure 11. Manuel García's laryngoscope. From Manuel García,
Hints on Singing (1894).

Manuel García II was born in Madrid in 1805, the son of Manuel
García I (1775–1832), a famous opera singer who had worked closely
with Rossini. The younger García sang for a time with his father's opera
company, and in 1825 the Garcías performed in New York City, where
they produced the first Italian operas in America. García II decided not
to pursue a singing career after an unsuccessful Paris debut in 1828
(Sadie and Tyrrell 2001, 522). Enlisting in the French army during the
1830 invasion of Algeria, García worked in military hospitals, where he
studied the larynx in cases of neck wounds. This experience helped spur
his investigation into the mechanics of the vocal instrument in conjunction with his work as a voice teacher, first in Paris and later in London.
Perhaps his most famous pupil was the "Swedish Nightingale," Jenny
Lind, whose voice he is credited with saving (Holland 1893, 68–70).[4]
    Lind's phenomenal international success increased García's renown,
but his most famous contribution to the study of the voice came from his
1854 invention of the laryngoscope: a small, angled mirror that was used
to view the vocal folds during singing (figure 11). Mackinlay's descrip-

tion of the moment of García's invention illustrates the shock of first seeing the glottis in action:[5]

> [García] placed against the uvula this little piece of glass, which he had
> heated with warm water and carefully dried. Then with a hand-mirror
> he flashed on to its surface a ray of sunlight. By good fortune he hit upon
> the proper angle at the very first attempt. Then before his eyes appeared the
> glottis, wide open and so fully exposed that he could see a portion of the
> trachea. So dumbfounded was he that he sat down aghast for several min-
> utes. On recovering from his amazement he gazed intently for some time at
> the changes which were presented to his vision while the various tones were
> being emitted. (Mackinlay 1908, 205)

The significance of this moment is better understood when one considers that the mechanics of the voice are hidden in the neck and so—
unlike other musical instruments—cannot be directly viewed and examined while in operation. As a result, early descriptions of vocal function
were often vague or incorrect. García claimed that "until our days the
physiologist possessed only some approximate notions, obtained by in-
duction, of [vocal] science. In order to make them precise he lacked a
means of direct observation" (1975, xx–xxi). Similarly, Mackinlay,
writing in 1908, argued that most people had become aware that "vibrations of the elastic bands" produce the sounds of the voice, that pitch
was "determined by their length and tension," and that "the 'breaking'
of the voice of a boy on reaching the threshold of adolescence is due to
the mechanical effect of the elongation of the [vocal cords]," but that "all
these simple facts were absolute mysteries previously to the enlightening
device of Manuel García" (1908, 210). The laryngoscope allowed the
voice to be observed in a way it never had before, which led to a more
modern understanding of vocal production.

García's revolutionary findings derived from the use of the laryngoscope were published in 1855 under the title "Observations on the
Human Voice," which was useful for scientists and medical doctors as
well as voice teachers. For example, a 1925 newspaper article noted how
the laryngoscope had "enabled the performing of operations that were
not even thought of before" ("Young García Passed Up Opera Career"
8). In fact, Stark argues that along with Hermann Helmholtz's 1862
work on the sensation of tone, García's theories "paved the way for the
modern study of vocal acoustics": "In many ways García can be considered the father of modern voice science whose legacy is no less present
today than in his own time" (1999, xxii).

The use of the laryngoscope to observe the voice led García to conclude that the primary source of sound was the glottis: "From what he witnessed it was easy to conclude that his theory, attributing to the glottis alone the power of engendering sound, was confirmed, and thence it followed that the different positions taken by the larynx in the front of the throat had no action whatever in the formation of the sound" (Mackinlay 1908, 205). García's conviction that the key to the voice was found in the glottis had grown from his experience in military hospitals, where he had had the chance to observe the larynx. Mackinlay described how, after his 1830 military experience, García began to investigate the workings of the voice, and he quotes his younger sister, who recounted how García brought home "the throttles of all kinds of animals—chickens, sheep, and cows," and would give her a pair of bellows, which she would "insert in these windpipes, one after another, and blow hard. Heavens! What extraordinary sounds they used to emit. The chickens' throttles would cluck, the sheep's would bleat, and the bulls' would roar, almost like life" (100).

This scene is worth noting because of how closely it resembles accounts of Alexander Graham Bell's experiments in the 1870s with the ear phonautograph, a device that was created by attaching a human ear taken from a cadaver to a mechanism that would etch sound waves. Authors writing about the cultural history of sound reproduction have made much of Bell's strange machine. James Lastra refers to the ear phonautograph as an illustration of how the simulation of physiological processes of perception was a "master trope" through which media technologies were understood in the nineteenth century (2000, 21). Jonathan Sterne sees the ear phonautograph as signaling a "shift from models of sound reproduction based on imitations of the mouth to models based on imitations of the ear" (2003, 33). Sterne also points to the ear phonautograph as a prototypical illustration of a tympanic mechanism whereby the perception of sound was understood as a vibrating membrane that worked through a process of transduction (35). According to Sterne, this was both an important step in the development of sound recording technology and an indication of modern conceptions of hearing.[6] García's experiments with the windpipes of animals must be seen in relation to the device Bell made some forty years later. García's experiments ultimately led to the laryngoscope: not a machine for recording or transcribing the voice, but a device for observing it. Nonetheless, as was the case with the ear phonautograph, the laryngoscope represented a modern reduction of a physiological process to a single mechanism, in this case voice production to the glottis.

García's laryngoscope and resulting theories were of use to doctors and scientists, but the effect of his work was most keenly felt in the field of vocal pedagogy. García developed his most controversial technique, the "coup de la glotte," or "stroke of the glottis," to focus voice production on the glottis. The coup de la glotte was a technique for beginning a vocal tone, something upon which no other previous vocal treatises had placed much importance (Stark 1999, 14). The coup de la glotte sought to establish firm glottal closure and so ensure the bright, ringing quality of chiaroscuro. García describes the technique as follows:

> hold the body straight, quiet, upright on the two legs, removed from any point of support; open the mouth, not in the form of an oval O, but by letting the lower jaw fall away from the upper by its own weight . . . hold the tongue relaxed and immobile (without lifting it either by its root or by its tip); finally, separate the base of the pillars and soften the entire throat. In this position, inhale slowly and for a long time. After you are thus prepared, and when the lungs are full of air, without stiffening either the [throat] or any part of the body, but calmly and easily, attack the tones very distinctly with a light stroke of the glottis . . . taken well at the bottom of the throat . . . in order that no obstacle may be opposed to the emission of the sound. In these conditions the tone should come out with ring and with roundness. (García 1975, 41–42)

García compared the coup de la glotte to the lips pronouncing the consonant "P" and the palatal arch articulating of the consonant "K" (42). The technique of the coup de la glotte resembles modes of modern efficiency since it involves isolating the "essential" part of the vocal mechanism through the use of modern instruments and increasing its efficient functioning.

The coup de la glotte was broadly interpreted, often misunderstood, and met with some vehement opposition from teachers and critics who claimed it damaged the voice. One famous critic of García's "scientific" approach was George Bernard Shaw, who wrote in 1892 that the voice trained in the coup de glotte was "objectionable"; Shaw claimed that he had "never heard a good singer who attacked notes explosively" (1931, 203). At the same time that Shaw criticized attempts to "base the art of singing on physiology" ("You can no more sing on physiological principles than you can fence on anatomical principles, paint on optical principles, or compose on acoustic principles"), he also had to concede that the modern, scientific conceptualization of the voice ushered in by García had become common coin: "Half a century ago every singing-master firmly believed that there were in the human body three glands—one in the head, immediately behind the frontal sinus; one in the throat; and one in the chest: each secreting a different quality of voice. Nowadays even an Italian singing-master must, on pain of appearing a gross igno-ramus to his pupils, know that all voice is produced by the same organ, the larynx, and that the so-called voices are 'registers' made by varying the adjustment of the vocal cords" (198). Despite his rejection of the coup de la glotte, Shaw's essay illustrates how García's work had brought about a modern way of conceptualizing and training the voice.

The modernity of the García school can also be appreciated by com-paring it to more traditional approaches of vocal pedagogy that relied on "resonance imagery," wherein "sensations of localized vibration are used as an indicator of good vocal function" (Stark 1999, 51). This type of vocal pedagogy used a language of "placing" or "focusing" the voice in different parts of the body. Indeed, Stark notes that the basic terms for the vocal registers, chest and head voice, reflect the influence of reso-nance imagery since they refer to where a tone is felt, not to where it is formed (52). García considered his techniques to be in opposition to some aspects of resonance imagery, as can be illustrated by an 1894 in-terview in which García explained why he did not believe in teaching "by means of sensation of tone":

> The actual things to do in producing tone are to breathe, to use the vocal cords, and to form tone in the mouth. The singer has nothing to do with anything else. Garcia said that he began with other things; he used to direct the tone into the head, and do peculiar things with breathing, and so on; but as the years passed by he discarded these things as useless, and now speaks only of actual things, and not mere appearances. He condemned what is so much spoken of nowadays, the directing of the voice forward or back or up. Vibrations come in puffs of air. All control of the breath is lost the moment it is turned into vibrations, and the idea is absurd, he said, that a current of air can be thrown against the hard palate for one kind of tone, the soft palate for another, and reflected hither and thither. (quoted in Stark 1999, 51–52)

In the wake of García's findings, techniques based on a scientific obser-vation of the vocal mechanism were pitted against a traditional approach more focused on bodily sensation. One might say that "seeing the voice" became a modern alternative to "feeling the voice."

It is important to note that proponents of resonance imagery did not vanish in the wake of García's invention. In fact, they have probably al-ways outnumbered more scientific or visually oriented teachers. Stark points to the practical reasons for this: "it is often more effective to suggest to the voice pupil, 'Get the voice forward,' than to say 'Try to get more second-formant resonance in your tone' " (55). Further, though García's laryngoscope allowed singers to see and understand their voices in a new way, it did not represent a rupture in terms of bel canto style. Recall how García was lauded for linking science and tradition, not for using the former to dethrone the latter. García represented a marriage of modern and traditional approaches to the voice, since the outcome of his scientific, instrumental technique was the same chiaroscuro tone of bel canto. If the laryngoscope allowed singers to see their voices for the first time, a few decades later the phonograph allowed them an equally novel way in which to hear themselves. García's invention provided a happy marriage between bel canto tradition and modernity, but Edison's did not. Indeed, recorded sound and, in particular, electronic recording had important consequences for many aspects of singing style, including vocal timbre.

HEARING VOICES

Like the laryngoscope, the phonograph allowed a singer to perceive her or his voice detached from the resonances of the body, an experience that was often described as being disturbing and unsettling. Erika Brady writes of how the phonograph allowed people to "hear themselves as others heard them," and she refers to accounts of famous musicians fainting during playback from the shock of the experience (1999, 38). There are physiological explanations for why our voices sound different to us than to others. For example, Sundberg notes that the higher frequencies of the voice don't radiate backward very effectively, making the timbre we perceive of our own voice sound more "bassy" than it sounds to those who hear us (1987, 159). A singer first hearing the playback of her or his recorded voice might be as "dumbfounded" and "aghast" as García had been at his first sight of the glottis in action: in both cases singers are confronted by the uncanny experience of their own defamiliarized voice.

By detaching the voice from both the body and the presence of a live audience, the phonograph helped spur new aesthetic protocols. Mark Katz has described a number of "phonograph effects," by which he means the "manifestations of sound recording's influence" on musical performance (2004, 3). For Katz, an important category of such effects arose in response to the fact that audiences could not see the performers they heard on records. Though it might seem an obvious point, Katz reminds us that this represented the loss of a powerful channel of communication, since musical performers "express themselves not only through the sound of their voices or instruments but with their faces and bodies" (20). Recording artists in the isolation of a studio, lacking the stimulus of audience feedback, often felt less compelled to use flamboyant gestures and expressive pauses. Performers thus took a less elastic approach to time in the studio than on the stage, which, along with the fact that early wax cylinders could record only around four minutes of music, led to "a noticeable move in classical performance toward steadier tempos" (23).

Michael Chanan makes a similar argument, noting that recording played a role in the shift from Romantic to modern styles of musical performance. As an example, Chanan compares Nikisch's 1913 recording of Beethoven's Fifth Symphony to Toscanini's 1921 recording, finding in the former remnants of Romantic style such as "the elastic treatment of pitch and tempo" (1995, 120–21). For Chanan, Toscanini's recording represents a more modern, "streamlined twentieth-century performance practice" in that it features a uniform, "geometrical" approach to pitch and tempo and so a general emphasis on "the more formal and abstract properties of music" (125). Chanan argues that this is indicative of wider stylistic changes and reflects the experience of recording. The pianist Glenn Gould also describes how recording could lead to the demise of Romantic flourishes, since it prevented performances from becoming "distorted by overexposure," and so "top-heavy with interpretive 'niceties' intended to woo the upper balcony, as is almost inevitably the case with the overplayed piece of concert repertoire" (1984, 336).

If studio performers were sometimes inclined to forgo certain "interpretive niceties," at other times they felt the need to add expressive techniques in order to make their musical performances more visible to the listener's imagination. In a fascinating chapter on recording violinists, Katz observes that the use of a strong vibrato became increasingly prevalent on recordings made after 1920. Katz offers this stylistic shift as a phonograph effect, suggesting that vibrato compensated for the loss of the visual dimension of performance by distinguishing individual performers on record, adding emotional cues, and, on the whole, offering "a greater sense of the performer's presence on record" (2004, 93).[7] Katz's connection between the invisibility of phonographic performance and the use of vibrato provides an opportunity to bring together two of the larger concerns of this book. Recall that the chapters in part 1 were concerned with the ways in which performers responded to their isolation from audiences. In part 2 we have been examining the importance of timbre and inflection in sound media performances. Katz's discussion of vibrato provides evidence that the separation of performer and audience could inspire expressive compensation in terms of timbre and inflection. Indeed, some of the same claims Katz makes about the function of vibrato could also be made about the performed laughter so prevalent on the early phonograph records described in chapter 1. We will return to the notion of the phonograph performer's "invisibility" later in the chapter. For now, it suffices to point out that the arguments of Katz, Chanan, and Glenn Gould suggest that, though García's laryngoscope allowed singers to observe their voices with scientific accuracy, the phonograph allowed singers to hear their voices in a modern, detached manner, and it also had more far-reaching implications for vocal technique.

Several of the topics that we have considered thus far in this chapter—bel canto, the laryngoscope, and the phonograph—serendipitously converge around the person and writings of Hermann Klein, a London-based writer and vocal teacher active in the first decades of the twentieth century. Klein studied with Manuel García II as a young man, and García even lived in Klein's parents' house in London for a time (Moran 1990, 17). García's influence on Klein is reflected in his 1923 bel canto instructional text as well as his work as a critic for the magazine *The Gramophone*. In fact, Klein planned to record and release a series of phonograph records in 1907 and 1908 called *The Phono-Vocal Method,* featuring vocal exercises based on Manuel García's *Hints on Singing* (301). In a reprint of the preface to his *Phono-Vocal Method* textbook, Klein wrote that he had until that time refused to write a book on singing "because of the extreme difficulty of offering effective instruction to would-be singers through the printed page alone, without the aid of the voice to illustrate my meaning." The gramophone, Klein wrote, had supplied "the missing link," since it reflected the voice "as faithfully as the mirror reflects the face" (303). As the mirrors of the laryngoscope had revealed the voice, so too apparently could the gramophone. Unfortunately, the Columbia factory where the master recordings were being stored burned to the ground, and the project was never completed (304).

One reason that Klein never returned to the *Phono-Vocal Method* was that he underwent a radical change of heart about the relationship between the voice and recorded sound. For Klein the advent of electronic recording and amplification meant that recordings no longer reflected the voice faithfully. The loud, projecting bel canto voice had been wonderfully suited to recording during the acoustic era when volume and

consistency of tone were paramount. As is well known, a sea change occurred in recording practice in the mid-1920s with the introduction of
radio microphones and electronic amplification. The implications of this
new technological context for singers and pedagogues in the bel canto
tradition can be indicated by an article entitled "The Distortions of
Over-Amplification," in which Klein described the "new sin of over-
amplifying a singer's voice in the making of a gramophone record": "I
cannot help regarding the process of enlarging or exaggerating the
human voice as a deliberate act of deception. It is not akin to the en-
largement of a photograph or a picture. It is not the same excusable device as that employed for increasing the volume of vocal, spoken, or instrumental sounds for the purpose of filling a large auditorium. It is done
simply in order to make the organ of the singer appear bigger, more resonant, more imposing and impressive, than it is in reality" (309). Klein
concluded that electronic amplification on records was "unfair to the
public" because it creates "a wrong estimate of the size of the voice, al-
ters its whole character, deprives it of its natural charm, and, as a rule,
exaggerates whatever faults there may be of enunciation, accent, and diction. In short, it converts the gramophone from a true witness into a false
one" (309–10).

Since records were no longer a true "mirror" of the voice, they could
not be used to teach singing, and they caused new problems when people
tried to imitate them. In an article called "The Penalties of Exaggera-
tion," Klein warned of the possible consequences of "too slavish and
exact" an imitation of the vocal sounds heard on "modern electrical records." Klein recounted an audition with a prospective student, a young
man who "did not know a note of music and had never had a lesson in
singing or music in his life" but owned a gramophone, on which he
played "records of the latest type, sung by Caruso and other favorite operatic tenors." When the student began to sing, he produced a sound that
Klein found "not quite easy to describe": "The young man, after fully in-
flating his chest, started by letting out a series of stentorian notes, which
he sustained at high pressure, his face distorted by glaring eyes and di-
lated nostrils. . . . It was tremendous; it was awful; it was also pitiful."
The cause of this pitiful display, according to Klein, was the man's effort
to reproduce "the gigantic sounds which he had heard issuing from his
gramophone": "He had been fascinated and led astray by the glorious
sonority of the tones that had filled his ears, and which he had unluck-
ily supposed to be of the normal strength given out by the average
singer." For Klein, this anecdote reflected the danger of "mistaking the

doctored article for the real thing," because "the microphone voice has ceased to be identical in volume and quality with its original" (377).

Klein has clearly naturalized bel canto as the "real thing," forgetting the structure of architecture, training, and personnel that made the original musical performance possible. But given his connections to García, it is perhaps not surprising that Klein seems to have understood the phonograph as an audio version of the laryngoscope: a modern tool that could be useful for displays of correct technique (his *Phono-Vocal Method*) and could, during the acoustic era of recording, accurately represent bel canto performance. In the tradition of bel canto singing, then, the laryngoscope was as pertinent a theoretical model for sound reproduction as photography or the telephone.

Though the student in Klein's anecdote reacted to microphones and electronic amplification by oversinging, a more successful and so more virulent threat to the bel canto tradition was the people who used amplification and the microphone to undersing: the radio crooners. Klein described crooning as "an inartistic and most vicious form of voice production . . . a distortion and misuse of the art of singing," and he hopefully asserted that the day of radio singers "with voices of infinitesimal volume . . . that would not travel half-way across a small concert room" was nearly over: "The full, free, ringing voice which is technically well produced endures!" (377). As we saw in the last chapter, crooners used electronic sound technology not to reproduce performances keyed to the concert hall, but to create new performance frames keyed to the intimate spaces of media reception.

Klein rejected the electric phonograph's ability to teach bel canto, but this was not the case with genres such as jazz and blues, which the phonograph disseminated to countless aspiring musicians. Evan Eisenberg points out the importance of records for spreading styles of blues performance: "Whereas Bessie Smith had needed to go on the road with Ma Rainey in order to learn from her, Victoria Spivey and Billie Holiday and Mahalia Jackson could learn from Bessie Smith by staying put in Texas or Maryland or Louisiana and playing her records. In the same way Johnny Winter could learn guitar from Robert Johnson when Johnson had been dead twenty years" (1987, 141). Along similar lines, Katz offers the example of the white jazz cornetist Bix Beiderbecke, whose career "is nearly inconceivable without the phonograph. Growing up in Davenport, Iowa, Beiderbecke had little chance to hear live jazz" (2004, 73). Beiderbecke was one of many white musicians captivated by the sounds of jazz performances that previously might have been heard only in certain parts of New Orleans or Chicago. Horn players like Beider-becke were inspired particularly by an influential performer who rose to fame in the jazz scenes of both of those cities and began making record-ings in the mid-1920s. Those records spread his audacious musical in-novations around the country and featured a vocal style that, like the whispering crooner, represented an alternative to bel canto imperatives. That performer, of course, was Louis Armstrong—the figure paired with Caruso as our double-voiced icon of phonography—and that vocal style was the throaty rasp.

THE RASP

In physiological terms, a raspy vocal timbre is created by loose glottal closure, a raised larynx, and relatively less resonance in the cavities of the head. This results in the creation of noise: "breathiness" from excess air passing through the glottis, and "throatiness" from a raised larynx. Fur-ther, the resulting tone lacks the spike in the high frequencies of the singer's formant that helped the bel canto voice to project. Indeed, a rough, raspy voice was considered the antithesis of bel canto. Recall how Pleasants's definition of bel canto emphasized that it involved "a disci-plined avoidance of shouting, nasality, harsh or open sounds" (1981, 20). Similarly, García's list of vocal shortcomings included guttural, nasal, and harsh timbres (1975, 1xii).[8] The bel canto tradition rejected many potentially expressive timbres of the voice in order to strive for an even, round chiaroscuro tone. In a culture in which bel canto was con-sidered the hallmark of good singing, a rasp would be understood to a large degree as reflecting a lack of training or sophistication. In Amer-ican musical culture, the rasp was also strongly associated with the African American voice.

A raspy style has been an aspect of several genres of African American singing, notably work songs, field hollers, gospel, and country blues. African American singing is certainly not reducible to this rasp, and even in a genre such as country blues one can hear a wide variety of vocal tim-bres. Nonetheless, many authors have connected the rasp to African American music and culture. Tricia Rose writes that African and African American music has tended to allow for "a wide range of vocal sounds," the rasp being one (1994, 66). Similarly, Roger Abrahams argues that one of the most distinctive features of "Black speaking behavior" is the use of a wider range of "paralinguistic features" than is found in "com-paratively stylized performance contexts" by white American speakers.

These paralinguistic features include pitch changes, the manipulation of cadences, and vocal effects such as "rasp, growl, falsetto [and] whine" (1976, 20).

Many authors have made connections between African American singing styles and African musical culture. In his influential book *Blues People,* Amiri Baraka stresses the importance of timbre in African performance: "Melodic diversity in African music came not only in the actual arrangements of notes (in terms of Western transcription) but in the singer's vocal interpretation. The 'tense, slightly hoarse-sounding vocal techniques' of the work songs and the blues stem directly from West African musical tradition" (1963, 26). He also quotes Ernest Borneman to the effect that "while the whole European tradition strives for regularity—of pitch, of time, of timbre and of vibrato—the African tradition strives precisely for the negation of these elements" (31).[9] Fales has elaborated on this last point, describing a predilection of African musicians to utilize "noise" as part of their sound: "While the manufacture of classical instruments and the performance practice of Western musicians has aimed toward reducing the amount of extraneous noise produced by an instrument, African musicians augment the natural noise potential of their instrument by attaching noise-makers such as rattling seeds or bottle caps on which the vibrations of the main resonator operate" (1994, 69).[10] In this context, a rasp might be considered not as untrained or unsophisticated, but as adding a degree of stylization and complexity to the tone.

The rasp was certainly just one option from a broad timbral palette available to African American performers, but it was one that took on heightened significance in a white musical culture where bel canto was the dominant yardstick for evaluating vocal performance. In such a context, the rasp stood out as a black expression against the white background of bel canto. In an African tradition, the rasp could be heard as a sophisticated stylization of tone, but white critics and audiences immersed in a turn-of-the-century musical culture dominated by bel canto would tend to hear it as "noise," interfering with the pure signal of the round tone. Nevertheless, there is evidence that the rasp could take on positive meanings to some white listeners, albeit only in the terms of racist notions of blackness so prevalent at the time. Consider an article on the "Negro voice" published in the *Washington Post* in 1903, in which the author asserts that "there is a peculiar vibrating quality in the negro voice due, perhaps, to a peculiar arrangement of the vocal chords [*sic*], which is not found in the white race. Its effect is absolutely unique and indescribable." The author notes that this "remarkable quality" of the black voice is "lessened by cultivation," and he goes on to make the atavistic tendencies in white thought painfully clear: "Unquestionably some of this music is almost as old as the world, for it has been chanted in the wilds of Africa to the accompaniment of rude drum and punctured reed ever since human beings could articulate. It still retains much of its original savagery, and when sung with the peculiar timbre which is the especial attribute of the negro's voice it produces an effect which sets the nerves tingling" ("Negroes as Singers" 6).

Black performers seeking successful careers in such a cultural context would need to develop styles that made use of a wide range of expressive techniques available in the African American tradition, while avoiding being considered "savage" or "unsophisticated" by the musical judgments of a dominant and oppressive white culture. Such a dilemma is, of course, only one aspect of the African American experience of a "double-consciousness," so famously identified by W. E. B. Du Bois: "One ever feels his twoness,—an American, a Negro; two souls, two thoughts, two unreconciled strivings; two warring ideals in one dark body, whose dogged strength alone keeps it from being torn asunder" (1903, 5). Popular recordings from the first decades of the twentieth century illustrate how some African American singers negotiated this difficult double bind.

In fact, recording technology played an important role in the development of African American vocal styles because it solved the problem of accurately notating the "peculiar timbre" of the black voice: William Francis Allen wrote in his 1867 introduction to *Slave Songs of the United States* that "the voices of the colored people have a peculiar quality that nothing can imitate; and the intonations and delicate variations of even one singer cannot be reproduced on paper" (Southern 1983, 151). Though bel canto's dominance was reified in the design of concert halls, the phonograph industry had the potential to open new avenues of access for black performers. Consider, for example, that the recording industry trade paper the *Phonogram* wrote in 1891 that "Negroes [record] better than white singers, because their voices have a certain sharpness or harshness about them that a white man's has not" (cited in Brooks 2005, 30). In fact, vocal performances of "blackness" were central to the early phonograph industry, although actual African American performers were allowed to participate only in very circumscribed ways.

As discussed in chapter 1, George Washington Johnson's *Laughing Song* and *Whistling Coon* were the first popular vocal recordings by an

African American. Listening to these records with an ear to timbre, we should note that Johnson's voice has a raspy edge, perhaps part of what made his performances stand out as particularly "authentic." Furthermore, the laughter and whistling that became the center of Johnson's career are expressive vocalizations that avoid easy categorization in terms of bel canto or rasp, and so they sidestep some of the dominant aesthetic judgments about the voice. Johnson divided his vocal performances between singing minstrel show material and wordless laughs and whistles, and so while he of necessity conformed to the racist stage conventions of the era, he also transcended them. Johnson was a pioneer, not only for his success in the phonograph industry, but also for developing a double-voiced approach that we will see was taken up by subsequent black performers.

Johnson's successor as the best-selling black recording artist was Bert Williams, a vaudeville comedian in the first decades of the century and "the first Negro entertainer to win the wholehearted admiration of white audiences" (Charters 1970, 9). Williams was born in the Bahamas in 1874, but his family settled in California, where he attended Stanford University. After leaving school, Williams entered show business, and he reluctantly began performing on the blackface minstrel stage with Martin and Seig's Mastodon Minstrels. It was there that he teamed up with another African American minstrel performer, George Walker. Walker and Williams struck out on their own and, billed as "Two Real Coons," they starred in a series of musicals on the New York stage between 1898 and 1909. After Walker retired from the stage owing to failing health, Williams went on to even greater fame, headlining the Ziegfeld Follies for a number of years beginning in 1910. Williams also made dozens of records between 1901 and 1921, and Tim Brooks describes him as "the best-selling black artist of the pre-1920 period by far" (2005, 105). As can be heard on his records, Williams had what Jim Walsh has called "a rasping, husky tone" to his voice (1950, 19). Williams's vocal performances, however, were not sung so much as recited in a half-spoken, half-sung style. As heard on records such as *All In, Out and Down* (1906) and *Let It Alone* (1906), Williams leaves the song's melody to the orchestra, while he bobs and weaves around it with his slow, off-kilter comic style. Williams's interplay with the orchestra can also be heard on his famous rendition of "Nobody" (1906), in which his slow, swooping delivery blends so well with the glides of the trombone that at times it is even difficult to distinguish his voice from the horn.

What can the idiosyncratic styles of Williams and Johnson tell us about the kinds of black voices that the phonograph industry would

permit at this time? Both men made use of a raspy timbre that fell outside the prerogatives of bel canto, but which could have served to authenticate their performances of "blackness" on the minstrel stage. Both
performers also used a range of vocalizations, including laughter and
recitation, and tended to turn their voices into instruments: Johnson with
his whistle, and Williams through his interaction with the orchestral accompaniment. Taken as a whole, we see that Johnson and Williams developed comic vocal styles that challenged the imperatives of bel canto
while both accommodating and struggling against the conventions of the
minstrel stage.[11] It is, of course, a sad irony not only that these singers
had to conform to minstrel show stereotypes, but also that the majority
of "black" material heard at this time was performed by white men:
Johnson and Williams were notable exceptions. In fact, their singing
styles are best understood in relation to the voices of the white minstrel
performers with whom they shared the stage.

Recordings of minstrel show performances from the turn of the century provide an avenue for examining the cultural meanings of the rasp
and the bel canto round tone for white singers. In what follows my goal
is not to establish a hierarchy according to which style or timbre more
closely approximates an authentic black performance style. In his discussion of the minstrel show, W. T. Lhamon warned against struggling
to prove whether minstrel songs were accurate depictions of African
American culture: "Until the cows come home, we might debate how
well or ill minstrels copied black culture. But that is a fruitless task and
always to be followed by such further imponderables as, What is authentic black culture? Is any authenticity there? What is 'black'?" (1998,
44–45). Instead of a chimerical pursuit of authenticity, I am interested in
mapping some of the meanings that adhered to vocal timbre in the context of the minstrel show, which enabled the creation of another kind of
vocal chiaroscuro: a white-black voice.

BLACKFACE, BLACKVOICE

White performers in blackface makeup began touring the nation in the
late 1820s, singing what were supposed to be "Negro songs and dances"
in venues such as circuses and theaters. Blackface entertainment became
increasingly popular throughout the 1830s and 1840s, during which
time minstrel performers created "a public sensation" (Toll 1974,
27–28). Certainly part of the charge of the minstrel show came from its
rejection of highbrow performance conventions. Eric Lott emphasizes

how the minstrel show functioned in terms of class distinction, arguing that it represented a "class-defined, often class-conscious, cultural sphere": "One of minstrelsy's functions was precisely to bring various class fractions into contact with one another, to mediate their relations, and finally to aid in the construction of class identities over the bodies of black people" (1993, 67). Lhamon agrees, stating that "precisely because middle-class aspirants disdained the black jitterbug in every region, the black figure appealed all across the Atlantic as an organizational emblem for workers and the unemployed" (1998, 44). "Blackface action," Lhamon asserts, was typically "slashing back at the pretensions and politesse of authority more than at blackness" (22).

The minstrel show's rejection of dominant culture and highbrow decorum was expressed in its raw, ecstatic style of performance. Toll describes the performance style of the Virginia Minstrels circa 1840s: "Once on stage, they could not stay still for an instant. Even while sitting, they contorted their bodies, cocked their heads, rolled their eyes, and twisted their outstretched legs. When the music began, they exploded in a frenzy of grotesque and eccentric movements. Whether singing, dancing, or joking, whether in a featured role, accompanying a comrade, or just listening, their wild hollering and their bobbing, seemingly compulsive movements charged their entire performance with excitement" (1974, 36). One might be led to conclude that the vocal performances heard on the minstrel stage would feature the raw, throaty rasp that had been associated with African American performance and that contrasted with the highbrow imperatives of bel canto. When one listens to recorded performances of minstrel material and so-called coon songs from the period between the 1890s and the 1920s, however, one hears exactly the opposite: those records feature a predominance of the bel canto round tone and a notable absence of the rasp.

Consider, for example, a record made by the Victor Olden Time Minstrels (Victor circa 1906) that features a typical abbreviated form of the stage minstrel performance, beginning with the minstrel "interlocutor" announcing, "Gentlemen, be seated," and then cuing the "grand opening overture." When this upbeat orchestral interlude ends, there is a burst of exuberant shouts and cheers—recall that the hearable audience of the broadcast era had its origins in the minstrel show. Next comes a section of comic interaction between the pompous interlocutor and the comic end man—in this case, the early recording artist Billy Murray. In spoken dialogue, Murray indexes "blackness" through a nasal, whining timbre and a sly, slow delivery. After the jokes, Murray sings the song

"Get Happy," which is in contrast to his spoken minstrel voice: here all "black" characterization is gone, and the song is performed with an even, projecting tone.

A record made by the Christy Minstrels (Victor circa 1907) reveals a similar dynamic. Here again is the introductory musical number, in this case an ensemble choral song, "College Life." After the perfunctory "Gentlemen, be seated," there is comic interaction between the interlocutor, S. H. Dudley, and two endmen, Billy Murray and Arthur Collins. In a manner similar to Murray's, Collins vocally indexes "blackness" through a slow delivery and a stifled manner suggesting that he is constantly on the verge of bursting into laughter; in fact, he does laugh after delivering his punch lines:

> *Dudley:* Answer me this question, were you ever in jail?
> *Collins:* I must say that I was in jail once.
> *Dudley:* Well, I'd be ashamed to own it.
> *Collins:* Oh, I didn't own it, I was just simply a boarder [laughter].

After an explosive bout of laughter, Collins goes into the song "My Kickapoo Queen." Like Murray's, Collins's sung performances are in contrast with his spoken ones: he sings the song straight, without characterization, and in a full, round tone.

Murray and Collins are particularly good examples of minstrel singers because they were both extremely successful early recording artists. The historian Tim Gracyk calls Murray "arguably the most popular recording artist of the acoustic era, with sales of his records probably exceeding those of any other artist" (2002, 233). Murray began his entertainment career in minstrel troupes in the 1890s, and he began recording for Edison in 1903 (235). He was primarily known for what were called coon songs—syncopated ragtime music with lyrics that featured crude racial stereotypes in the minstrel stage dialect—although he was also associated with the songs of George M. Cohan (238). Arthur Collins was "among the half dozen most prolific recording artists during the acoustic era" (65). He began recording in the late 1890s and was, like Murray, known as a coon singer. Collins was most closely associated with the song "The Preacher and the Bear," which he first recorded in 1904 and which became such a perennial favorite that versions of the song recorded by Collins were still being released as late as 1941 (71). Although he was one of the most successful performers of "black" material, one hears little timbral diversity in Collins's performances. Instead, his records feature his trademark rich baritone voice and a round tone.[12]

There are several ways to explain the prominence of bel canto style on minstrel records from this era. First, Toll argues that a shift occurred in minstrel performance after the 1850s toward more genteel, "sentimental, emotional material" typified by the music of Stephen Foster: "By 1845, minstrelsy in New York City drifted toward the 'refined' melodic approach to minstrelsy and away from the earthy vitality of its folk roots" (1974, 37). Minstrel troupes such as the Ethiopian Serenaders "sought the respectability of 'high' culture," and so a growing emphasis was placed on the romantic balladeer who sang sentimental love songs (53–54). When the phonograph industry got off the ground in the 1890s, it had access to this latter stage of the minstrel show. William Howland Kenney has further argued that recordings of folk and traditional songs were often sung with an operatic voice because of the importance of European classical music for a phonograph industry trying to legitimate itself as highbrow entertainment suitable for middle-class homes (1999, 61). There were also technical reasons for the predominance of bel canto. As we've seen, bel canto's ability to project was well suited to recording during the acoustic era, when singers had to etch their voices into wax. Further, at a time when mass duplication was difficult, the studio was, according to Andre Millard, "the place to mass-produce recordings rather than make one faultless master," and so singers often had to perform the same songs again and again (1995, 263). In that context, raspy-voiced singers would be more prone to lose their voices.[13]

But there is another explanation, one related to Katz's notion of the "invisibility" of phonographic performance. Note that the lines of racial identity that were already unstable in blackface performance were made even more tenuous on records. For white singers, the faux–African American minstrel dialect, occasional whoops and laughs, and a syncopated delivery were the markers of an authentic African American voice, whereas timbre tended to remain in the European musical idiom. This timbral inflexibility goes hand in hand with the overdetermination of the laugh and the minstrel dialect as markers of authenticity. Singers such as Arthur Collins vocally marked themselves as "black" through those devices: Tim Gracyk notes that one of Collins's trademarks was "a short laugh, often interjected between lines in songs" (2002, 66). In this context the laugh and dialect took on increased importance as an acceptable means of indexing blackness without breaking too many of the protocols of "good singing." As images of minstrel troupes on posters and in catalogs often sought to reassure the white audience that the blackface performers were white, so the bel canto round tone functioned as an assurance that the racial masquerade went only so far.

An exception to that pattern that may prove the rule can be found in the performances of Billy Golden (figure 12). Born William B. Shires in 1858 in Cincinnati, Ohio, Golden started a career in blackface comedy on the vaudeville stage in the 1870s (Gracyk 2002, 143). One of his trademarks was using the "cane pat" as part of "buck-and-wing dancing" (J. Walsh 1944, 25). Golden began recording with Columbia in 1891, and his most famous record was *Turkey in the Straw,* a song that he introduced to the public (Tim Gracyk 2002, 144). His numerous recordings of coon shouts were an enormous success. Jim Walsh, writing in the magazine *Hobbies* in 1944, recalled that Victor catalogs had advertised that "no other Negro specialty records have ever approached the popularity of those by Billy Golden" (1944, 26). Walsh goes on to quote the Victor catalog as claiming that Golden's performances were "so real" that "the listener forgets all about Golden and hears only a jolly old darky with an infectious laugh." Walsh was quick to agree: "That statement is literally true. As perfect representations of 'before de wah' darky types, it seems impossible that Golden's work could be excelled" (26).

What made Golden's vocal performances so convincingly authentic to listeners? Consider his 1905 record *Rabbit Hash* (Victor), which features a solo vocal performance by Golden, who, over the course of its roughly two and a half minutes, presents an astonishing range of vocal timbres, registers, and characterizations. The record begins with a long cry of "Yeah!" that bends up into a falsetto yodel at the end, after which Golden goes into a rhythmic, singsong delivery that is punctuated by hysterical laughter that rockets from a low chest tone up to a high falsetto: "Yeah! Down south old rabbit had a mighty bad habit [laugh], of slippin' through the turnip patch, a-cuttin' down the cabbage [laugh], did you ever see such a rabbit? Well I never did. Dat am the worst rabbit ever I see'd [laugh]."

In what comes next, Golden's style becomes more complex and polyphonic. First, he speaks directly to the rabbit he's been describing, unleashing a stream of malapropisms and nonsense that recalls the parodic "stump speech" of the minstrel show: "Look here rabbit, you am too scandinavious, son-a-bodest, sun-a-bo-titious, unexclusive dus-en-atious." Continuing to address the rabbit, Golden says, "Now you get away from here," but he quickly turns around to respond as the rabbit: "I ain't a gwyne to do it." Next comes another lightning change in timbre, this time to a fantastically heavy rasp: "Ahhhh, go on! [laugh]" This kind of

Figure 12. The blackface comedian and early recording
star Billy Golden.

crazy-quilt vocal collage continues throughout the record. He scolds,
"Rabbit, ain't you 'shamed?" The rabbit replies, " 'Deed I am," and then
his voice jumps up to an exaggerated falsetto "Mmm-hmmm." The repeated hook of the record is a propulsive rhythmic chant that embodies
the radical shifts in timbre and register featured on the performance as a
whole: "A rabbit, a hash, a polecat mash, a rat coon mush, a jaybird
soup, and [falsetto] a peck-a-peck-a-peck-a-peck-a-peck-a-peck-peck-
peck-a [heavy rasp] good gravy! [laugh]" The heavy rasp heard on the
lines "Ahhhh, go on!" and "good gravy!" is a recurring trope not only
on this record but on Golden's other recorded performances as well. His
1902 recording of "Turkey in the Straw" (Monarch) begins with and is
punctuated by ecstatic laughter that includes both falsetto and a throaty
rasp. The middle of the song features a vocal break during which Golden
performs malapropisms and then, speaking as the turkey, delivers the
line "Go 'way, back and sit down" with an exaggerated rasp.
    The rasp lent distinction to Golden's performances in a context in
which even minstrel vocal performances were characterized by the round
tone of bel canto.[14] In fact, Golden's style on records such as *Rabbit*

Hash represents a rejection of several of the central imperatives of bel canto. Besides striving for a pure tone, one of the goals of that tradition was to create a smooth, consistent tone and a graceful movement between vocal registers. A vocal register is a "series of consecutive notes that can be produced with nearly identical quality," in the male voice the primary two being chest (or full voice) and head (or falsetto) (Sundberg 1987, 50). A central aspect of bel canto pedagogy was to "reduce or even eliminate timbral variation between registers," so that the shift into a different register would be marked "by the smallest possible timbral differences" (51). The goal of achieving continuity across the vocal registers is roughly analogous to Hollywood's filmic language of continuity editing, whereby the inherent discontinuity of moving from shot to shot was smoothed over via techniques such as eyeline matches and matches on action. By contrast, Golden offers the vocal equivalent of Soviet montage: a performance of constant collision and juxtaposition in terms of chest voice and falsetto, language and laugh, spoken dialogue and singing, clear and raspy vocal timbres.[15]

Wayne Koestenbaum has written that transgressing the smooth break between vocal registers can represent other transgressions for male singers, in part because falsetto has been so strongly gendered female: "The failure to disguise this gendered break is fatal to the art of 'natural' voice production. The singer schooled in bel canto will avoid eruptions by disguising the register breaks and passing smoothly over them. The register line, like the color line, the gender line, or the hetero/homo line, can be crossed only if the transgressor pretends that no journey has taken place" (1993, 167). Golden boldly crosses this vocal line, and I would argue that it was the resulting polyphonic and ecstatic quality—as well as the use of a raspy delivery—that made Golden's performances seem to index an authentic "black" style. Walsh's assertion that Golden faithfully represented a before-the-war "darky" might be understood as meaning that his vocal style retained conventions of the antebellum minstrel stage. The vocal style heard on Golden's records might be considered an analog to the frenzy of "grotesque," "eccentric," and "seemingly compulsive" movements that Toll describes as aspects of minstrel show style circa 1840.

Recall how Walsh stated that Golden's style was such that one "forgets all about Golden" and sees only the "jolly old darky." The rasp was a central feature of a kind of vocal performance that could make the white performer disappear into the minstrel stereotype. Here, then, is another reason for the white minstrel singer's use of bel canto: to be sure that vocal performances were understood and evaluated according to the performer's vocal mastery, and to be sure that the bright outline of white would remain visible in an otherwise "black" performance. Golden demonstrates how the rasp could be an important technique for creating authenticity for some minstrel singers on early phonograph records. A story told by Jim Walsh suggests the effect of Golden's style: "I well remember that, as a small boy, I was playing [Golden's recording of the song] 'Yaller Gal' on the Victrola one day when I saw the Methodist preacher approaching. Suspecting he wouldn't approve my taste in music, I snatched the record off, and by the time he neared the house, the recorded voices of Anthony and Harrison were wailing, 'Looking This Way,' a tried-and-true Gospel hymn" (1944, 27). This quote suggests some of the transgressive resonance of a raspy timbre for white singers at this time.

The records of black and white minstrel singers reveal a varied and complex range of styles, and they demonstrate that choices about vocal timbre were intricately bound up with the performance of race. Two of the most successful minstrel performers of the first decades of the twentieth century were chosen to be featured on one of the earliest double-sided records released by Columbia Records: Bert Williams's "All In, Out and Down" coupled with Billy Golden's "Turkey in the Straw" (J. Walsh 1950, 19). These two singers developed very different vocal styles, both of which were combined and redefined in performances by the most influential popular singer of the 1920s and 1930s: Louis Armstrong.

HEARING DOUBLE

I have argued that African American singers in the early years of the phonograph industry faced a dilemma in that the timbral variations permitted by African and African American musical traditions were often defined as different from bel canto and so heard in negative or atavistic terms. In response to this situation, George Washington Johnson and Bert Williams found ways to double their voices to encompass a range of timbres and expressive techniques. Louis Armstrong represents the apotheosis of that kind of vocal doubling, since, as Giddins writes, he was "the only major figure in Western culture who influenced the music of his time equally as an instrumentalist and a singer" (1988, 33). That is, Armstrong the instrumentalist and Armstrong the singer represent two voices whose dialogue comments on the stylistic duality of rasp and bel canto.

Armstrong stated in a 1962 interview that "singing and playing is the same," and his trumpet playing is a stunning example of the vocal nature of much African American instrumental performance (cited in Berrett 1999, 26). Many innovative techniques in blues and jazz instrumental style—bending notes, adding vibrato and rasp, using mutes on horns—aim to endow Western instruments with a timbral flexibility akin to the human voice's.[16] Indeed, the ability to "sing" through an instrument is one solution to the stylistic bind faced by African American performers: recall George Washington Johnson's recourse to the whistle, and Williams's interplay with the trombone on "Nobody." In fact, Armstrong's trumpet works as a kind of bel canto translation device, encrypting his melodic and rhythmic invention into the kind of round tone that he was unable to achieve with his singing voice.[17]

In what follows, however, I will focus on Armstrong's singing voice, which was given its gravelly tone largely as the result of a physical condition called leukoplakia, in which growths develop on the vocal cords (Collier 1983, 239). Leukoplakia is exacerbated by overindulgence in activities such as smoking and drinking, and it is worth noting that in addition to being associated with black performance, the rasp is also an index of "bad living," which perhaps adds to its status as a sign of outlaw authenticity. Armstrong's voice was extremely influential—his biographer Gary Giddins relates an anecdote about musicians "sticking their heads out the window trying to catch colds" in order to sound like him—which certainly reinforced the cultural association between African American performance and a raspy tone (1988, 87).

Though he was most famous for his wordless scat singing, Armstrong's use of language was an important part of his style and was well suited to the recording studio. For example, consider Armstrong's performance of "Lazy River" (1931) in relation to Roman Jakobson's notion of the "speech event." Jakobson describes six factors that make up any speech event: an addresser; an addressee; a message that is sent; a code that the addresser and addressee share; a common context or referent for the message; and a channel of physical and psychological contact between those in dialogue (1980, 81). All these factors are present in any speech event, but one or another can be emphasized, resulting in what Jakobson calls the six basic aspects of language. Armstrong's recorded performances reveal a remarkable agility in bringing these various aspects of language in and out of momentary dominance.

Lazy River begins with an instrumental section during which Armstrong makes his vocal entrance in a playful call-and-response with the horns ("yeah, uh-huh, sure"). Armstrong's voice functions in what Jakobson calls the "phatic" mode: a type of speech act that is oriented toward maintaining the channel of contact and is typified by various ritualized verbal formulas ("good morning," "have a nice day," and so on). Armstrong provides a phatic channel of feedback in "conversation" with the band, heightening our perception of the vocal quality of the instruments. Before beginning to sing the first chorus, Armstrong lets out some quick instructions to the band ("Way down, way down!"). Imperatives such as these are examples of what Jakobson refers to as "conative" speech events, which are predominantly keyed toward the addressee (83). Armstrong can be heard in the conative mode when he directs the band here, as well as at the end of the song ("Swing out!").

Armstrong proceeds to sing about going up a lazy river and lingering in the shade of "a kind old tree," ending with an unaccompanied line: "Throw away your troubles, dream a dream of me, dream a dream of me." Armstrong's delivery of such expressive song lyrics is best understood as being oriented toward the message itself: what Jakobson terms the "poetic." Note that Armstrong's delivery of lyrics is not so much like the recitation of poetry as like a film narrator who at times appears within the narrative. Take the last verse, in which Armstrong starts with the title line ("Up the lazy river"), but then breaks it down to the single word "mmm river," and then seems to speak to the river itself ("Oh, you river! Oh, you dog!"), as though he had stepped into the narrative world of the song.[18]

From so far within the poetic frame, Armstrong abruptly rekeys his performance with a last injunction to his fellow musicians ("Look out, swing out there!") before the final trumpet solo. In fact, we should note how frequently he breaks the performance frame: as we have seen, breaking frames has been an important technique used by studio performers to provide their recordings with a sense of immediacy. A dramatic example of such a moment occurs in this recording of "Lazy River" when Armstrong delivers his trademark exclamation, "Oh, you dog!" which is low and extremely raspy. Such asides and laughs resemble phatic speech acts in which a channel of contact is maintained not with his band but with the listener. That sense of collusion continues when, after an off-the-cuff laugh signals that he has flooded out of the performance frame, Armstrong self-reflexively comments on his own performance ("Boy, am I riffin' this evening!") before going back into the song. Here Armstrong is speaking in direct address to the listener about the "code" of his speech itself, what Jakobson calls the "metalingual" function.

Armstrong's rapid-fire rekeying recalls Billy Golden's frenetic *Rabbit Hash*. Indeed, the two men share some common techniques: Armstrong's "Oh, you dog!" resembles Golden's "Ah, go on!" in that both function to highlight excesses of vocal rasp. The listener, however, never gets the sense of frantic discontinuity from Armstrong's "Lazy River" that one finds on Golden's records. This is in part because of the way in which Armstrong tends to connect his notes in smooth, fluid lines, even during his most gymnastic phrases. Also note that Armstrong, unlike Golden, never goes into falsetto, instead using his horn to access high notes. Golden's register breaks lend him a certain gender ambiguity and add to the overall sense of vaudevillesque comedy in his frantic style. By contrast, Armstrong's unbreakably confident delivery, fluid phrasing, and consistently raspy tone provide his performances with a sense of continuity and allow him to use a range of vocal techniques and timbres as wide as Golden's, but for the purposes of emotional expressivity.

Jakobson's framework has allowed us to appreciate the flexibility of Armstrong's voice as an instrument of language. But Armstrong is best known for using his voice to go "beyond" language, as we hear in the second chorus of "Lazy River." Here Armstrong delivers one of his most famous scat performances, his voice becoming an elegant instrument of expression and so emphasizing what Jakobson calls the emotive or expressive function, when a speech act is oriented toward the addresser. "The purely emotive stratum in language," Jakobson writes, "is presented by the interjections" (1980, 82). Popular singers make great use of devices that are or approximate interjections ("Oh, yeah!") to convey immediacy and emotion, and Armstrong uses his various "mmms," "ohs," and scatted syllables to great emotive effect.

The scatting on *Lazy River* is also a vivid illustration of how Armstrong revises the original rhythm and melody of his material: a form of African American expression called "signifying." The term *signifying* can be used to refer to a range of playful verbal manipulation through the use of creative indirection (Abrahams 1976, 50).[19] Henry Louis Gates Jr. has argued that signifying represents a kind of black double-voicedness because it typically entails referring to and revising preexisting utterances (1988, 51). This means that the juxtapositions of signifying tend to have a critical edge akin to parody. Bert Williams's sly tiptoeing around the orchestral melody line can be heard as a subtle form of musical signifying, but Armstrong's style provides a more vivid example. That is, even when Armstrong sings alone, we always hear two

voices; the original melody is always suggested and simultaneously cri-
tiqued by Armstrong's revisions.

Because signifying of this kind is a verbal technique that "turns on the
sheer play of the signifier," it tends to focus the listener's attention on the
materiality of language (78). In Lindon Barrett's terms, this marks an important distinction between what he calls the singing voice and the "signing voice." Barrett argues that the singing voice is best seen in contrast
to the signing voice in a Western culture that promotes the transcendent
nature of speech: "Singing amplifies generally overlooked and seemingly
meaningless physical dimensions of the signing voice, or speech. . . . The
singing voice foregrounds and plays upon bodily dimensions of vocal action usually taken for granted" (1999, 78). Barrett argues that the
singing voice has been of particular importance for African Americans
because of how it situates the voice in the body, "a signal cultural moment and revision for those who would be confined, according to dominant wisdom, to the supplementary realm of the body. Singing in its
physicality reclaims the voice for the body" (79). The emphasis on the
materiality of the voice is, for Barrett, "the paramount aesthetic of
African American vocal performance" and is heard most vividly in scat
singing (79–80).

The grain of the singing voice is certainly emphasized over its linguistic function in Armstrong's scatting, which also happens to amplify our
experience of the raspy materiality of his body. Indeed, Armstrong's self-
assertive style projected a powerful masculine sexuality, and Krin Gabbard writes that he "used his trumpet to express phallic masculinity along
with a great deal of the sexual innuendo that was already an essential element of jazz performance" (1996, 139). Alan Lomax's work on folk
singing can help illuminate the role of the rasp in Armstrong's masculine
persona. Lomax claims that "in most cultures males perform in harsher,
heavier, noisier voices than women" (1968, 192). Lomax argues that
women's singing styles tended to feature egalitarian group interlock or interplay, and hence a clear, nonraspy vocal style in order to facilitate a co-
hesive group sound.[20] By contrast, the rasp was a type of vocalizing that
Lomax claimed would cut through and dominate musical performances,
and so it stood for "the commanding masculine leader, the voice of authority, the tone of the chief or the military commander" (73).

Rasp was held by Lomax and his circle to be an index of self-assertion
as well as masculinity. In Lomax's *Folk Song Style and Culture,* his assistant, Edwin E. Erickson, wrote that "rasp, whenever it appears as a

prominent feature of singing style, is the universal sound of self-assertion" (205). Lomax claimed that raspy singing was generally associated with "masculine training for assertion," since "the irregular acoustical features of vocal noise militate against the production of good blend" (192–93). Similarly, Erickson stated that "any departure from a clear, relaxed tone, is expressive of the individual and his concerns": "Rasp, defined loosely as harsh guttural vocalization, appears to have an especially strong association with social diffuseness and personal assertiveness" (205). Perhaps one way to explain the connection between this vocal timbre and the concept of self-assertion is to note that the creation of noise in the throat more clearly indexes the individual body of the singer than a tone that resonates in the chest and head and is projected out to fill a performance space, as is the case with bel canto.[21] Along these lines, in his 1923 bel canto instructional text, Hermann Klein described how the sensation of bel canto singing is such that "the tone is coming not from the throat at all, but existing ready-made in the area to which it is reflected" (Moran 1990, 29). The bel canto style sought to transcend the body, not surprising since bel canto arose in a Western culture that tended to divide mind and body and saw the voice as being in the domain of the former. The rasp in this context could represent a self-assertive performance of embodiment.

Lomax's stark demarcations between male and female modes of vocalizing are certainly overgeneralized. A raspy vocalization is available equally to men and women, although overt performances of self-assertion have often been easier for men in patriarchal societies. Nonetheless, Lomax's work suggests gendered associations tied to the rasp that helped provide Armstrong's vocal performances with a sense of self-assertive masculine sexuality. Armstrong's rasp becomes most pronounced in those moments of excessive laughter and reflexive asides when he breaks the performance frame. Such moments are typically referred to as Armstrong's "mugging," what Giddins calls "a kind of body English done with the face . . . a way of acting out the music." Some critics and audiences have found Armstrong's mugging to be extremely problematic, both because such clowning could undercut his status as an "artist," and because it invited accusations of being an "Uncle Tom" (Gabbard 1996, 206–15). I would like to consider these performance excesses from another angle: their function in relation to the dynamics of phonographic performance.

Giddins stresses the intensely visual nature of Armstrong's mugging, which he writes was "so much a part of his vocal performances that it is impossible for anyone who has seen him to listen to his records without imagining his facial contortions" (1988, 111). It follows that Armstrong's excesses should be considered techniques that were particularly able to compensate for the lack of visual communication in phonographic performance. Consider Armstrong's recording *Laughin' Louie* (1933), a very strange record, made even stranger by the fact that several writers have singled it out as epitomizing the paradoxes of Armstrong's career. One such paradox had to do with Armstrong's relationship to the songs he performed. Giddins argues that one of Armstrong's innovations was to assert the creativity of the performer over and above his material—an example of the "singer, not the song" dynamic described earlier in this chapter. That is, Armstrong often elevated mediocre material through his unmistakable and irrepressible approach. Nowhere is that irony "more breathtaking," Giddins writes, than on *Laughin' Louie* (38).

The record begins with a frantic eight-bar opening vamp, after which the band abruptly stops and yells, "Yeah! Give it to 'em, Laughin' Louie!" Armstrong speaks quickly in his gravelly voice: "Before I swing for you, I gotta do a little practicing on this little Selmer trumpet." He laughs, introduces the song, laughs again, and counts off the band. They launch into a fairly nondescript number, Armstrong singing what Giddins calls a "rum tune": "Laughin' Louie, I'm Laughin' Louie, yes, boy, it ain't no hooey, mmm, that's me." After a saxophone solo, the music abruptly stops again, and the band laughs. Armstrong says that he's going to play "a beautiful number," and we hear him back off the mike to get to his trumpet position. A band member yells out, spurring more laughter. After a pause, Armstrong produces a single staccato note. The same band member who spoke before offers an exaggerated "Mellow!" and both the band and Armstrong laugh. Next we hear another pause, another ridiculous toot, and more laughs from all involved.

You may have noticed that *Laughin' Louie* bears more than a passing resemblance to the genre of laughing records discussed in chapter 1, in which a laughing audience member interrupts a musician who proceeds to crack up, and so is unable to finish the performance. Recall that the Okeh company released a string of successful laughing records in the early 1920s; the first of these featured a comically thwarted trumpet performance and false starts much like those heard on *Laughin' Louie*. Okeh also happened to be the label that released Armstrong's most influential recordings with the Hot Fives and Sevens beginning in 1925. Armstrong may well have been familiar with Okeh's big-selling laughing records and decided to make his own. Hearing *Laughin' Louie* as a laughing record helps situate Armstrong's style of mugging in relation to genres and techniques that played an important role in defining the performance parameters of the recording studio. In other words, while his mugging certainly recalled the conventions of the minstrel stage, it also made for striking and dynamic records that revealed the expressive potential of the phonograph.

But Armstrong puts his own twist on the laughing record genre. In fact, *Laughin' Louie* is best seen as a sublime instance of signifying, which reveals the constructed nature of cultural assumptions about the voice and race. For one thing, Armstrong interacts with his fellow musicians in the context of a band jam session, not with an audience at a formal performance or music lesson. Further, Armstrong's flubs are intended to produce laughter in his audience, not the other way around. But the most marked difference between *Laughin' Louie* and laughing records is the way in which Armstrong's record concludes. Though the standard laughing record ends with a convulsing musician unable to catch his breath, Armstrong regains his composure and delivers a gorgeous solo as the band listens in rapt silence. Armstrong's notes climb to the top of his range in tones that, while pure and clear, still index the physical struggle required to make them. Armstrong sustains a stunning high note, the band plays a quick chord beneath him, and a cymbal crash abruptly signals the end of the record.

The overwhelming beauty and sheer virtuosity of this closing performance, when juxtaposed with the "rum tune" that has preceded it, are what make the record stand as such a paradox for critics. Giddins describes the "immutably stark and haunting beauty" of the end melody and asks, "What manner of man is this Laughin' Louie who can play music to make the angels weep?" (1988, 38). Stanley Crouch finds in this finale "a chilling pathos" that "achieves a transcendence in the upper register that summons the cleansing agony of the greatest spiritual." "The feeling one is left with," Crouch writes, "is one of great mystery" (1978, 45). Perhaps part of the mystery Crouch hears on *Laughin' Louie* involves the fact that Armstrong's double-voiced balancing act seems to be stretched to the breaking point. Armstrong's style indexes the dialogue between rasp and bel canto by taking each one to its extreme: the hyper-gravelly gruffness of his singing voice and the horn's round tone whose clear, high notes register a sense of sublime artistic transcendence—note, for example, the way in which both Crouch and Giddins describe his solo on *Laughin' Louie*. Though the tradition of bel canto pedagogy defined these timbres in stark distinction from each other, Armstrong's most successful records interweave the two until distinctions blur. But on *Laughin' Louie* the center will not hold: his raspy laughter and mugging present an earthy humor too reminiscent of lowbrow genres like laughing records and the minstrel show to integrate with the transcendent coda. Perhaps this is exactly the desired effect: Armstrong signifies on the laughing record, with all its troublesome connections to the performance of race, in order to explode those assumptions.

What is certain is that one is still left at the end of *Laughin' Louie* with a sense of great mystery because of the many paradoxes of Armstrong's career. One of these is the fact that Armstrong's performances seem utterly free and without compromise, and yet they—like those of George Washington Johnson and Bert Williams—were made at a time when many limitations were placed on black expression. In fact, while Armstrong remained an influential singer through the 1950s and 1960s, a generation of black musicians of the bebop generation criticized Armstrong for what they saw as his stylistic concessions to white audiences. Crouch writes of how his father, who had been "baptized in Lunceford, Ellington, and bebop," considered Armstrong "an embarrassment, a return to an unpleasant identity, or a man who had allowed white people to impose a ridiculous mask on him. In short, an uncle tom" (45). This was a period of transition in the performance of race in America, when the conventions of white vocal performance of "black" material changed as well. In the final section of this chapter I will address cultural associations tied to the raspy vocal timbre of white singers in a post-blackface era.

SHOUT AND SCREAM

Blackface entertainment in America largely came to an end in the 1950s, its overt racism increasingly unacceptable in an era when the Civil Rights movement was gaining steam, when the NAACP began to be able to exert pressure on the media industries, and when, in the face of the Cold War, there was a desire to improve the country's reputation for the treatment of African Americans (Rogin 1996, 196–99). Krin Gabbard, however, has argued that blackface did not so much end as change its form; he points to Marlon Brando's interest in jazz culture and use of improvisation in his psychoanalytically inflected Method acting to suggest that Brando was perhaps "the first American actor to practice minstrelsy in whiteface" (1996, 19). Similar arguments could certainly be made about Elvis Presley and the emergence of white rock and roll in the

1950s.[22] I have argued that there had been a notable lack of rasp on recordings of white minstrels, and so some of Presley's early performances become particularly notable. Elvis's whoops, hiccups, and edgy rasp on a track like "Baby Let's Play House" (1955) recall Golden's *Rabbit Hash* more than the performances of white crooners such as Bing Crosby and Frank Sinatra, and his recordings of "Hound Dog" (1956), "Jailhouse Rock" (1957), and "One Night" (1958) feature a full-blown, razor-edged rasp.[23]

White minstrel performers were visually marked by the mask of burnt cork, but they had typically maintained a traditional bel canto vocal timbre since at least the 1890s. The round tone of their voices was an island of whiteness in a sea of pseudo-black performance. Without recourse to blackface, Elvis had to indicate "blackness" through his clothes, the movements of his body, and the timbre of his voice. One might argue that after the end of blackface, the voice took on new importance in white renderings of blackness.

For Elvis and, later, the Beatles, the rasp resonated with some of the same transgression it had held during the era of the minstrel show: it was still a vocal performance that was coded as black and was a means of revolt against highbrow standards of vocal production. John Lennon was a white singer from this era who embraced African American blues and R&B records, and whose own shouted performances show the extent to which he made a rasp a part of his vocal style. "Twist and Shout" features Lennon's famously tattered lead vocal, performed at the end of an all-day session on February 11, 1963. The Beatles chronicler Mark Lewisohn is not alone when he describes this performance as "arguably the most stunning rock and roll vocal and instrumental performance of all time; two-and-a-half minutes of Lennon shredding his vocal cords to bits" (1988, 26). The centrality of the throaty cry on Beatles records is demonstrated in the breakdown sections of the song when Lennon, George Harrison, and Paul McCartney layer their sung "aahs," building to their ecstatic screams. Though certainly influenced by a tradition of black performance (the song had, after all, already been a hit for the R&B group the Isley Brothers), Beatles performances such as this one also resonated with other layers of cultural meaning concerned with gender and sexuality. To grasp these meanings, contrast the effect of "Twist and Shout" with Michel Chion's writing on the function of the female scream in narrative film.

Chion makes a distinction between the "shout" and the "scream" that can be useful in a consideration of the gendered meanings of the rasp.

Chion writes that "we tend to call the woman's cry a scream, and the man's cry a shout" (1999, 78). The difference, according to Chion, is that the man's shout "is a shout of power, exercising a will, marking a territory, a structuring shout," whereas the woman's scream embodies "an absolute, outside of language, time, the conscious subject" (78). Thus, "the man's shout delimits a territory, the woman's scream has to do with limitlessness" (79). Chion reasons that this is due to the fact that for men, "the woman's scream poses the question of the 'black hole' of the female orgasm, which cannot be spoken or thought" (77). For Chion the timing of the woman's scream in a cinematic narrative is of the utmost importance: it "above all must fall at an appointed spot, explode at a precise moment, at the crossroads of converging plot lines, at the end of an often convoluted trajectory, but calculated to give this point a maximum impact." "It is amazing," Chion adds, "to consider the extravagant luxury of the means devoted to the screenplay and production mobilized in order for everything to be lost and spent in a woman's scream" (77).

As was the case with the work of Alan Lomax, Chion's stark demarcations between male and female modes of vocalizing are certainly overgeneralized. In fact, Beatles records reveal an interesting gender reversal on Chion's structure. Here it is the male scream that explodes at a precise moment, usually before the guitar solo. Also note the "extravagant luxury of means" on "Twist and Shout" when the layered "aahs" build an overwhelming tension that is "lost and spent" in the band's exuberant cries.[24] The visual style and long hair of the Beatles have often been mentioned as transgressing gender norms of the time, but their vocal performances represent a certain degree of gender-bending as well, since they resemble what was a traditionally female function in the cinema.[25]

It is important to note that their self-assertive male vocalizing was the catalyst for a wave of screams from a largely female audience. Film footage of Beatles concerts from the height of the Beatlemania era reveals the importance of screams, both from the band and from the audience. Barbara Ehrenreich, Gloria Jacobs, and Elizabeth Hess note that "in no setting, at any time, was [the Beatles'] music audible above the frenzied screams of the audience" (1992, 86). These authors go on to assert that "when screams drowned out the music, as they invariably did, then it was the fans, and not the band, who were the show" (104). They suggest that the screams of those female fans were a form of cathartic release from sexual repression: "Adulation of the male star was a way to express sexual yearnings that would normally be pressed into the service of popularity or simply repressed. The star could be loved noninstrumentally, for his own sake, and with complete abandon. Publicly to advertise this hopeless love was to protest the calculated, pragmatic sexual repression of teenage life" (97). Susan Douglas writes that "without being able to put it into words, but quite able to put it into screams, girls instinctively recognized the Beatles as a Trojan horse, smuggling androgyny, a contempt for middle-class conventionalism, and sexual release into their protected, middle-class worlds" (1994, 117).

These arguments recall Lomax's claim that the singing voice is "a remarkably accurate indicator of the cultural level of [sexual] tension" (1968, 194) and that "control of female sexuality" was "symbolized by the introduction of disturbing and idiosyncratic noise into vocalizing" (198). Again, Lomax's sweeping assertions must be tested in specific cultural and historical contexts, but they are suggestive when applied to the screams of Beatles fans. No matter what the limitations of their theories, when coupled with the observations of Ehrenreich and her colleagues and Douglas, Lomax's and Chion's work suggests that in post–World War II America the rasp of the white male singer had not only racial but also gendered associations. In those remarkable performances during the height of Beatlemania, the scream became a complex language of its own, a form of wordless mass communication. In the next decade, both Lennon and the generation of screaming fans that attended his concerts further redefined the cultural meaning of the rasp.

A SCREAM AWAY FROM HAPPINESS

The Beatles stopped touring in 1966, becoming, as Ehrenreich and her coauthors put it, "the first musical celebrities driven from the stage by their own fans" (1992, 86). As is well known, the band retreated to the recording studio, where they made some of their most critically respected records.[26] Lennon became uncomfortable with the acclaim given to *Sgt. Pepper's Lonely Hearts Club Band* (1967), and he reacted against its conceptual structure and classical orchestration with his subsequent noisy and self-consciously primitive work on the 1968 *White Album*. His first solo record, *Plastic Ono Band* (1970), is even more stripped-down and gritty. A central component of the record was the influence of Lennon's work with the therapist Arthur Janov. That influence is most clearly heard on the long sections of Janov's primal scream therapy on tracks such as "Mother" and "Well, Well, Well."

Despite his claims to have invented a radically new approach to therapy, Janov was part of a larger movement of cathartic group therapy during the late 1960s and early 1970s in which the scream often played a central role. A number of group therapies collectively known as the "human potential movement" began to make a splash on the American cultural scene in the late 1960s. These approaches were often defined in opposition to conventional techniques of one-on-one psychotherapy, and one therapist at the time described their emergence as "a post-Freudian revolution" (Hoover 1967, L8). In one of several mainstream press articles chronicling the rise of group therapy, the *Washington Post* described in 1970 how "the human potential movement attempts to put people in touch with their own feelings": "The groups value candor and honesty, try to make people respond emotionally rather than intellectually, and to lower their conventional, social masks" (Lundberg 1970, 171).[27]

Michael P. Nichols and Melvin Zax, in their book, *Catharsis in Psychotherapy*, trace elements of the human potential movement to Freud's work with hysterics and the influence of his contemporary Wilhelm Reich, who was "concerned with the treatment of physical blocks against the expression of emotion" (1977, 105). The origins of institutional group therapy can be found in post–World War II treatment of disturbed soldiers, and in particular in the work of Kurt Lewin at the MIT Research Center for Group Dynamics in the 1940s and the National Training Laboratories (NTL) in the 1950s (Lundberg 1970, 171). The techniques developed in these group settings were spread through courses in "sensitivity-training" used by U.S. businesses as "a means of sharpening up communication among executives" (Hoover 1967, L8). Nichols and Zax describe how a range of therapies such as Stanley Keleman's bioenergic work, Rolfing, Alexander technique, and Gestalt therapy emerged on the American cultural scene in the late 1960s. All of these therapeutic schools shared the view that repressed feelings such as anger that are not fully experienced and expressed can accumulate and create "psychic abscesses" that lead to emotional disorders and pathological behaviors (1977, 151).

One of the key techniques for draining those psychic abscesses was screaming. Wilhelm Reich's patients had been asked to shout and scream as part of "non-verbal work," since Reich felt that language was "often used as a defense to block affective expression" (109). Screaming was also a recurring technique for many of the practices in the human potential movement. A 1971 *New York Times* article described how an all-day workshop run by the Esalen Institute began with "a technique for releasing tension in which each person stood and screamed as loudly and

mindlessly as he could" (Malver 1971, SM4). One of the most successful therapists at this time, Daniel Casriel, described his "New Identity
Therapy" as "a kind of group therapy that uses screaming as a tool to
help patients express long-buried emotions" (1972, 1). Casriel's techniques were made widely known in his 1972 book, *A Scream Away from
Happiness*. The expression of feelings with nonverbal screams was the
centerpiece of Casriel's therapy: "Often the words end up in sounds that
are shrieks or wails, sounds beyond words, arising from depths of pain,
anger, fear, or from the need for love" (2). Casriel's goal was to overcome the "anaesthetization of basic emotions and encapsulation of the
feelings behind a defensive shell that is extremely hard to penetrate in traditional psychotherapy situations" (3). Casriel's techniques, like those
used in many other therapies in the human potential movement, represented a rejection of the speech-centered approach of Freudian psychoanalysis and were instead focused on cathartic, emotional, nonverbal exercises in group settings.

The importance of the scream was especially clear in anger exercises,
which Casriel divides into different levels of intensity based on the location of the anger in the body, which bears an interesting parallel to traditions of "resonance imagery" in bel canto vocal training. Casriel
claims that the first level of anger comes "from the head, an 'intellectual'
anger, quietly thought and expressed." The second level "emerges as a
loud scream" and is connected to the throat. The third "delves deeper,"
emerging as "a murderous rage" from the chest, and the fourth level of
anger "rumbles loosely and rhythmically from the depths of the belly"
(263). This final level Casriel refers to as "identity anger": "It is the assertion of an individual who is fully connected to his feelings and aware
of what he is entitled to feel as a human being. . . . This fourth level of
anger is felt throughout the body. You feel aware of a total you, a total
identity" (263). Casriel describes the experience of "identity anger":
"Usually the person stands up, with feet planted firmly, head thrown
back, fists clenched at his sides. . . . Eventually the feeling takes over. He
becomes a mass of angry energy, throwing out the words again and
again—'I'm angry, I'm angry!' They vibrate even deeper in his belly. You
can hear the difference as someone begins to connect. It is no longer a
choked-up, red-faced scream from the throat or an hysterical, frustrated
roar. Instead, the words and finally the sound of the feeling roll forth
from the belly, easily and forcefully, in deep, assured tones" (264).

Casriel provided transcriptions of group sessions that indicate how
these techniques played out in actual practice:

Casriel: Okay, who has a feeling? Who wants to work?

Vilma: I do. I don't feel good. I don't feel sexual at all. When I don't want to screw, my boy friend gets mad and stomps out. It's happened twice this week.

. . .

Nancy: Happened last month, too, didn't it?

(There is no response. Vilma nods yes.)

Nancy: What did the group tell you, Vilma?

Vilma: That I was angry, because Mitchell wouldn't marry me. And that I didn't want to screw because I was angry.

Casriel: Is it true? What do you think?

Vilma: But I've told him several times I'm angry. It doesn't do any good. He doesn't pay any attention to me.

Casriel: You don't seem angry. Are you angry right now?

Vilma: Yes, I think I am.

Cathy: (Screaming) Vilma, I can't stand your turned-off tone—you never get to a feeling. Scream, you bitch! If you're angry, GET ANGRY!

. . .

Vilma: (Standing up to scream) I'm angry. I'm ANGRY. I'm ANGRY.

(Vilma continues to scream for thirty-five seconds. She is performing an exercise she has seen others do in group.)

Peter: The hell you're angry! You're about as angry as a pussy cat! (Leaping to his feet) If you're angry, sound angry! Like this . . . !

(Peter lets out an intense scream that lasts ten seconds, then a second ten-second scream, and finally a third that lasts about twelve seconds.)

Cathy: That's not all, Peter. Go on.

(Peter continues to scream, looking at each group member as he does so. His screams get increasingly higher-pitched and filled with pain. Before he is finished, he has screamed for over three minutes.)

Casriel: Go on, scream it all out Peter.

(Peter screams again, this time with some tears in his eyes. Cathy rises and takes him in her arms, and he begins to scream with pain. Finally, there is only the sound of his sobs.)

Casriel: That's your pain, Peter. It's okay. It brings people close to you when you show it. Look around the room and see for yourself. All your life you felt alone because you couldn't show your real feelings. Now you're not alone." (15–17)

The scream in Casriel's sessions played a double function: it was both a vehicle to and a sign of catharsis, a supposed indication of hidden pain and a path to healing. Arthur Janov's therapeutic system worked along similar lines, but where Casriel focused on group settings, Janov typically worked with individuals. He introduced his concept of the primal scream in a 1970 book of the same title. Janov emerged from the pack of quasi-celebrity group therapists as a particularly glamorous figure; he was singled out for some of the harshest criticism by the mainstream psychology community for his pretentious and unfounded claims about his methods, as well as his utter disregard for their clear historical precedents.[28] Janov's therapy was based on the idea that hidden "primal pains" are created in childhood that make people numb to all real feeling. As a cure, Janov devised "primal therapy," the climax of which occurred when the patient emitted the primal scream: "Finally, out it will come: a scream—'Daddy, be nice!' 'Mommy, help!'—or just the word 'hate': 'I hate you, I hate you!' This is the Primal Scream. It comes out in shuddering gasps, pushed out by the force of years of suppressions and denials of that feeling" (1970, 83–84).

For Janov, the scream is important because of its relation to pain: "It is not the scream that is curative, in any case; it is the Pain. The scream is only one expression of the Pain. The Pain is the curative agent because it means that the person is feeling at last" (90). Janov claimed that the effect of the scream was to make the patient "become whole again," to "unify the person" and attain a "feeling of power" (41, 119).[29] The discourse and practice of group therapy as represented by Casriel and Janov brought with it a conception of the scream as a vehicle of catharsis. This articulation of the scream, seen most clearly in Janov's primal scream, made the raspy cry resonate with European intellectual movements such as psychoanalysis, existentialism, and expressionism (as represented by Edvard Munch's painting *The Scream*). This might seem far removed from the realm of popular music, but the primal scream was merged with the rock shout in a performance by the most famous and influential musical performer of that era.

PRIMAL SCREAM

The most important factor in Janov's rise to semicelebrity status was the fact that John Lennon worked with him in the summer of 1970, spoke of the experience in fairly grandiose terms, and soon after released an album, *Plastic Ono Band,* that clearly bore the influence of Janov's thought. Take, for example, the song "Mother," which kicks off the album. It features the stark, minimalist arrangements heard throughout the record: a driving rhythm section of bass and drums, and a piano hammering simple, sustained chords. Over the top of this backing track, Lennon's voice features an echo effect reminiscent of Elvis Presley's work at Sun Studio in Memphis. The lyrics of the song reflect Janov's interest in facing the primal pains of childhood trauma: "Mother you had me, but I never had you. I wanted you, you didn't want me. So I, I just gotta tell you, Goodbye." After three verses, the song stretches out to become a stage on which Lennon demonstrates Janov's primal scream. Lennon repeats the line "Mama don't go, Daddy come home," eventually swooping up on the words "don't go" with a searing rasp. Each bar at the end of the repeated phrase drops two beats, making the pattern spiral in on itself and so build in intensity. Coupled with the dropped beats, the increasingly painful rawness of Lennon's voice seems to represent a deepening experience of pain and the quest for catharsis.[30]

Though I find there to be a raw, emotional power to these performances, the pretensions of the record, particularly given the limitations of Janov's thought, make it an easy target for parody. On National Lampoon's 1971 album, *National Lampoon's Radio Dinner*, Tony Hendra plays John Lennon on a track called "Magical Misery Tour," supposedly taken from the album *Yoko Is a Concept by Which We Measure Our Pain*. The track features Lennon reciting bitter recriminations against his former bandmates taken from actual *Rolling Stone* magazine interviews ("Paul wasn't the walrus, I was the walrus, I was just saying that to be nice but I was really the walrus") and then launching into cries of "Genius is pain!" and "Ow!"

Whatever its pretensions, Lennon's performance on "Mother" reflects the role of the scream in the human potential movement: the rasp indexes emotional truth and catharsis meant to unify a divided self. In the context of his career as the singer of R&B barn burners such as "Twist and Shout," Lennon's vocal performances on *Plastic Ono Band* bridge the gap between a cathartic scream and a shout traditionally associated with black genres of performance, serving to redefine the rasp. We have seen that the raspy voice of a white singer often had only superficially to do with a commitment to black experience: minstrel singers were more concerned with thumbing their noses at elitist conventions, albeit in carefully circumscribed ways. But the transgressive power of records by white performers from Billy Golden to Mick Jagger was in large part due to that timbre's association with blackness, whether via jazz, blues, or the early American minstrel stage. Lennon's immense fame and influence at this time helped assure that, after *Plastic Ono Band*, the raspy shout of a white rock singer would signify not so much a commitment to African

American style as an existential cry of pain at modern life. This is most clearly demonstrated by the performances of the white art rock most influenced by Lennon: Johnny Rotten of the Sex Pistols, Black Francis of the Pixies, and Kurt Cobain of Nirvana. In all these cases, the screams of white singers signify the revelation of inner truth or cathartic release, not black performance.

It should be noted that all this vocal shredding relied on sound technology. First, the ability to mass-produce records meant that singers did not need to do marathon performances of the same songs: note that Lennon's famous performance of "Twist and Shout" was captured in one take. Lennon could go for broke in a way that a singer in the recording studios of the turn of the century could not. Further, many raspy delivery styles are just as dependent on microphones as was Rudy Vallee's quiet crooning. Just as the crooning style could not have filled an auditorium as the full-voiced bel canto could, neither could the raspy voice of singers such as Armstrong or Lennon be projected without electronic assistance.[31] Indeed, contrary to common sense, raspy singing is not necessarily very loud, and some singers known for a hypermasculine shriek actually manage this style through a relatively quiet manipulation of vocal timbre that is achieved, of course, with a closely held microphone.

PART THREE

Bugging the Backstage

CHAPTER 5

The Act of Being Yourself

Allen Funt's *Candid Microphone* made its network radio debut in 1947, establishing a model of broadcast entertainment that has been on the air in various forms ever since. *Candid Microphone* involved the secret recording of a victim who was provoked to respond to an absurd or irritating situation. To use a phrase coined by Erving Goffman, this format involves "bugging the backstage": "We expect that some places will exist where privacy is ensured, where only a known number of persons will be present, and where such persons will be only those of a given category. Here, presumably, the individual can conduct himself in a manner that would discredit his standard poses were the facts known; and, of course, it is just these places that are the best ones to bug" (1974, 168). In the context of the arguments I've been developing in this book, it should be noted that forms of entertainment based around the act of bugging the backstage are dependent on the technology of sound recording, making performances so captured "modern," much like the singing of crooners such as Rudy Vallee, whose style relied to such an extent on radio microphones, was "modern."

Indeed, the performances captured by secret recording will be seen to have important affinities with some of the tendencies in modern vocal performance that I have characterized thus far. For example, in part 1 I demonstrated how the vocal performances characterized by flooding out found on laughing records and broadcast laugh tracks have functioned to help overcome the separation of performer from audience. In chapters

165

5 and 6 I point out similar dynamics of flooding out in performances captured by secret recording. This chapter will be concerned with the types
of performances found on Funt's shows, and the ways in which they have
been understood in the culture at large. In addition to furthering my
analysis of modern styles of vocal performance, Funt's shows present the
opportunity to examine the ways in which a format structured for radio
changed in its move to television—a comparison that can help to define
some of the formal properties of performance in those media.

TAP JITTERS

When it debuted in 1947, Allen Funt's *Candid Microphone* was often described in terms of "eavesdropping." A review in the *New York Times*
stated that "eavesdropping is the devious métier of these gentlemen, at
which they have developed uncommon proficiency" (Stewart 1947, 85).
Variety, in a negative review of the show's pilot episode, wrote that
"eavesdropping is a dull hobby except in rare situations" ("Candid Microphone" 27). Funt (figure 13) didn't shy away from this label, entitling
the book he published in 1952 on the workings of his show *Eavesdropper
at Large*. The eavesdropping on *Candid Microphone* was facilitated by
hidden microphones and new recording technologies, which made it
closely akin to wiretapping, a practice that was the subject of national legal
debate and that held a particular fascination for the American public.

The term *wiretapping* is typically associated with the surreptitious
recording of telephone conversations, but its use predates the telephone.
Samuel Dash, in a comprehensive 1959 study of wiretapping, noted that
California had legislation prohibiting the interception of telegraph messages as early as 1862 (1959, 23). A *New York Times* article from 1883
relates how the term was being used in the nineteenth century to describe
the interception of telegraph messages: "Another telegraph wire-tapping
scheme was discovered on Tuesday afternoon, this time at Coney Island,
by which pool-sellers and patrons of pool-sellers at that place were swin-
dled out of about $15,000" ("Pool-Sellers Robbed Again" 1). Wiretap-
ping continued to be an issue for emerging national telephone services.
Dash writes that New York police were actively tapping telephones in
criminal investigations in 1895, and in that same year Illinois enacted
legislation prohibiting wiretapping for "the purpose of intercepting
news dispatches" (1959, 25).

Wiretapping has been a widespread practice since the nineteenth century, but it has remained mysterious and confusing to the general pub-

Figure 13. "Fortyish, a little overweight, and balding": Allen Funt, creator of *Candid Microphone* and *Candid Camera*. © Reuters/Corbis.

lic, in large part because of the contradictions of wiretapping legislation. Dash observed that even in 1959, people were not to be blamed if they did not understand the laws about wiretapping: "There is no uniformity among states and there is conflict between the laws of several states and the federal law" (4). A brief overview of the often complex legal history of wiretapping will help provide a cultural frame of reference for the debut of *Candid Microphone* in 1947.

Discussions of wiretapping legislation usually begin with a 1928 Supreme Court case, *Olmstead v. United States* (277 U.S. 438).[1] In this case the Supreme Court decided by a slim majority that wiretapping by federal agents was not a violation of Fourth Amendment protection against illegal searches, since law enforcement officers did not physically enter a house. Chief Justice William Howard Taft, in delivering the opinion of the court, stated that "the language of the [Fourth] amendment cannot be extended and expanded to include telephone wires, reaching to the whole world from the defendant's house or office. The intervening wires are not part of his house or office, any more than are the highways along which they are stretched." In a precedent that would hold for the next forty years, the court ruled that the Fourth Amendment protected places, not people.[2]

Although the case officially gave the green light to wiretapping, perhaps its greatest legacy is in the famous dissenting opinions of Justices Oliver Wendell Holmes and Louis D. Brandeis. Holmes referred to tapping as a "dirty business" and stated that though it was "desirable that criminals should be detected, and to that end that all available evidence should be used," it was also "desirable that the government should not itself foster and pay for other crimes, when they are the means by which the evidence is to be obtained." Brandeis declared that "the evil incident to invasion of the privacy of the telephone is far greater than that involved in tampering with the mails": "Whenever a telephone line is tapped, the privacy of the persons at both ends of the line is invaded, and all conversations between them upon any subject, and although proper, confidential, and privileged, may be overheard. Moreover, the tapping of one man's telephone line involves the tapping of the telephone of every other person whom he may call, or who may call him."[3] The conflicted legal history of wiretapping is well illustrated by the fact that the most famous aspects of this decision, which allowed the practice, are these eloquent and often-cited dissenting opinions.

The *Olmstead* case involved Prohibition Bureau agents tapping the phones of a gang suspected of smuggling illegal liquor into Washington State. Fitzgerald and Leopold note that the Prohibition Bureau was "probably the only domestic agency to make regular use of phone taps," and even the FBI did not have approval from the attorney general to tap phones at this time (1987, 166). I will return to the importance of the association of wiretapping with a "moral" issue such as Prohibition, but for now it should be pointed out that the practical result of the *Olmstead* case was to lead to the expansion of wiretapping from the Prohibition Bureau to other agencies, including the FBI (167).

The next important development in wiretap legislation came as a result of the 1934 Federal Communications Act, which set the stage for a reversal of the Supreme Court's 1928 decision. Section 605 of that act stated that "no person" could intercept and divulge "any communication" to any person (Dash 1959, 388). The wording of the act is lifted from the Radio Act of 1927, which sought to prevent the pirating of messages by rival communications companies. In a 1937 Supreme Court case, *Nardone et al. v. United States* (302 U.S. 668), however, the legislative language created for media companies was applied to individuals. Referring to Section 605's prohibition against intercepting communications, the court ruled that evidence intercepted by tapping telephone wires was inadmissible in federal courts. But despite being technically illegal on the federal level, wiretapping was still allowed in many state courts, and in fact it became increasingly prevalent in law enforcement throughout the 1930s. This created a strange situation in which the law didn't prohibit the bare act of wiretapping, provided the information was not divulged or published.

This brings us to the 1940s, a time when Dash claims wiretapping "reached a high point" because of the fact that there was "little or no enforcement of laws prohibiting or restricting wiretapping, and wiretapping techniques had been perfected" (30). Wiretapping became a hot topic in the popular press in the late 1940s and early 1950s. One reason for this was the intensification of the Cold War and anxiety about foreign espionage. The temper of the times can be illustrated by the Judith Coplon case, which involved a former Department of Justice analyst whose jury conviction on espionage charges in 1949 was reversed because the FBI illegally tapped conversations between Coplon and her lawyer. New York Mayor William O'Dwyer's claim in March 1949 that his enemies were tapping the phones of city officials was another event that fueled the wiretapping discussion ("Wire-tapping Mystery" 34). It was, however, the arrest of Nancy Fletcher Choremi that was, according to Dash, "the most notorious case" of wiretapping reported at this time (1959, 33). Choremi, the daughter of the U.S. consul general to Casablanca, was found guilty through wiretap evidence of loitering and prostitution in July 1948. High-profile cases such as these helped spur widespread discussion of the pros and cons of wiretapping in the popular press.

Wiretapping was often defended as a necessary tool in the fight against a new kind of organized crime. A *Time* article published in January 1954 describes how "the telephone greatly reduces the effectiveness of such old police methods as shadowing a suspect and checking on his contacts": "It is hard to trail a criminal who uses the telephone for communication unless the police follow him technologically, i.e. tap the wires over which his messages pass" ("Debate on Wiretapping" 12). The article goes on to describe how "the modern tendency toward elaborate organization" made for a new kind of criminal, the most dangerous of which were Communist spies who were recruited "on an ideological basis." Wiretapping is presented as being central to the "new counterbalancing powers" the police required in the fight against organized crime and communism (12).

But opponents of wiretapping still argued that the practice was an invasion of personal privacy. For example, Harold Ickes wrote in a 1950 *New Republic* editorial that "it could be argued that tapping telephone wires to hear what a client may say to his lawyer is a more outrageous offense than violating a confessional" (1950, 17). Indeed, wiretapping represented a difficult balancing act between equipping law enforcement and preserving individual rights. One way that writers and legislators dealt with that tension was to make a distinction between public and private tapping: tapping was acceptable only if done by the state, not by the private sector. In a dissenting opinion in the *Nardone* case, Supreme Court Justice George Sutherland emphasized the "manifest difference between the case of a private individual who intercepts a message from motives of curiosity or to further personal ends, and that of a responsible official engaged in the governmental duty of uncovering crime and bringing criminals to justice." Summing up his 1959 study of wiretapping, Dash wrote that "the basic problem" and "the real controversy" of wiretapping were "whether law-enforcement officers should be allowed to tap even though private individuals may not" (1959, 385).

Writers and pundits in the popular press often relied on a similar distinction between public and private tapping. For example, though *Time* warned that "sooner or later, free societies must deal with the danger that increasingly sensitive electronic eyes and ears may destroy personal freedom by annihilating privacy," its solution was to authorize wiretapping by the FBI and "forbid all other wiretapping." This strategy was a magic bullet whereby the government could deal with "the Communist conspiracy" while also supposedly controlling the "chilling potentialities of technological surveillance" ("Debate on Wiretapping" 13). Similarly,

Newsweek argued that though wiretapping was required for espionage and kidnapping cases, it was being widely abused in its use in connection with marital investigations by private eyes, and that this had "contributed to the disgust which many people have for wire tapping" ("Hot Wire-Tapping Debate" 20–21). In a 1949 *Saturday Evening Post* article called "I Was a Wire Tapper," a former government tapper, William Mellin, declared that he was "deadset against" the private tapping typified by "divorce lawyers, blackmailers, bookmakers," and "politicians wanting to dig up dirt" (1949, 19).

References such as these to divorce lawyers and the "marital investigations of private eyes" are typical examples of the way in which private tapping was negatively connected to prurient voyeurism. Supreme Court Justice Sutherland contrasted the wiretapping done by "sworn officers of the law engaged in the detection and apprehension of organized gangs of criminals" with "the odious practices of the town gossip, the Peeping Tom, and the private eavesdropper." The wiretapping private eye was an oft-cited scapegoat: "A husband who suspects that his wife isn't quite as faithful as she should be can hire [wiretappers] to put a tap on his apartment phone" ("Busy Wiretappers" 31). Private tapping was also connected to the debauched lives of the rich and famous: "In Los Angeles, movie stars seeking grounds to divorce their mates are the best customers for the wiretappers" (32).

But the clear line between public and private tapping starts to erode when one considers evidence that suggests how frequently "official" tapping was used in cases involving prostitution and Prohibition. Recall the *Olmstead* case of 1928 and the fact that wiretapping was originally used almost exclusively by the Prohibition Bureau. Prostitution was another crime that seems to have attracted a disproportionate amount of wiretapping. *Time* magazine described in a 1954 article how "the cops tap public phones, listen in on hundreds of conversations in the hope of picking up leads on bookies or prostitutes" ("Debate on Wiretapping" 13). In a public hearing on wiretapping spurred by the Nancy Choremi case of 1948, it was suggested that "75 to 90 per cent of all wire-tapping by the police in New York was in bookmaking and prostitution cases where the alleged offense was not a felony" (Grutzner 1948, 30). A focus on prostitution and the voyeuristic nature of government wiretapping are made explicit in a March 7, 1955, story in *Life:* a flow chart, "How Wiretap Is Worked," starts with a photo of "former stripper Ann Corio," whose apartment had been bugged ("How Wiretap Is Worked" 45). This article illustrates how the voyeuristic possibilities of wiretapping were part of public, official business as usual at the same time they were being associated only with "private" tapping.

Larger questions of wiretapping's infringement on personal privacy were sidestepped by making a distinction between "good" wiretapping, done by the government in its fight against conspiratorial crime, and "bad" private wiretapping, characterized by its seedy sexual dimensions. In practice, those two categories were not so easily separated. What is certain is that all the press coverage of wiretapping in the late 1940s and early 1950s led to a general state of anxiety about this little-understood practice. One name given to this anxiety was "tap jitters": "the very lack of definitive knowledge [of who is tapped] has given rise to a disease which might be called 'the wiretap jitters' " ("Busy Wiretappers" 31). The jitters were the result of the fact that any wire could be tapped without any audible evidence of it: "No reliable electrical devices are available to detect taps" (31). Mellin, the ex-tapper, wrote that "more and more people, especially in public life, are getting what we call 'tap jitters.' It's a rather new nervous ailment" (1949, 38).[4]

Funt's *Candid Microphone* reflected the culture of wiretap jitters when it went on the air in 1947. The recurring slogan of the show plays directly on uncertainty about wiretapping: "No one ever knows when he's talking into the candid microphone." At the end of the show, the announcer warned that "until next week the candid microphone goes back into hiding, the better to catch you in our act. Nothing is off the record when the man with the hidden mike crosses your path, with a microphone that hears without being seen: the candid microphone." Funt's show played the tap jitters for laughs, both recognizing and defusing postwar anxiety and uncertainty about wiretapping. Andrew Ross has connected Funt's television show *Candid Camera* to "national paranoia about Communism" (1989, 108). Ross reads the message of that show as being that "no one ought to think that their own actions . . . could ever go completely unnoticed or unheard. Everyone and everything could be monitored" (108). *Candid Microphone* reveals this connection both earlier and more directly, since its debut came at the height of the "tap jitters," and its mode of production was, like the surveillance techniques prevalent at the time, the surreptitious recording of conversations.

Funt's show navigated between the categories of public and private wiretapping that I've been discussing. *Candid Microphone* exploited the private, voyeuristic possibilities of wiretapping that were being demonized by the popular press, a fact that Funt tried to downplay. Indeed, even the choice of the word *candid* to describe his recordings can be read as a strategy to inoculate his program against the pervasive anxiety about wiretapping. Funt stated that since his gags took place in a public place and never depicted anything a person wanted to conceal, they were "candid, rather than secret": "I never touch on any confidential areas of a person's life" (Flagler 1960, 90). But if Funt resembled the voyeuristic private tapper in some ways, the technological origins of his show were to be found in the U.S. military. Indeed, the technologies and approaches that made Funt's show possible were the direct result of changes connected to World War II that were to have major effects on broadcast entertainment.

SPOILS OF WAR

The recording technology used to create *Candid Microphone* was itself a point of interest for the public. Funt writes how "in those days, the late forties, the public was fascinated by the idea of recording equipment that was so small it could be hidden" (1994, 35). That fascination was evident in the popular press coverage of wiretapping, which breathlessly listed such things as voice-activated recorders, parabolic microphones that could listen to conversations three hundred yards away, and small recorders hidden "between basement rafters and in manholes" ("Busy Wiretappers" 34). The development of techniques that exploited audio technologies such as these was largely the result of World War II.

During the 1940s the army used new sound recording technologies such as magnetic wire recorders, which were used by reporters to gather eyewitness reports and interviews (Morton 2000, 61). Funt described his time in the Signal Corps during World War II, when he used a German wire recorder: "Up to that point any sound recordings were usually made in a studio using bulky equipment. This wire recorder, though enormous by today's standards, was the smallest, most advanced portable recorder of that time" (1994, 23). Using this technology, Funt began producing shows for army radio like *The Gripe Booth*, in which "soldiers could come into the studio and complain about anything in the army without fear of repercussions" (26). *The Gripe Booth* was Funt's first involvement with secret recording: "As soon as the red light came on [the soldiers] became tongue-tied. My solution was to disconnect the red light and record them secretly. The conversations I obtained under these conditions were invariably more candid" (26). Notably, the "candid" format relied on the use of portable and concealable recording technology, and so could not be broadcast live.

New kinds of sound recording devices allowed Funt to record candid
material, and he could broadcast that prerecorded material over the air-
waves thanks to the policies of Armed Forces Radio. Until that time,
radio networks had instituted policies "intended to restrict the playing
of commercial phonograph records on the air" (Morton 2000, 50). The
"live imperative" of network radio broadcasting was originally established by Federal Radio Commission legislation in the late 1920s, legislation that encouraged the dominance of live broadcasts on radio: "Stations broadcasting live entertainment would be given precedence in the
allocation of air space because that material presumably remained unavailable in any other form" (Hilmes 1990, 27). Since only the networks
could afford top-of-the-line talent on live variety shows and the AT&T
landlines that made widely disseminated live programming possible, this
legislation functioned to bolster network dominance of radio. The historian David Morton describes how the Armed Forces Radio Network
(AFRN) was helping to "undermine the argument that live radio was
somehow special, and made recorded programs seem more acceptable"
(2000, 60). This was due to the fact that the AFRN did not have the "restrictive policies or formal regulations regarding the use of recordings"
that the networks did (60). The widespread use of recorded V-Discs during the war is one indication of the more liberal use of prerecorded material by the AFRN (William Howland Kenney 1999, 197).

After the war the American radio networks increasingly broadcast
prerecorded material as well. In the same issue of *Variety* that reviewed
the debut episode of *Candid Microphone*, several articles describe the industry shift to transcription. Louis G. Cowan's article "Disk Shows Win
Their 'D' " described how "millions of dollars are going into the production of transcribed shows. Some of the greatest performing talents are
now doing their radio stints on wax." Again, this shift in production is
linked to wartime improvements: "A good part of radio transcription development took place during the war years when local and regional
sponsors sought to add prestige via radio with important shows and
names" (1947, 28). Frederic W. Ziv, who would go on to play an important role in the early days of filmed television, wrote an article called
"Doin' What Comes Naturally—By Transcription," in which he argued
that "listeners love a good show. They get the best shows on transcription. Artists and producers love to produce good shows. They can get
their best performances on transcription" (1947, 35). Finally, an article
called "An Afternoon at the Waxworks" described how Bing Crosby's
use of transcription on his ABC show permitted him to develop a flexi-

ble, "piecemeal production technique" whereby "every segment of the stanza is as near perfect as they want it. There's no taking chances on distasteful fluffs. The process encourages adlibbing, which, if it comes off well, is left in, if it doesn't, it's sliced out of the final wax" ("Afternoon at the Waxworks" 37). Crosby would go on to pioneer the use of another wartime development that had important effects on broadcasting: German magnetic tape recorders brought to America after the war. In a move that signaled an important change in radio production practice, Bing Crosby began using Ampex tape recorders on his popular radio show in 1947, the same year that *Candid Microphone* went on the air.

Funt's candid format, then, is best understood in the context of technological developments taking place in radio broadcasting and sound recording during the 1940s. Funt's show consisted entirely of prerecorded material, and its production and success were made possible by Armed Forces Radio, trends in postwar radio production toward transcription, and the portable sound recording equipment made available to the U.S. Army. An interesting paradox of recording technology becomes evident when one considers both Funt's show and Bing Crosby's use of transcription as described in the *Variety* article referred to above. In both cases, recording techniques were employed to provide performances that seemed to heighten a sense of immediacy and spontaneity: recall how Crosby utilized transcription to add more ad-libbing to his show. Similarly, despite being inseparable from technologies of recording, *Candid Microphone* managed to produce a striking sense of immediacy. That is, the fact that the show provided a sense of eavesdropping on private conversations and situations was paradoxically provided by recording. Part of that sense of immediacy was due to the fact that *Candid Microphone* lacked a studio audience, which gave the show more of a sense of clandestine eavesdropping. A reviewer noted that Funt's technique was "preferable to that of some quiz programs. The people of whom he makes use at least are not subjected to a gaping studio audience" (Stewart 1947, 85).

As an example of the "purest" type of eavesdropping heard on Funt's show, consider a sequence called "Veteran's Views." The fact that it was included both on a phonograph collection of the show's highlights and on a "Best of " broadcast from July 1948 suggests that this sequence was particularly successful with the listening audience. On the liner notes for the record, the track is described this way: "A blinded colored veteran talks to his legless buddy in a waiting room of a Veteran's Administration Office about soldiers, civilians, and life." At one point the amputee asks, "Were you married before you went into the service?" "No, no," replies the blinded veteran, "I got married after I come out." "That's the question everybody asks me, too," says the amputee. "I don't know why they ask that. I guess they . . . they want to know if we were married after we become disabled or before." "Oh, yes," agrees the blinded vet, "a lot of people ask me . . . was my wife, was I going with my wife before I went in the service? No, I've never seen my wife." The amputee continues, "I don't know, I guess they're waiting to see, ahh, if a, if a one-legged man is capable of getting married or if a blind man is capable of getting married. I think that's what they're looking to find out." "That's true," the blind vet agrees, "a lot of them don't think you're capable of doing these things, but you can do them."

The subject matter of this sequence illustrates how the origins of Funt's work were in wartime programs like *The Gripe Booth*. But this frank discussion of postwar male crisis also demonstrates the potential strangeness of secret recording as broadcast entertainment, as well as the show's unlikely combination of voyeuristic and quasi-governmental wiretapping. "Veteran's Views" can stand as an example of the rawest kind of "fly-on-the-wall" eavesdropping presented on *Candid Microphone*; it was a mode that would not, however, become the norm on Funt's show. Another approach to secret recording came to predominate *Candid Microphone,* and to understand the sense of immediacy produced by the show, one must consider not only the technique of secret recording and the lack of a studio audience, but also the nature of the performances frequently captured by Funt's tape: people losing their tempers.

THE RILE

When planning *Candid Microphone,* Funt wrote that he had initially wanted to create a program that "would simply record the beauty of everyday conversation. The notion of having a chance to record people talking when they didn't know anyone was listening—pure eavesdropping—was what fascinated me" (1994, 26). Funt discovered that this approach produced the "most uninteresting garbage you could imagine" (28). Indeed, as "Veteran's Views" demonstrated, turning secret recording into broadcast entertainment presents some particular challenges, one of which is giving a recorded sequence some semblance of formal shape or narrative closure. In that regard, Funt decided to step in, taking on the role of the "provocateur": "someone was needed to take the ordinariness of an everyday situation and push it one step further, into a scene, and in some cases even a spectacle" (28). A formal structure developed wherein Funt would lie in wait and record his victims as he attempted to incite them to anger.[5] Funt described how this dynamic of the "rile" became the central focus of the show: "Although we planned for variety, it soon became apparent that the thing we did best, and the thing our listeners liked most, was making people blow their tops" (1952, 24).

Reviewers of the show frequently commented on the way Funt tried to "rile his subjects." R. W. Stewart wrote in the *New York Times* that Funt's "deportment and remarks, as they become progressively provoking, are calculated to incite the beset person to a state anywhere between the sputtering stage and mayhem, all in behalf of the unremitting endeavor to produce radio entertainment" (1947, 85). Take for example a skit in which Funt posed as a shoe salesman who has mislaid a female customer's shoe. Funt makes half-baked attempts to find the missing shoe, and then starts asking such questions as, "Are you sure you came in here with two shoes?" Funt keeps egging the woman on, suggesting she leave the store wearing a pair of sneakers and come back later. The sequence ends when, after Funt has asked the woman if she'd like a cigarette or some gum, she blurts out, "Aw, shut up!"

The structure of pleasure on *Candid Microphone*, then, is largely a matter of inciting people to flood out. As I described when discussing laughing records in chapter 1, that term has to do with Goffman's conception of maintaining an understanding of the nature of a social interaction. Flooding out occurs when an individual "capsizes" as a social interactant by, for example, dissolving into "laughter or tears or anger" (1974, 350). I have shown how this kind of vocal performance played an important role in the early life of recorded sound: for instance, laughing records helped overcome the dislocation of performer from audience in media performances and provided a powerful index of authentic presence. The flooding out of Funt's victims might be seen in similar terms, since outbursts of anger were often the central source of voyeuristic pleasure on the show. The climax of many segments, as we can see in the shoe salesman gag, is not when the gag is revealed, but a moment of flooding out: the woman telling the salesman to "shut up." To borrow a term from Richard Bauman's study of the narrative reenactment of practical jokes, the fabrication on *Candid Microphone* is usually not discredited: the gag is not revealed on air to the victim (1986, 45).[6]

Not just anyone was heard flooding out: the victim was typically the member of a marginalized group, either a woman or a person with a

marked ethnic accent. Funt alluded to his interest in capturing different
ethnic types when he wrote that *Candid Microphone* "painted a portrait
of New York in that era" (1994, 32). A *TV Guide* story stated that "Funt
does not toss out people with foreign accents or garbled grammar. He
seeks them out" ("Is Candid Camera Just Clean Fun?" 15). An example
can be heard in a gag involving a fruit seller. Funt's "great experiment"
was to ask this question: "How many grapes can a customer sample before he gets tossed out on his ear?" Again, the segment involves Funt
pushing his victim to the limit, trying to get him to flood out in anger or
frustration. The fruit seller has an accent, possibly Italian or eastern European. The climax of this segment is when, after devouring huge
amounts of food and haggling with the fruit seller, Funt suggests that the
seller go and help other customers while he continues to "look around."
The fruit seller replies, "You look around but not with the mouth!" Not
only is this the closest we get to flooding out in this sequence, it is also a
moment when the fruit seller's accent is most pronounced. In another
segment found on an LP anthology of the show, a waiter with a foreign
accent is infuriated by Funt's constant demands to make substitutions on
his order, finally blurting out, "Take it or leave it!"[7]

This focus on ethnic and social types works in a manner reminiscent
of nineteenth-century texts called "physiologies." Robert Ray describes
these texts, written between 1839 and 1842, as "the first best-selling
mass-market paperback books," providing "an immediately legible account, however misleadingly simplified, of the cosmopolitan crowd" divided into "pseudo-scientific portraits of social types" (1995, 26–27). Ray
quotes Richard Sieburth, who writes that the physiologies "served to reduce the crowd's massive alterity to proportions more familiar, to trans-
form its radical anonymity into a lexicon of nameable stereotypes, thereby
providing their readers with the comforting illusion that the faceless con-
glomerations of the modern city could after all be read—and hence
mastered—as a legible system of differences" (28). The physiologies presented a mode of pleasure based on identifying others in a modern urban
context. Seeing *Candid Microphone* as an extension of this project makes
one of the show's slogans take on a slightly different meaning: Funt's victims are "caught in the act of being themselves" in that they are made legible as types. The fruit seller is "caught in the act" both by flooding out
and by letting his "foreign" accent come to the fore so that he can be more
easily classified as a type: the immigrant fruit stand owner.

Ray goes on to compare the physiologies to photography, arguing
that the latter "produced the opposite effect" because of the way it could

capture the contingent detail (29). Whereas the physiologies tended to foreground social types, photography powerfully presents the individual, accidental, and unique. As such, Ray describes "the candid snapshot" as "the triumph of the photographic sensibility" (32). Indeed, photography's ability to capture the unique individual can be illustrated by the way in which it was mobilized for law enforcement purposes. Tom Gunning writes that "photography, through its indexicality, iconic accuracy, and mobility of circulation, provides the ultimate means of tying identity to a specific and unique body" (1995, 20). For Gunning, the photograph could become the ideal witness of crime, able to identify the unique criminal: "The camera captures the guilty one in a moment of unconscious self-betrayal. As an index of guilt, the camera penetrates behind conscious concealment and uncovers a guilty image that the criminal cannot obfuscate, not only because of its indexicality and iconicity but also because the criminal remains unaware that a photo was being taken" (36).

As I did in my examination of the categories of stage and film acting in chapter 3, I want to suggest that the comparison of physiologies and photography can be enriched by including a consideration of vocal performance in the sound media. How does recorded sound fit into this contrast between written and photographic modes of representation? We have seen how Funt's strategy of the rile gravitated toward ethnic typing. In fact, it may be argued that purely audio modes such as radio and phonography have tended toward ethnic typing because of the way they emphasize the ethnic or regional accents of their performers. In his discussion of the influence of radio style on the theater of the 1950s, Bruce McConachie argues that radio writers, directors, and actors "had to rely more on 'type characters' than their counterparts in film and the theater did" (2003, 39). Broad ethnic accents were an effective form of character development when actors could not convey visual information with gesture, costume, or makeup. Ethnic caricature was also a useful strategy on the "descriptive specialties" of the early phonograph industry, since performers had to establish a dramatic scene quickly: recall that phonograph records at this time could contain only about four minutes of material.

Of course, such ethnic caricature was not unique to the sound media. Ethnic typing was equally prevalent on the nineteenth-century vaudeville, burlesque, and minstrel stages, where performers often faced time restrictions like those encountered in phonograph recording.[8] Pamela Robertson Wojcik argues that a form of typecasting was the standard practice of most American stock companies at this time as well, via the "lines-of-business" tradition of casting. In that system, actors maintained specialized roles with fixed interpretations that included ethnic types (2004, 171–73). Considering the prevalence of ethnic caricature across a range of popular entertainments around the turn of the century, we should avoid claims that the sound media represented a radical departure from other performance practices.[9] There are, however, compelling reasons for the continuation of ethnic typing in early phonographic and radio performance.

Although Funt's rile technique often relied on the recognition of types, it should be noted that his stated goals sound a lot like Ray's characterization of photography. For example, Funt introduces a phonograph album collection of *Candid Microphone* sketches as "candid portraits in sound" made of the "plain, everyday" people that history "counts, sorts, and lumps together." These people have "no single name except Americans," and their voices are remembered only "as a chorus." What *Candid Microphone* does, according to Funt, is make these people heard "as individuals." Further, in his 1952 book Funt described how his show sometimes captured voices that went against type in ways that made listeners uneasy: "I remember how many hundreds of letters of disbelief we received after we used a recording of a policeman who sounded like a college student. But without an Irish brogue and the other standard equipment, he just wasn't accepted as the real thing" (1952, 137). Part of Funt's stated progressive agenda was to break down stereotypes, partly through editing ("we won't use scenes in which a member of a racial or religious minority comes through in a manner that might be objectionable to anyone"), and partly through the way in which recorded sound could capture a unique, individual voice (115).

Funt's show emerges as something of a hybrid or transitional text in which tendencies in representation are in tension. Sound recording, like photography, can capture the unique individual, and yet the recorded or broadcast voice is often called on to overcompensate in terms of regional or ethnic accents in order to stand for other visual signifiers of identity. At the same time, Funt sought to use secret recording to break down stereotypes, and so he went against the grain of long-standing tendencies in sound media performance practice. One way to test some of these assertions is to gauge changes that occurred in Funt's program when it moved from radio to television. On TV, Funt's victims would still be "caught in the act," but perhaps in a different way.

THE REVEAL

On August 10, 1948, *Candid Microphone* debuted on television, becoming *Candid Camera*. At first, it seems to have stuck fairly close to the radio model I've been describing. In an early episode set in New York City's Empire Mills Coffee Shop, there is an overwhelming emphasis on ethnic and minority victims. The victim of the first gag is an African American man. After the gag is revealed, Funt describes how the coffee shop is in the part of the city that used to be Hell's Kitchen, which explains it's very "colorful kind of patron." The next victim is a man Funt describes as being "unintelligible" because of his manner of speaking, and the female victim who follows also speaks with a heavy European accent.

Two differences, however, can be found between this early television text and its radio predecessor. First, the fabrication is revealed more often: victims are sometimes told they are on television and that the situation is a prank. Second, this show features a more complex mix of the live and the prerecorded. While there is still no studio audience, Funt's hosting of the show and interviews with the shop's owners are done live, interspersed with prerecorded gag sequences. In fact, the Empire Mills Coffee Shop program illustrates how awkwardly the live and the prerecorded coexisted during this era of television. After Funt sets up a gag sequence, there is a technical problem with cutting to the taped segment, and Funt is forced to ad-lib for several minutes while the problem is corrected and the taped sequence can roll.

Throughout the 1950s, *Candid Camera* moved from network to network, and it was periodically off the air altogether, finding a permanent slot on CBS prime time only in 1960. During that time, Funt redefined the format of the show in several important ways, which led to its greatest level of popular success in the early 1960s. For one thing, the show came to be performed in front of a live studio audience. Second, the network forced Funt to take on Arthur Godfrey as a more polished cohost. Also, prerecorded sequences were increasingly accompanied by live narration: Funt stated that he had realized that "people needed to be told when to laugh" (1994, 65). The blending of the live and the prerecorded became even more complex, as live narration and the reactions of a studio audience accompanied prerecorded segments. It is difficult to imagine how these elements would have been possible on the radio, where it would have been much more difficult to distinguish between taped segments and live studio responses. The fact that these changes made the

show more palatable for prime-time television might be connected to the
fact that they also took the edge off the voyeuristic aspects of secret
recording, making the taped segments seem more like a public event or
a variety show.

In 1961 *TV Guide* described another vital change in the show at
around this time: "Through the years, the tone of Funt's shows has become more sensitive to the feelings of his subjects. In the early days he
often drove people to the brink of profanity and mayhem—and sometimes over the brink. Now he is less interested in how abrasively he can
rub a person the wrong way than in how a man reacts to the unexpected
or, simply, how he copes with the realities of everyday life in the mid-
20th Century" ("Is Candid Camera Just Good Clean Fun?" 16). Funt described how this was in part a public relations move, since many in the
audience felt his provocations went too far: "As our audience grew, we
became aware that a significant group of listeners felt the show was
cruel—an opinion that persists to this day" (1994, 33). The solution was
a careful emphasis on showing heroic and universal behavior, as well as
giving victims a medal that read: "You were caught in the act of being
yourself and were big enough to enjoy it." These moves were meant to
demonstrate to the audience that Funt "really liked people" (34).

Funt was still concerned with capturing people flooding out, but in a
way oriented to the visual medium: "It was the faces of ordinary
people—confronted by ordinary events—that would captivate viewers
for years. These faces were filled with surprise, with bewilderment, with
thought—and, at times, with anger" (41). To this end, by the early 1960s
the show had developed a new visual technique that Funt called "the reveal": "This was the moment we told the subjects it was all a joke and
they were going to be on television. (In later years it was done with the
trademark phrase 'Smile! You're on *Candid Camera!*') This required delicate handling, but if done right, it was the best moment of the scene"
(48). The importance of the reveal is illustrated in the intricacy of Funt's
description of the development of this visual technique:

> The reveal was hard to capture on film because the zoom lens had not been
> perfected yet. To go quickly from a wide shot to a close-up, the cameraman
> had to actually remove the wide-angle lens and attach a telephoto. This
> wasted valuable seconds. I dreamed up a turret-style attachment for our
> cameras which held three lenses—wide, medium, and close—and hired an
> expert in the field to build it for us. The turret could be turned by the assis-
> tant cameraman just as the subject was told he was on "Candid Camera."
> We got so good at using the turret that we only lost six frames between the
> wide and close-up shots. (48)

The reveal recalls *Candid Microphone's* interest in the dynamics of flooding out, but with an obsessive focus on the face.[10] Funt noted a wide range of responses when victims were let in on the joke, and he was often surprised by understated reactions. On some occasions Funt had to physically "latch onto" people in order to "keep them in front of the camera" (48). The image of Funt physically restraining his victims in order to capture their faces recalls Gunning's discussion of representations of early twentieth-century criminals grimacing in order to resist having their identity fixed by photography (1995, 27). Caught in the act, indeed.

The reveal, like the rile, worked as a strategy for giving secretly recorded performance a formal shape and a sense of closure. As *Candid Microphone* became *Candid Camera,* the emphasis shifted from the rile to the reveal. This is not to say that there were never reveals on *Candid Microphone,* but they occurred much less frequently, and when they did occur, they often did not provide closure. For example, in two sequences, one called "The Lady from the Lecture Bureau," and another "Testimony Dinner for a Nobody," the gag is revealed, and yet the victim continues on, nonplussed. The radio reveal also lacks the immediate effect of its visual counterpart, since it is often quite hard to gauge the nature of the victim's response when the listener has recourse only to sometimes ambiguous vocalizations.

There is one *Candid Microphone* reveal, however, that will reward closer analysis. Funt sets up a sketch entitled "Two Boys and a Watch" by describing "two grimy shoeshine boys" whom he saw looking at the watches in a New York store where Funt posed as a watch salesman. Funt describes the two boys as being about six and eight, and their accents strongly suggest that they are African American. In a secretly recorded interview with Funt, we learn many facts about the boys: they work around Times Square, singing and dancing to draw crowds; they must stay at their work to avoid a beating from their father; and they want a watch so that they can get to school on time. "Listen, kids," says Funt, "have you ever been on the radio?" Confused, they answer no. "You see this?" We hear a brushing sound as the microphone is revealed. "That's a microphone; we just made a record of everything you said." There is a pause, and then the little boy's heartbreaking reply: "I'm scared." Funt quickly reassures them, and when he gives them a free watch to share, they shout with delight.

The first thing this complicated performance can illustrate is how *Candid Microphone* functioned as an update on the physiologies: here we are presented with the stereotypical "grimy," singing and dancing

African American shoeshine boy. Second, the sequence demonstrates how ambiguous the moment of the reveal could be on the radio, since it is quite difficult to determine the boys' response when they come face-to-face with the microphone. But in the sound of the revealed microphone, the following awkward pause, and the boy's frank admission of fear, "Two Boys and a Watch" also represents a retelling of a very old story about recording technology, one that can suggest other layers of meaning to Funt's reveal.

Michael Taussig, in his book *Mimesis and Alterity,* has described an American and western European "fascination with the Other's fascination with the talking machine," as demonstrated in "frontier rituals" in which the white man's phonograph is used to awe the natives (1993, 207). For example, Taussig points to the famous sequence in Robert Flaherty's *Nanook of the North* (1922) when, in wonderment at the white trader's phonograph, Nanook puts the phonograph disc in his mouth (201). Taussig argues that the appeal of narratives featuring the "savage" awed by recorded sound stem from the fact that "the magic of mechanical reproduction" had, for most modern Western people, become a mundane part of everyday life while still retaining its aura of mystery and magic:

> Vis à vis the savage they are the masters of these wonders that, after the first shock waves of surprise upon their invention and commercialization in the West, pass into the everyday. Yet these shocks rightly live on in the mysterious underbelly of the technology—to be eviscerated as "magic" in frontier rituals of technological supremacy. To take the talking machine to the jungle is to emphasize and embellish the genuine mystery and accomplishment of mechanical reproduction in an age when technology itself, after the flurry of excitement at a new breakthrough, is seen not as mystique or poetry but as routine. (208)

Similarly, Erika Brady describes the use of the phonograph in anthropological fieldwork, as well as in humorous accounts of the first experience of the phonograph by country "rubes." Brady argues that, in contrast to the suggestion of these pervasive narratives of "technological supremacy," it was "participants in American mainstream culture" who maintained "an attitude of mythically charged wonder" toward the phonograph and its inventor, the "Wizard of Menlo Park" (1999, 31). In fact, Brady claims that mainstream Americans found it harder to come to grips with a talking machine than did many members of native cultures, owing in part to the fact that Americans tended to have no spiritual explanation for disembodied voices, whereas other cultures did.

Brady concludes that these narratives are more a projection of "the fantasies and anxieties of the tellers' culture" than "an accurate picture" of native or nonmainstream cultures (30).

Once placed in the context of this problematic narrative lineage, the pleasures of "Two Boys and a Watch," and, indeed, Funt's reveal more generally, start to seem more complex. Arguably, the pleasure of witnessing the shock of the revealed microphone is quite similar to the frontier ritual described by Taussig. Another clue that Funt's format is closely linked to anxieties about recording technologies can be found in the origins of *Candid Microphone*. In his 1952 book Funt describes the scene in 1943 at Camp Gruber, Oklahoma, when he first considered a show based on secret recording. While waiting in line to make a record of his voice to send home to his parents, Funt noticed that the soldier in front of him was particularly anxious: "I know I'm going to louse up this thing although I've been practicing all morning. I don't know why the hell I'm so nervous, but my hands are all wet" (1952, 11). Funt was struck by what he called "one of the worst cases of microphone fright I had ever seen," and he recalled thinking that a microphone could be "more frightening than a machine gun" (12). This anecdote reveals how the seed for Funt's program was the realization of the irrational anxiety that still surrounded sound recording, even in the 1940s.

The reveal then, is the moment not only when the victim is let in on the joke, but also when he or she comes face to face with the apparatus (the mike or the camera), and by extension with the much larger apparatus of national network broadcasting. Indeed, with the establishment of the reveal, Funt's show became an elaborate game of hide-and-seek with recording technology—first it is hidden, then it is revealed. "Two Boys and a Watch" brings the colonial dimensions of this narrative to the surface—Funt becomes the white anthropologist, infiltrating the Others' space, interviewing them and recording their performances, awing them with his display of technological supremacy, and finally offering them paternalistic charity. Buried within the pleasures of the reveal, then, is a reenactment of the "magic of mechanical reproduction" for an American population that still struggled to understand it, even as it was part of the texture of their everyday lives. The more dramatic and unambiguous televisual reveal focused on the face of an individual subject caught in a moment of inhibition, and so it can also be understood in relation to a tradition of hidden amateur photography.

Tom Gunning describes a culture of amateur photography at the end of the nineteenth century that was "light-hearted" and "mischievous," emphasizing "visual curiosity" and a search for knowledge that was "more voyeuristic than scientific." Importantly, the work of these amateurs helped to create "a modern sense of the everyday body and its behavior." Early photographs in this mode portrayed "the human body when frozen in mid-action and caught unawares," and it often violated aesthetic standards and "concepts of bodily propriety." Gunning notes that these photos, as well as films by the Lumière brothers, presented "casual bodily postures of everyday life" and thus "created a new modern self image, a casual self presentation diametrically opposed to the formal, almost allegorical poses of studio portraiture" (2001, 88–90).

Candid Camera clearly has affinities with this tradition of amateur photography. Indeed, Funt's persona was that of the amateur everyman. TV Guide wrote that "one reason Funt is able to get the most out of uneducated types is that he appears to be one of them" ("Is Candid Camera Just Good Clean Fun?" 15). In a 1948 article, Newsweek referred to Funt's "graying hair," "perpetually harried expression," and "ordinary New York manner and dialect," which allowed him to "easily pass for just about anybody" ("Funt's Fun" 62). Besides this amateur persona, Funt's dedication to capturing people off guard, and his recurring injunction to smile, can be seen as a continuation of the amateur fascination with, and creation of a modern conception of, the casual body.

Funt's use of secret recording brought temporal aspects of performance to that project. Notice how, in the following quotations, Funt discusses his work in terms of performance, contrasting "candid behavior" with conventional acting:

> The major part of candid behavior is miles away from the dramatic conception. I have seen cold anger expressed with nothing more than a limp smile. I have watched a man get the surprise of his life without the slightest visible change of attitude. We have photographed joy that looked like dismay, sorrow that resembled gaiety, and terror that could easily have passed for elation. This is why it has been a long, slow task to convince people that our candid studies are genuine. Generations have been educated to accept the characterizations of the stage and screen. (1952, 138)

> Stage "business"—the insignificant gestures and actions used so widely in the drama—differs greatly from what happens in real life. Even where dialogue and major action have some of the quality of true realism, the hero, at the careful instruction of the director, still taps his cigarette on the case during a lull in conversation. The pensive businessman studies his fingernails. The nervous housewife rearranges the flowers on the mantelpiece. The gangster impatiently flips a coin. But the real-life counterparts of these same people don't indulge in any such stylized gestures. They rub

their eyes, pick at threads in their clothing, and scratch their heads and other areas. (140)

These quotes demonstrate how Funt's camera could capture gestures and expressions that made conventional modes of acting seem contrived. Funt made similar claims about vocal performance, contrasting dramatic dialogue to secretly recorded dialogue. Characters in fiction, according to Funt, speak in an "orderly, concise way," and a line of dialogue is "a neat little package of words, painstakingly selected and assembled by the author to serve some neat little purpose" (122). Fictional characters express themselves "in a straightline fashion, using a nice simile or a neat allusion here and there for color" (123). "Real-life dialogue," Funt asserts, "is almost never like that": "In real life there is a great deal of overtalk and three-way talk—the kind of conversation in which three individuals will talk almost simultaneously, and yet each one will hear as much as he wants to of what the other two are saying" (123, 125). Interestingly, Funt describes this kind of overtalk by comparing human hearing to the microphone: "The explanation of this phenomenon lies in the versatility of the human ear. Unlike a microphone, which indiscriminately picks up everything it hears, the ear 'tunes in' what it wants and 'tunes out' what it doesn't want" (123–25). For Funt, then, secret recording not only captured conversation with unprecedented fidelity, it even allowed people to hear speech in an entirely new way.

Funt described other aspects of the beauty of candid speech through the example of the secret recording of a woman in a baseball stadium who spoke "in an urgent, almost raucous voice." In his attempts to describe the beauty of her speech, he refers to "the haphazard way the woman's thoughts formed into words—not always the right words—and then tumbled out. That's a quality that characterizes a great deal of the candid speech I've recorded. The brain is attempting to communicate by means of a vocal mechanism which is often unreliable, and that may account for the strangely untidy quality of so much candid speech. Words are misused, tenses change, plurals become singulars. And yet the total effect of [it] . . . conveys a mood and a meaning seldom encountered in fiction" (128–31).

It is interesting to note that the two elements of performance that Funt singles out as being more "real" than conventions of the stage and screen were already at that time a part of some schools of realist acting. For example, Naremore describes how overlapping dialogue had been heard on the Broadway stage since the 1920s as well as in some films of the classical Hollywood era (1988, 44). Similarly, the "untidy" quality of candid speech recalls improvisational techniques typical of the Method acting made famous by the Group Theatre in New York. Indeed, the Method became well known at exactly the same time as Funt's emergence in broadcasting: Marlon Brando's famous performance in *A Streetcar Named Desire* hit national screens in 1951. As an indication of the common cause between the Method and secret recording, consider that the Group playwright Clifford Odets sought Funt's advice about how to secretly record his family: "[Odets] wanted to create more believable transitions between sections of dialogue. After playing the tapes, he told me, 'When I listen to the conversations of real people, they don't use transitions. They change the subject in a flash. And yet, it's still believable.' He went on to use that style in his writing, and it was magic. When you heard an actor on the stage jump from one thought to another without the slightest concern for continuity, it created an electrifying sense of reality" (Funt 1994, 51).[11]

Secret recording of vocal performance might be considered a factor in the development of realist acting styles such as the Method. As the amateur photographer had, Funt's programs played a role in the creation of a modern casual body and voice. But the centerpiece of *Candid Camera* was not so much a casual body as a body in the convulsive grips of shock and surprise. Since its goal was the production and capture of an involuntary response, the reveal can be connected to Linda Williams's descriptions of "women in spasm" in early film pornography (1989, 48). Notably, Funt's camera often revealed the uninhibited reactions of a male victim. Funt said that "if you asked me to describe the perfect person for 'Candid Camera,' I'd say he's fortyish, a little overweight, and balding" (1994, 44). Besides sounding a lot like a description of Funt himself, this demonstrates the show's notable emphasis on male spectacle. For example, a *Candid Camera* classic sequence features a provocatively dressed woman at a department store. The woman browses near male shoppers, and Funt's camera captured their leering gazes. Here the male gaze becomes the subject of an invasive male gaze.

Underlying structural similarities to pornography were brought to the surface in a film project Funt began when *Candid Camera* was canceled in 1968. Not coincidentally, that was the same year that Hollywood introduced its new ratings system. This was a time when the ratings system was still in flux: in 1968 *Midnight Cowboy* won the Oscar for best picture with an X rating, and, as Jon Lewis points out, in 1972 and 1973 hard-core porn features like *Deep Throat* outearned "all but a handful of the major studios' legit releases" (2000, 192). Funt made the film *What Do You Say to a Naked Lady?*, which was released in 1970 with an X rating. In a typical scene, the eponymous naked lady steps off an elevator, much to the shock of a man waiting to get on. The camera zooms not to the naked body of the woman, but to the facial reactions of the man. As was true of the sequence described above, the reveal is turned primarily on the male face, and so a strange kind of voyeuristic tension is manifested where the presence of the female body becomes secondary to the flooding out of the man's face.[12] The reveal in this film, and in a series of similar "adult" shows Funt made for the Playboy Channel, takes the erotics of that technique to its logical extensions, and yet it all the while focuses on the display of male affect.[13]

The success of Funt's candid format on television and film relied on his adaptation of a formal structure designed for radio. This meant moving from a mode of incitation, the identification of type, and an unmediated address to the home audience to one presented to a studio audience and based on the erotics of the reveal. Both *Candid Microphone* and *Candid Camera* offer instances of modern performance made possible by portable sound technologies and featuring dynamics of flooding out. The preceding discussion will help us consider a therapeutic discourse to which Funt's work has been put. The "candid" format has not only been remarkably successful and durable in broadcast entertainment, but has also accrued to itself discourses of realism, social science, and therapy.

THE REAL

In addition to depending on portable sound equipment, the pleasures of the rile and the reveal were also made possible by editing. That is, secret recording as a mode of entertainment relies on recording huge amounts of material and editing out all but the few moments of interest. Again, the technological context of the 1940s becomes important, since magnetic tape was much easier to edit than previous forms of sound recording. Indeed, each sequence of *Candid Microphone* is peppered with edits, sometimes even in mid-sentence. The same holds for *Candid Camera*. Funt described how his crew "often filmed forty hours a week, because it took as many as thirty tries to get a single piece that was usable. Then the lengthy editing process began" (1994, 49). *TV Guide*, like many popular press accounts of the show, also discussed the editing process, stating that *Candid Camera* "exposes 50 feet of film for every foot televised"

("Is Candid Camera Just Good Clean Fun?" 15). Portable sound equipment and extensive editing—these two aspects of production were central not only to Funt's shows, but also to influential styles of documentary filmmaking.

As was the case with *Candid Microphone* and *Candid Camera,* new
forms of documentary filmmaking such as direct cinema and cinema verité were made possible in the 1950s by "the availability of very portable
synchronous sound recording equipment" (Nichols 1991, 44). In another similarity to Funt's programs, portable sound equipment inspired
new levels of interaction between subject and filmmaker: "Speech need
no longer be reserved for postproduction in a studio, far removed from
the lives of those whose images grace the film. The filmmaker need not
be only a cinematic, recording eye. . . . The filmmaker's voice could be
heard . . . in face-to-face encounter with others" (44). Like Funt, documentary filmmakers could thus function as "mentor, participant, prose-
cutor, or provocateur" (44). In terms of editing, the direct cinema of
Frederick Weisman was dependent on editing ratios similar to Funt's; his
"footage shot usually totaled some thirty hours for each hour used"
(Barnouw 1974, 246). Although it might seem an unlikely comparison,
What Do You Say to a Naked Lady? has some additional formal similarities to the landmark cinema verité film by Jean Rouch and Edgar
Morin, *Chronique d'été* (1961). Like Funt, Rouch and Morin were "on-
camera participants in the venture, and evolved procedures that seemed
to serve as 'psychoanalytic stimulants' " (254). Additionally, both *Naked
Lady* and *Chronique d'été* contain self-reflexive "screening room" sequences where the film is shown and discussed, that discussion itself becoming a part of the film (254). In both cases this is a technique mobilized to provide a sense of complete disclosure and an accompanying
amplification of realism.

It is worth noting the use of these cutting-edge documentary techniques in such a non–avant-garde setting as American network television. That Funt's candid format predates these documentary movements
suggests that the movement of influence may not be as clear as one might
think. In terms of innovation, Funt may be placed alongside not only
Rouch and Morin, but also Andy Warhol. Peter Weibel, in an analysis of
Warhol's work such as *Screen Test* (1965) and *A: A Novel* (1968), argues
that Warhol was the first to suggest that "surveillance is enjoyment; observation is entertaining." "Warhol was a pioneer, paving the way for the
soap operas, game shows, and reality shows" (2002, 218). It should be
noted that Warhol's work came almost twenty years after *Candid Mi-*

crophone, and several years after *Candid Camera* had been a massively successful network program. The fact that Funt's program shared techniques in common with these modes of documentary and art filmmaking might have helped provide the show with a heightened sense of realism and cultural weight. Funt's use of techniques associated with cutting-edge documentary filmmaking helped frame the show in terms of "reality," despite the fact that it was the product of massive amounts of editing. But the cultural resonance of Funt's work goes beyond a sense of documentary realism, and it has consistently been framed by a discourse of social science.

The most famous example of this might have been when the sociologist David Riesman wrote in *The Lonely Crowd* that Funt was, after Paul Lazarsfeld, the "most ingenious sociologist in America" (Funt 1952, 13). In a 1961 *TV Guide* cover story on *Candid Camera,* Funt is described as "practicing his own brand of psychology": "An orthodox psychologist might collect data by running rats through mazes. Funt is interested only in human beings. He sets up situations . . . and records people's reactions—with a hidden camera" ("Is Candid Camera Just Good Clean Fun?" 12). Considering the cultural context of the wiretap jitters that existed when *Candid Microphone* debuted, one might consider this scientific discourse as a strategy for making his show seem less like the work of a voyeuristic private eye and more like an academic study. Indeed, that helps to explain Funt's insistence on referring to the people caught by his mike and camera as "subjects" and not "victims" (Flagler 1960, 59).

What is clear is that this aura of social science has provided Funt's shows with a remarkable life beyond broadcast entertainment. For example, episodes of *Candid Camera* have become a staple of undergraduate psychology courses. Funt donated the noncommercial educational rights to *Candid Camera* to Cornell University, where the show has been used for research and educational purposes, and candid sequences from the show have been compiled in educational videos and textbooks. In a 1978 article James Maas, the Cornell professor of psychology with whom Funt worked, described the show's potential as scientific data: "While the films were not meant to serve a formulated scientific purpose, the parameters of the situations were planned, the situations allowed for a variety of responses, and the behaviors were recorded systematically. Behavior was not influenced by experimenter bias or expectancy, by the characteristics of the laboratory setting itself, or by the subject's willingness to report" (1978, 114). Maas found that clips from the shows had their greatest potential in their value as "supplementary instructional material": "They can be utilized to visually portray lecture topics without absorbing an inordinate amount of valuable lecture time and to clarify materials that often leave the student confused or unstimulated" (115). In a quote that nicely reaffirms the importance of the television laugh track, as well as the precariousness of secret recording as a mode of entertainment, Maas wrote that "when one removes the canned laughter, even the funniest of scenes becomes a serious object of study for students who have been adequately prepared to note scientific phenomena" (115).

Anna McCarthy, in her insightful discussion of *Candid Camera* as a first wave of reality television, describes the numerous points of "institutional, biographical, and intellectual contact between social scientists and Funt" (2004, 28). Foremost among these, McCarthy notes connections between Funt's work and the "obedience" studies of Yale University's Stanley Milgram (34).[14] On the level of performance, one might explain the resonance of Funt's work with social science by noting the close proximity of the practical joke and the kind of experimental hoaxing often found in social scientific research. Goffman describes a type of interaction he calls fabrication: "the intentional effort of one or more individuals to manage activity so that a party of one or more others will be induced to have a false belief about what is going on" (1974, 83). Fabrication creates different understandings of a situation, as opposed to "keying," which "leads all participants to have the same view of what it is that is going on" (84). Of the different forms of fabrication described by Goffman, the practical joke is "a more or less elaborate fabrication of a bit of the victim's nonverbal environment in order to lead him into a misconception of what is happening, often at a moment when the perpetrator is not present to see the result" (89).

Another of Goffman's forms of fabrication is called "experimental hoaxing": "the practice of conducting human experiments which require on methodological grounds (as almost all human experiments do) that the subject be unaware of what it is that is being tested and even unaware that an experiment of any kind is in progress" (92). Here, often for scientific purposes, strangers are chosen as subjects. Notably, Goffman states that these kind of experiments are "quite similar to the hoaxes that Allen Funt and his *Candid Camera* program appeared to present, except that Funt was obliged to obtain legal consent for use from the victim" (92). McCarthy also notes the similarities between Funt's reveal and scientific debriefing (2004, 34). When looking only at dimensions of performance, one finds reasons for the scientific discourse that has surrounded Funt's show.

Another illustration of the thin boundaries between Funt's work and some aspects of postwar social science can be found in the work of the sociologist Harold Garfinkel. One of Garfinkel's most influential scholarly contributions was his pioneering exploration of "ethnomethodology": the study of "the body of common-sense knowledge and the range of procedures and considerations by means of which the ordinary members of society make sense of, find their way about in, and act on circumstances in which they find themselves" (Heritage 1984, 4). Garfinkel's work leading to the coining of this term took place in the 1960s; his influential *Studies in Ethnomethodology* was first published in 1967. Garfinkel noted that the "background expectancies," or everyday social assumptions, were so familiar and routinized that they were typically unavailable for sociological study (1984, 36). His goal was to bring these "stable social structures of everyday activities" to the surface, often by setting up situations in which the assumptions of everyday activities were broken: "Procedurally it is my preference to start with familiar scenes and ask what can be done to make trouble. The operations that one would have to perform in order to multiply the senseless features of perceived environments; to produce and sustain bewilderment, consternation, and confusion; to produce the socially structured affects of anxiety, shame, guilt, and indignation; and to produce disorganized interaction should tell us something about how the structures of everyday activities are ordinarily and routinely produced and maintained" (37–38). The manipulation of familiar scenes to provoke bewilderment and confusion was known as "breaching experiments" (Heritage 1984, 78).

If this is starting to sound a lot like the setup for one of Funt's programs, consider a few of Garfinkel's experiments. In one, students were "instructed to engage an acquaintance or a friend in an ordinary conversation and, without indicating that what the experimenter was asking was in any way unusual, to insist that the person clarify the sense of his commonplace remarks" (Garfinkel 1984, 42). A female student reported the following interaction with her husband when the two were watching television. When he remarked that he was tired, she asked, "How are you tired? Physically, mentally, or just bored?" "I don't know," he answered, "I guess physically, mainly." "You mean that your muscles ache or your bones?" she continued. "I guess so. Don't be so technical," he scolded. Later, the increasingly bewildered husband stated, "All these old movies have the same kind of old iron bedstead in them." Continuing the experiment, the woman said, "What do you mean? Do you mean all old movies, or some of them, or just the ones you have seen?" "What's the matter with you?" asked the exasperated husband; "You know what I mean." "I wish you would be more specific," she replied. Ending the report of the experiment in a way that would have fit seamlessly on a *Candid Microphone* broadcast, the husband floods out: "You know what I mean! Drop dead!" (43).

This experiment was useful for Garfinkel because of the way in which it exposed the degree to which speakers assume their listeners share their assumptions about what they are talking about and expect them to fill in gaps in their often vague communication (Heritage 1984, 81). But the surface similarities to Funt's methodology are hard to miss, as is the case with a Garfinkel experiment that would have worked particularly well on *Candid Camera,* in which students were instructed "to select someone other than a family member and in the course of an ordinary conversation, and without indicating that anything unusual was happening, to bring their faces up to the subject's until their noses were almost touching" (Garfinkel 1984, 72). Secret recording was even a motif in several of Garfinkel's experiments. Take, for example, one in which the experimenter "engaged others in conversation while he had a wire recorder hidden under his coat. In the course of the conversation the experimenter opened his jacket to reveal the recorder saying, 'See what I have?' An initial pause was almost invariably followed by the question, 'What are you going to do with it?' " (75). Garfinkel's ethnomethodology, an influential mode of sociological inquiry that rose to prominence during the decade of Funt's greatest success, provides another example of the many overlaps between the candid programs and postwar social science, in particular on the level of performance.

As a final illustration of the candid format's remarkable ability to cross over into semiscientific realms, consider the case of Norman Cousins. In 1964 Cousins, the editor of the *Saturday Evening Post,* contracted a rare, crippling, and seemingly irreversible disease while traveling abroad. In his book *Anatomy of an Illness* (1979), Cousins describes how he cured himself by taking charge of his own treatment. The cure Cousins devised consisted of large doses of vitamin C and laughter provided in large part by watching episodes of Allen Funt's *Candid Camera.* Later, when the legendary director John Huston was suffering with cancer, his friend Paul Newman contacted Funt to ask for tapes of the show for Huston's treatment. Newman reported that every thirty minutes of the show gave Huston four "pain-free hours" (Funt 1994, 225). In the wake of this attention, Funt began a fund called Laughter Therapy, in which tapes of *Candid Camera* were sent to patients in chronic pain.

Funt wrote that he was interested in how laughter "eases the suffering of pain," and "might prove to have a healing effect as well": "I wanted to establish a foundation to help others in pain and to collect more evidence in the form of actual patient testimonials" (225). In a remarkable second act after its run on network and cable television, Funt's show has been posited as scientific data in college-level psychology education and has also been thought to imbue laughter with a particularly medicinal quality.

The therapeutic function of television has recently received some scholarly attention. Mimi White describes a therapeutic model of television narrative based on Foucault's discussion of confession. She studies the rise of therapy and counseling TV shows such as Dr. Ruth's *Good Sex* in the 1980s (1992, 25).[15] Barbara Klinger describes the therapeutic function that results from repeated viewing of certain films on home VCRs and DVD players. Klinger refers to the recent use of the term *cinematherapy* in self-help psychology books and film guides to refer to the use of specific films as emotional "self-medication" for specific situations or emotional states (2006, 169–70). *Candid Camera* offers a model of TV therapy similar to cinematherapy, but one that works through the supposedly medicinal properties of laughter. The show's resonance with discourses of realism and social science seems to amplify its medicinal effects. In the larger context of this book, the therapeutic uses to which Funt's work has been put can serve as another indication of the powerful cultural resonance of both flooding out and secret recording as modes of modern performance.

Besides illustrating some of the cultural meanings of modern vocal performance, Funt's candid format is also a productive case study for thinking about the uses of recording. I've discussed Funt's shows in terms of new sound recording technologies, a shift in radio away from live broadcasting, as well as connections to wiretapping and documentary filmmaking. *Candid Microphone* and *Candid Camera* were hybrids of the live and recorded that experimented with integrating the two in innovative and influential ways. Funt's pioneering model for turning "bugging the backstage" into broadcast entertainment has proven to be remarkably resilient. Indeed, Funt's cultural capital has spiked recently because of recognition of the candid format as an important precursor to the reality TV programming that has become a central feature of American television since the 1990s. Some recent shows that work along Funt's lines include *New Candid Camera, The Jamie Kennedy Experiment,* MTV's *Punk'd,* Comedy Central's *Trigger Happy TV,* HBO's *Da*

Ali G Show, and Spike TV's *The Joe Schmo Show.* Analysis of the candid format can provide ways to describe formal aspects of these shows. For these purposes, I'll narrow down my discussion of Funt's candid format to three dimensions: the reveal, the practice of taking "normal" people as victims, and the use of secret recording.

TO REVEAL OR NOT TO REVEAL

The presence or absence of the reveal plays an important role in shaping the meanings of a show based on secret recording. Comedy Central's *Trigger Happy TV* eschews the reveal as well as Funt's invasive zoom onto the face of his victim, instead keeping the camera in a long shot. This means that the viewer's focus is less on the reaction of the victim than on the comedic performance of the provocateur, thus making the show feel more like a British sketch comedy than a psychology experiment. In fact, Funt always required the actors he hired as provocateurs to remain in the background, insisting that they keep their back to the camera, and let the "subject" be funny: "The audience must focus on the subject, not the actor" (1994, 106). One function of the reveal, then, is to help define who is doing the performing in a secret recording, the actor or the subject.

Spike TV's *The Joe Schmo Show* offers a quite different variation on Funt's format, essentially taking the gag-reveal dynamic and blowing it up to mammoth proportions by stretching a single prank across an entire television season. The gimmick of *The Joe Schmo Show* is that only one contestant on a ridiculous reality show called *Lap of Luxury* is for real; the rest are actors and all the contests are scripted. The season builds up to the colossal revelation to Matthew Kennedy Gould, the one "real" person in the house, that the entire show is a put-on. The final episode plays this super-reveal for all it's worth, lingering on the moment when Gould is told that "the only real thing on this reality show is you." We are repeatedly shown Gould's shocked and tearful expressions and hear audio loops of his desperate, falsetto voice asking, "What is going on?" Stretching the fabrication to these proportions brings to the surface ethical issues that were always present in Funt's model of "bugging the backstage." Over the course of the series, Gould develops a genuine friendship with "Brian" (Brian Keith Etheridge), who is an actor playing the role of "the Buddy" as well as a writer on the show. Gould's relationship with Brian becomes the most emotionally charged aspect of the reveal. The hoax is revealed to Gould on the final episode when Gould's housemates begin to admit, one by one, that they are actually actors. At one point, Gould turns away in confusion, and Etheridge grabs his arm to keep him on camera. When it becomes clear that all the cast members are in fact actors, Gould turns to Brian, pushes his hands away and asks insistently, "Are you an actor? Are you an actor?"

The tangible sense of betrayal and resentment that Gould feels when Brian owns up is forgotten in the excitement of the oversized check for $100,000 that is quickly brought on the set and the earnest tributes to Gould from the cast. (Recall how Funt learned that he needed to accentuate the positive and even gave his victims a medal to prove that he "liked people.") Still, when Gould was interviewed later, after the shock of the reveal had faded, he said that his relationship with Brian was the hardest part of the experience for him to reconcile, and that he still struggled with feelings of resentment: "I wanted Brian to be a real person so bad." The issues of betrayal, deception, and resentment that are an inherent part of secret recording as a mode of performance become explicit on *The Joe Schmo Show,* but they were always present on Funt's programs. Hence Funt's catchphrase, "Smile! You're on *Candid Camera!*" came to accompany the moment of the reveal. In this light, it can be seen as a subtle reminder to the victim that he or she had best hide any sense of resentment until after the cameras are off.

NORMAL PEOPLE

As James Friedman notes, one of the most distinguishing features of reality TV is the use of "seemingly 'normal' real people rather than professional actors" (2002, 8). Indeed, television scholars have argued that reality TV is better understood more as a mode of production than a genre, one that cuts production costs by sidestepping union labor and expensive star performers. Chad Raphael describes the emergence of American reality TV in the late 1980s as a response to an economic restructuring of U.S. television caused by the growth of cable, an increasingly fragmented audience, loss of advertising dollars, and resulting cuts in production costs (2004, 121). Some of the largest costs of television production were contracts for above-the-line talent, which made reality formats an appealing cost-cutting option (123). Both reality TV and Funt's programs featured everyday people instead of professional actors, but for different reasons.

Though MTV's *Punk'd* uses secretly recorded pranks à la *Candid Camera*, the show's victims tend to be celebrities, often the Hollywood-insider

friends of the show's host, Ashton Kutcher. What is lost is Funt's progressive attempt to show the nobility of "plain, everyday" people, and
the resulting aura of scientific experimentation. Making celebrities the
butt of televised pranks can be appreciated for the reasons outlined by
Jeffrey Sconce in his description of the critically maligned reality show
Celebrity Boxing: "In a society that closely monitors the length of Brad
Pitt's beard and allows Tom Cruise venues to opine on war with Iraq,
any attempt to humiliate the celebrity class should be embraced and celebrated" (2004, 256). More than raw celebrity humiliation, however,
Punk'd resembles the voyeuristic pleasures of the outtake reel, on which
the viewer hopes to catch a glimpse of the "real" bodily presence of the
star as revealed in a moment of flooding out in surprise or laughter.

SECRET RECORDING

Although they appear to have much in common with *Candid Camera,* it
is important to note that HBO's *Da Ali G Show* and *The Joe Schmo
Show* do not feature secret recording. On *The Joe Schmo Show,* Gould
was very much aware of the fact that he was being filmed; he just thought
it was for a show with a very different premise, called *Lap of Luxury.*
Similarly, the victims of comedian Sacha Baron Cohen's *Da Ali G Show*
know that they are being filmed, but they are not aware of the real context of the show. Cohen's shtick is to present himself as one of three fictional television hosts: Ali G, a hopelessly dim hip-hop wannabe and
host of a "street-level" English television show; Bruno, an Austrian fashion journalist; or perhaps his most famous character, Borat, an Andy
Kaufman-esque "foreign man" figure and reporter from Kazakhstan.
Posing as Ali G, Cohen pulls off the amazing feat of nabbing interviews
with the likes of Boutros Boutros-Ghali, Noam Chomsky, Newt Gin-
grich, Ralph Nader, and C. Everett Koop. The televised encounters between Cohen and his interviewees rapidly become ridiculous (as happens, for example, when Ali asks a surly C. Everett Koop whether it
would be possible to surgically install a cell phone in his body).

In the painfully awkward interviews and panel discussions hosted by
Ali on topics such as sex, religion, and the media, *Da Ali G Show* provides not the Funtian, quasi-scientific revelation of the way real people
behave when captured by a hidden mike or camera, but the ways in
which a visible mike and camera affect behavior. That is, watching the
show, one marvels at the absurd situations and offensive lines of ques-
tioning that people will endure when sitting before a camera crew. John

Corner has described how performances on reality TV shows such as *Big Brother* often seem to involve a process he calls "selving," whereby " 'true selves' are seen to emerge (and develop) from underneath and, indeed, through, the 'performed selves' projected for us, as a consequence of the applied pressures of objective circumstance and group dynamics" (1999, 261–62). Like other reality TV programs, *Da Ali G Show* and *The Joe Schmo Show* play on this mode of textual pleasure. The viewer tries to discern subtle degrees of "selving" and performance in order to distinguish the role played in that process by the media apparatus. Perhaps this shift in emphasis—from the desire to capture real people behaving in authentic ways through the use of a candid mike or camera to formats that instead scrutinize the interplay of identity and performance in the face of an omnipresent camera—can be connected to a post–9/11, post–Patriot Act culture of surveillance, or even to the loss of a modernist faith in the ability to capture a "real self."[16] On closer inspection, however, both Funt's influential shows and these postmodern variations on them illustrate how "the act of being oneself " has always been just that: an act.

CHAPTER 6

Phony Performances

In the early 1990s a team of unknown amateur entertainers from Queens, New York, released two comedy albums that sold nearly one million copies each. Their second release entered the *Billboard* chart at number 12, the highest debut ever for a comedy record, and was nominated for a Grammy Award as best comedy album of 1995 (Ehrlich 1995, H28). The success of these recordings led to a feature film, also released in 1995. John Brennan and Kamal Ahmed, known professionally as the Jerky Boys, attained this degree of media success not through years of stand-up appearances in comedy clubs or by paying their dues in the film or television industry, but by tape-recording their prank telephone calls. The Jerky Boys are only the most striking demonstration of the way in which prank phone calling has become a prominent form of comedy performance in recent decades. One can buy a multitude of commercially manufactured cassettes and CDs of prank calls, hear phone pranks on talk radio broadcasts, watch a television program on Comedy Central called *Crank Yankers* that is entirely devoted to prank calling, peruse large numbers of phone pranks available on the Internet, even download "do-it-yourself" digital audio files to use on one's own prank calls.

Like Allen Funt's "candid" radio and television programs, tapes of prank calls are an example of secret recording as a mode of media entertainment and, as such, feature vocal performances that can be considered modern in that they were made possible by sound technologies—in this case, affordable home recording equipment that became available in the 1970s. In light of the last chapter, the pranksters who have made these tapes might be considered the descendents of private-sector wiretappers and Allen Funt's "everyman" persona—they are amateur comedians whose performances were produced and distributed via cheap recording technologies to a grassroots network of listeners.

In the previous chapter I demonstrated how Funt's secretly recorded performances came to have cultural uses beyond entertainment, functioning in some cases as social science and therapy. Similarly, the performances captured by phone pranksters walk a fine line between comedy entertainment and more troublesome forms of media practice such as obscene and harassing phone calling. These latter uses of the telephone have typically taken women, ethnic and racial minorities, and the working class as their targets. Indeed, recordings of prank calls all too frequently reveal the obsessions and small-minded worldviews of postadolescent white males. By taking tapes of prank calls seriously as comedic texts, I do not want to validate their sometimes hateful content or make light of their connection to other, more venomous forms of nuisance calling. But the best pranks transcend harassment to become something else—wonderful hybrids of ad-lib comedy, social experiment, and absurdist guerrilla theater. In a book on college pranks, Neil Steinberg observed that "a prank is never the product of apathy," and that the best become known "because of their cleverness, their planning, and the energy required to bring them to being" (1992, xiv).[1] Similarly, even the most childish and offensive phone pranks are planned, recorded, and distributed performances that are enjoyed by listeners as entertainment, and so they can provide insights into such things as the role played by the sound media in the construction and performance of identity.

For example, a common tactic of phone pranksters involves the performance of race or class impersonation in order to cross boundaries of urban space. Here the transgressive pleasure of the prank hinges on the vocal performance of a social or ethnic type as well as an exploration of the modern city via the telephone network. Gender is another center of gravity for many prank calls, which is not surprising given that many scholars have argued that the telephone is a gendered technology, one that has often been considered a female domain (Rakow 1992, 1). In that light, the male dominance of prank calling since the 1970s stands as a notable exception. Indeed, the most prevalent spectacle on prank recordings is a male caller inciting a male victim to anger, often involving verbal performances that have traditionally served as a prelude to physical violence. The humor of these pranks is derived from the way in which traditional measures of masculine status are made to seem ridiculous. Besides shedding light on the interaction of identity, performance, and media practice, prank calls can serve as an index of historical changes in the cultural experience of the telephone. My evidence for the latter will largely be taken from representations of prank and obscene phone calling in press coverage and film narratives.

My approach to telephone conversation is the result of the influence of two academic fields. The first of these is the work on telephone interaction done by scholars of sociolinguistics such as Harvey Sacks, Emanuel Schegloff, and Robert Hopper. The telephone has been an important resource for the field of conversation analysis because it allows for easy recording of a type of interaction that is remarkably similar to face-to-face communication: "Researches designed to contrast telephone and face-to-face conversation have displayed instead their essential similarity" (Hopper 1992, 10). Scholars working in the field of conversation analysis have made their conclusions based on the study of "normal" telephone talk. Taking phone pranks as an object of study can be compared to the "breaching experiments" of Harold Garfinkel, wherein assumptions and expectations about social interaction were tested by blatantly upsetting them. Along these lines, there is much that can be learned about telephone interaction by looking at how its rules are flouted by pranksters. Hopper wrote that "the sound of telephone conversation is the poem of North American industry" (xi). If that is the case, then the prank call is its dirty joke: a mode that is less prestigious, but potentially just as culturally revealing.

If the telephone has played a surprisingly important role in the study of conversation, it has been one of the least examined areas of media studies. The scholarly neglect of one of the largest media industries, as well as one of the most frequent points of everyday interaction with electronic media, is certainly notable, and it can be explained in several ways. Lana F. Rakow has argued that the telephone has only recently been taken seriously by scholars because of the way in which it has traditionally been associated with women: "That the telephone has been seen as a trivial and beneficent technology says more about scholars' perception of women than about the telephone or women's experiences with it" (1992, 2). Another reason for the lack of attention paid to the telephone is the fact that telephone interaction does not typically offer up tangible texts or performances for a formal analysis. Indeed, recent work on the telephone by media scholars gets around this lack by focusing on the cultural life of the telephone in terms of social practice, the apparatus, or the industry (Marvin 1988; Sterne 2003; Rakow 1988, 1992; and Green 2001). Recordings of prank calls provide a way to bring performance to the study of telephone interaction since they are comedy texts in addition to secretly recorded telephone conversations. Indeed, the study of the phone in terms of performance can help bridge the gap between the work of conversation analysis, with its fantastically intricate examinations of mundane telephone conversations, and the social, cultural, and technological analysis found in the work of media scholars.

My debt to the cultural histories of media studies will become clear as I begin my analysis by placing recordings made in the 1970s and 1980s in a larger context. A short cultural history of prank phone calling will establish how changes in the telephone system helped to determine changes in the culture of the phone that have, in turn, shaped the performances heard on prank calls. I will demonstrate that the prank call is a performance that has, since the 1950s, been associated with contradictory cultural meanings: understood both as a form of comedy entertainment and as a serious social problem that became a trope of urban legends as well as horror films.

A BRIEF HISTORY OF THE PRANK CALL

Anxieties about dubious uses of the telephone seem to have existed from the earliest years of its national implementation. One indication of this can be found in the folk etymology of the word *phony:* a word widely held to be derived from the word *phone.* For example, Marshall McLuhan cites a 1904 article that stated that "phony implies that a thing so qualified has no more substance than a telephone talk with a supposititious friend" (1964, 232). Counter to this widespread belief, Peter Tamony has persuasively shown that the word *phony* preexisted the telephone in the form of *fawney,* a word associated with a swindle called the fawney rig. This involved a ring or pocketbook that was dropped by the swindler who, when the victim picked it up, would run to claim half its worth. Of course, the ring proves to be valueless, a fact that "the swallower of the bait" discovers too late (1990, 103). To refute the theory that *phony* originated in the use of the telephone "to lure victims to false appointments in order that a criminal operation might be carried on," Tamony points to evidence that the word *fawney* had been "synonymous with ring-dropping since the middle of the nineteenth century" (101). Still, many people seem to have made this connection between the phone and the phony: in popular parlance, the fawney ring of the nineteenth-century con artist became the phony ring of the telephone prankster.[2]

Though anxieties about telephone misuse existed at the turn of the century, anonymous prank calling would have been difficult in that era of operator switchboards and party lines. During the first decades of the century, telephone service involved routing calls to a central office where the caller would speak to an operator who would manually connect the two parties. Operator switching made anonymous calling difficult if not impossible, since the operator knew the source of any incoming call. Further, it was widely believed that operators eavesdropped on conversations (Green 2001, 17). Operator switching would also have made evident the way in which the phone exchange represented a modern technological and social network, or what Tom Gunning, in his analysis of how the telephone functions in the films of Fritz Lang, describes as a "technological web" (2000, 97).[3] Colin Cherry has discussed the importance of the telephone as social network: "It was the [telephone] exchange principle that led to the growth of endless new social organizations, because it offered *choice* of social contacts, on demand, even between strangers, without ceremony, introduction, or credentials, in ways totally new in history. The exchange principle led rapidly to the creation of *networks,* covering whole countries and, since World War II, interconnecting the continents" (1977, 114).[4]

A genre of popular phonograph records recorded in the first decades of the twentieth century can illustrate some ways in which the social and technological network of the phone was experienced at that time. "Cohen on the Telephone" was a popular comedy skit that was recorded by numerous performers and record labels between 1910 and 1930. "Cohen" records are an example of the ethnic stereotyping typical of the vaudeville stage and heard on much of the early output of the phonograph industry. Cohen is a Jewish immigrant whose comic monologues are motivated by telephone conversations in which he is unable to accomplish his goals, most often because of misunderstandings produced by his thick European accent. What follows is an excerpt from a version of the skit as performed by Monroe Silver, circa 1920 (Aeolian Vocalion):

> Hallo! Are you there? Hallo! Hallo? What number do I want? Well, what numbers have you got? Excuse me, my fault. I want central 5050, please; yes, that's right, 50 . . . fifty-fifty. I say, Miss, am I supposed to keep on saying, "Are you there?" and "Hallo!" until you come back again? Well, don't be long. Hallo? Are you there? Oh, yes—you are the bank? Yes, I want to

see the manager, please; I say I want to see . . . What did you say? This is not a telescope, it's a telephone? You're very clever this morning, ain't it? Well, do me a favor. Hang a small piece of crepe on your nose, your brain is dead, and if I have any more of your impertinence, I'll speak to the manager about you. I said . . . Oh, I am speaking, Oh, you are the manager? I beg your pardon, I'm much obliged.

For the remainder of the record, Cohen tries to get his shutter repaired, but can't make himself understood ("that blew the shutter out . . . the shutter . . . No, I didn't say 'Shut Up!' ").[5] The form of this record is representative of the majority of Cohen records in that we hear only Cohen's side of the conversation; this is a technique for motivating a comedic monologue employed more recently by performers such as Shelley Berman, Bob Newhart, and Lily Tomlin. An interesting variation on that form can be heard on a record featuring Joe Hayman, a performer credited as the originator of the Cohen character. Note how, on *Cohen 'Phones for a 'Phone* (Columbia), we are presented with a more complex range of characters in order to suggest the "technological web" of the telephone network:

> *Cohen:* Hallo! Hallo! Are you there? I'm phoning about getting a new phone installed.
> *Female Operator:* Ring up John 22202.
> *C:* Hey, are you giving an imitation of a locomotive or what? Besides, who is John?
> *FO:* That's the number: 22.
> *C:* Oh, two-two yourself and see how you like it.
> *FO:* That's the plant department.
> *C:* Plant department, heh-heh. She thinks I want to start a garden. Well, all right. Give me 22202 Jacob—I mean John. Hallo. I want the flower department.
> *Male Operator:* Oh, you mean the plants department.
> *C:* Yes, I want to speak to someone about getting a new telephone.
> *MO:* I'll connect you, then ask for equipment.
> *C:* Thank you. Hallo? Are you there? I want . . . what that other fellow told me to ask for.
> *Female Operator:* Don't be funny, what do you want?
> *C:* I want a new telephone, you see . . .
> *FO:* Ring up commercial, main operator.
> *C:* I don't want an operation.
> *FO:* Ask for commercial, main operator official.

> C: Hallo! Hallo! Are you there? I want to see the commer-
> cial official, the main one, about an operation.
> *Male Voice:* Have a good time last night, kiddo?
> *Female Voice:* I'll say I did, it was just grand. See you again tonight,
> huh? Same place.
> C: Ah, you see it's about a new phone.
> FV: What's that? You want to take me home?
> MV: Sure, if you like, and, say, listen, Mabel, no foolin'—let's
> get engaged and I'll give you the nicest ring.
> C: Hey, Mabel, I give you two rings already but I don't
> want to marry you. I want a telephone, not a wife. You
> see, I'm trying . . .
> FV: Some . . . guy on the wire.
> MV: Hey, mister, don't butt in. You asking for trouble?
> C: I'm asking for a new telephone, maybe it's the same
> thing though.
> MV: Ring up commercial, TBX.

The expanded cast is used to represent the social network of the tele-phone as tangled, confusing, and overwhelming. We laugh at Cohen's difficulty in navigating through a bureaucratic telephonic space where vi-sual cues are absent and standards of social status and decorum become uncertain.

Cohen records must have functioned for their listeners much like Cal Stewart's Uncle Josh recordings. That is, Cohen makes clear how *not* to behave on the telephone, demonstrating Jonathan Sterne's assertion that "early telephone conversation was a learned skill," and enacting a cau-tionary tale for an immigrant population struggling to learn the codes of modernity (2003, 261).[6] But Cohen is not presented solely for ridicule: after all, he has the best lines and his sardonic wisecracks and asides work to forge a sense of camaraderie with the listener. Indeed, part of the popularity of these sketches, presumably with immigrants very sim-ilar to the hapless Cohen, can be traced to the way in which Cohen's fail-ures can be due as much to the deficiencies of the telephone as to his in-ability to cope with modernity. Either way, the Cohen sketches demonstrate how telephone service with operator switching was experi-enced as an entry point to, and reflection of, larger social networks of the modern city: the phone is Cohen's connection to his landlord, the phone company, the plumber, the health department, and the gas company. *Cohen 'Phones for a 'Phone* also illustrates another reason that anony-mous calling would have been difficult at this time: party lines. One might never be sure when "some guy on the wire" might "butt in," or simply listen in on a personal conversation. Cohen records represent telephonic space as a confusing urban grid as well as a crowded modern street.

When we consider the Cohen records, it is notable how popular press stories about early phone pranks often describe pranksters exploiting the telephone's ability to function as a gateway to larger social networks. Consider three news stories from the *Los Angeles Times*. The first, from April 28, 1904, describes how a woman "found the telephone an excellent ally in carrying out her scheme for the discomfiture of her victims." The woman ordered flowers and food for an elaborate wedding feast to be delivered cash on delivery to a family that lived in a "tent" and that "professed to know nothing whatever" about the matter ("Wedding Feast Not Wanted" A1). A second story, found in the March 11, 1909, issue, describes how "ministers, doctors and tradespeople, through the medium of a Home telephone, have been made victims of a practical joke." "Men of the cloth" and "doctors of every school" hurried to 27 Thornton Avenue as the result of telephone calls, only to find it a tenantless house. Throughout the rest of the day, "many called to deliver goods, ranging from a leg of lamb to an upright piano, and representing practically every line of business along the way" ("Owner of Voice Vainly Sought" H10).

Note the similar tactics found in this final example from June 29, 1924: "First came the undertaker. He was disappointed. Then came the ambulance, engine roaring, gong clanging, only to return empty. And then in quick succession came grocers, more undertakers, detectives, plumbers, electricians, firemen, hardware men, milk men, butchers and florists, some with their wares and others without them. All left fuming, fretting and vowing vengeance." In this case, the perpetrators were discovered: they were two sixteen-year-old schoolgirls: "one was Evelyn Bellows, daughter of C. B. Bellows, wealthy automobile dealer" ("Two Girls Play Telephone Joke" E10). Unlike the pranks I will examine below, none of these situations involved prying into the backstage experience of an individual victim. Instead, they exploit how the telephone functioned as a powerful interface with modern social networks, the same networks that Cohen was unable to master. Indeed, the fact that the pranksters in the last story were upper-middle-class teenagers who were capable of manipulating those networks on "a lark" offers an indication of how social hierarchies could alter the experience of the telephone.

If operator switching and party lines revealed telephone service to be
a complicated network, the shift to automatic switching concealed that
fact. Automatic switching allowed the caller to dial a private line directly,
without the intervention of an operator. The first fully automated telephone office debuted on December 10, 1921, but the shift to automatic
switching and dial phones occurred gradually. Venus Green has shown
that it was not until the end of the 1930s that dial telephones had reached
a majority of the American population (2001, 162). The implementation
of automatic switching, coupled with the gradual decline in party lines,
allowed for truly anonymous phone calling. This in turn led to an increase in prank and nuisance calls in the 1950s and 1960s.

One way to gauge that increase is through a parallel increase in the
press coverage of nuisance calls throughout the 1960s—coverage that
makes clear how prank calls caused something of a moral panic. A July
9, 1961, article in the *Los Angeles Times* called "Terror on the Telephone" indicates new trends in prank calling that were emerging at this
time. The article recounts how a woman received a call at four o'clock
in the afternoon and heard a "sobbing, moaning" voice on the line: "Oh,
it's terrible, it's terrible . . . it's your husband. . . . There's been a terrible
accident." The female voice identified herself as "one of the girls that
works in the factory," and hoarsely described how "a piece of machin-
ery" fell on the head of the victim's husband. "The doctor tried to save
him, but he wasn't able to. . . . He's dead." The poor woman was
stunned, "on the very edge of hysteria, shocked beyond anything that
had ever happened before in my life," and waited to talk to a doctor for
news of her dead husband. Then, suddenly, "a shrill burst of laughter"
was heard, followed by "girlish laughter and shrieks in the background":
"Oh, your husband's all right. It's just a big joke. Don't get too upset"
("Terror on the Telephone" TW7).

This was not an isolated event, but an instance in a larger national
trend that was spreading among a particular demographic: "From all reports it seemed clear that groups of teen-age girls were behind the calls"
(TW8). The gender of the pranksters is worth noting, as is the fact that
they were teenagers—a group that became increasingly identified with
the use of the telephone in the 1950s. A 1956 story in the *New York
Times* described how telephone usage among teens had recently been
growing, until, "in some cases, it has become a consuming passion":
"Telephoning is actually rivaling televiewing as a recreation in some
sets" (Barclay 1956, 245). The article described how teenagers had come
to monopolize the telephone to such a degree that an increasing number

of families were investing in separate, private lines exclusively for their use.

The identity of the pranksters described above reflects changing demographics of telephone usage, and their tactics reflect other changes in the experience of the telephone. Compare the "Terror on the Telephone" call to the account of Evelyn Bellows, the daughter of the wealthy automobile dealer who was caught making prank calls in 1924. The 1961 call does not use the telephone to activate social networks of the city, but instead involves an actorly performance by the prankster to facilitate an intense one-to-one interaction that involves the emotional exploitation of the victim. In fact, the 1961 article noted that acting was a primary motivation for the pranks: "Apparently the girls took turns to see which could be the best 'actress'" ("Terror on the Telephone" TW8). Melodramatic performances during pranks such as these were certainly aided by improvements in telephone receivers that made audible more subtleties of the voice. Further, these pranks relied on anonymous calling that was made possible by automatic switching.

"Terror on the Telephone" makes clear that this type of prank was considered a serious social problem. The article includes this statement from George S. Stevenson, "M.D. President-elect, World Federation for Mental Health": "The shocking hoax described here is no joke—it is a sign of potential trouble. The young person who could play such a trick may well have a serious emotional problem. If you ever find your child is involved in an incident like this, it is your duty to get competent counseling about it. . . . Don't make the mistake of dismissing it as a youthful prank" (TW8). The girls' pranks helped raise public concern about nuisance calling to a fever pitch, which eventually led to U.S. Senate hearings.

Those hearings, on abusive and harassing telephone calls, were held in 1965 and 1966, largely the result of widespread concern about "malicious calls to the families of Vietnam servicemen" (Rakow 1988, 223). Some of these calls were remarkably similar to the 1961 example described above: wives and mothers of servicemen abroad were told that their husbands and sons had been hurt or killed. An April 1966 article in the *New York Times* described how some anonymous callers gloated over the death of a relative in Vietnam: "In one case, in a call to a home where the widow of a captain killed in Vietnam had been staying, a man and a woman said in unison over the telephone: 'Slaughtered sheep sound like this . . .' The words were followed by a bleating noise" (Baldwin 1966, 4). There was much speculation about the origins of these mysterious and sadistic calls; the *Times* article stated that servicemen believed that "Communists or left-wing sympathizers in the United States" were responsible (4). Another newspaper article that year described how "every day a faceless horde of cranks is using the telephone to gain access to homes across America. With a spin of the dial, this growing menace in many instances is turning the telephone into an instrument of terror" (Buck 1966, 11). Calls to the families of soldiers in Vietnam received the most media attention and sparked the most governmental concern, but nuisance calls of all kinds were skyrocketing at this time. By 1967 a survey by Frank Murray and Lynda Beran found that 47 percent of their respondents had received an obscene or nuisance phone call (1968, 107).

The increase in nuisance calls and speculation about sinister conspiracies behind some of them cloaked prank calling in an aura of dread and anxiety, a fact that is reflected in depictions of anonymous calling in certain horror films of this era. Take, for example, William Castle's *I Saw What You Did (And I Know Who You Are!)* (1965), based on the novel *Out of the Dark* (1963) by Ursula Curtiss. The marketing of the film made clear how central was the telephone to its depiction of terror. Castle described how huge plastic telephones were placed in front of theaters, and newspaper ads around the country encouraged people to call a phone number for a special message: "Upon dialing, a girl's voice answered and whispered sexily, 'I saw what you did, and I know who you are,' and made a date to meet the potential customer at whatever local theatre was showing the picture" (Castle 1976, 181).

Further, consider the theatrical trailer for the film, where we see a ringing white phone by a bed, and a woman's hand reaching toward it. The movement of the hand is halted in a freeze frame and a man's voice blurts out, "Don't answer it!" Next we see a black phone on an office desk with a man's hand reaching for it. Again, the image freezes and this time we hear a woman's voice warn, "Don't answer it!" A third vignette features a female hand reaching for a phone on the wall of what appears to be a kitchen. One thing that these brief representations make clear is how strongly the use of the phone was gendered—the woman's telephone is by the bed and in the kitchen, the man's telephone is in the office. Shots of a woman's hand frozen while reaching for the phone are also remarkably similar to images used in telephone company advertisements about obscene phone calls dating from this same time. Castle's film plugged into anxiety about anonymous calling in general and nuisance calling in particular, and he even claimed that his film sparked an in-

Figure 14. Terror on the telephone in the era of anonymous calling: William Castle's *I Saw What You Did (And I Know Who You Are!)* (1965). Source: BFI.

crease in phone pranks among teenagers: "It seemed that almost every teenager in the country was on the phone, making crank calls by the thousands, jamming the phone lines" (1976, 181). In light of evidence from the press such as the 1961 "Terror on the Telephone" story discussed above, it seems less likely that Castle's film started a prank-calling fad and more likely that it fanned the flames of an already existing and controversial practice.

The film follows two teenage girls, Libby (Andi Garrett) and Kit (Sarah Lane), who are left in charge of Libby's younger sister when their parents go to a dinner party. Left on their own, the girls begin to make prank phone calls along lines very similar to the one described in the 1961 *Los Angeles Times* article: the pranks are played on victims chosen at random from the phone book and involve actorly vocal performances (figure 14). The importance of the phone book is indexed in the film's trailer, where we are shown the flipping pages of the telephone book under the voice-over: "Your name is in this book. It could happen to you!" Once a random victim is chosen, the girls use a low, breathy voice to impersonate an older, seductive woman in order to confuse and provoke their victims, who are frequently married women: "Hello, is Bill there? This is Alice. I've been waiting for him almost an hour. Yes, at the Green Garter club."

Although the girls' pranks begin as harmless fun (for example, calling "John Hamburger" to ask for "six with pickles and onions") the film quickly shifts gears to present prank calling as a dangerous social problem. Libby tries out a new approach, saying to random victims, "I saw what you did, and I know who you are." Unfortunately, one of her victims is a psychopathic killer, Steve Marak (John Ireland), who has just brutally murdered his wife in a shameless shot-for-shot rip-off of the shower scene from Alfred Hitchcock's *Psycho* (1960). Libby delivers the title line with a sexy, breathy voice, and in further conversations she convinces John that she is a woman named Suzette. Libby is entranced by her performance with John, whose voice she finds exciting and sexy: "His voice was so deep, so exciting. It's like he was running his hand down my back, really slowly." Desperate to see what John looks like, the girls take their parents' car to his house, and Libby peers in his windows. She is apprehended by John's neighbor Amy (Joan Crawford), who is in love with John, and has overheard his conversations with "Suzette." Amy frightens Libby away, but not before taking her driver's permit. John ends up killing Amy, finding Libby's address on the driver's permit, and going to her house for the suspenseful finale.

The fact that Libby and Kit's phone pranks lead to mortal danger drives home the film's moral lesson about prank calling. Libby tearfully says, "We're not going to be using the phone for a long, long time." What follows is a strange coda that is unmotivated by the narrative; sped-up voices chatter over an eerie, low-angle shot of a telephone pole, and a recording of an operator intones, "Sorry, you have reached a disconnected number," as the final title appears: "The End of the Line." This ending is in part an ostentatious final flourish that works to underscore the film's telephone gimmick. But it also points to how the effect of the film is derived not only from anxiety about phone pranks, but also from the impersonal, inhuman dimensions of automatic telephone service, here mobilized to instill an eerie sense of the uncanny.[7]

Though the marketing and narrative of *I Saw What You Did* clearly index anxieties about prank calling, a comparison to other narratives that centrally involve the telephone will help further demonstrate what was terrifying about the telephone at this time. The first of these is D. W. Griffith's classic film *The Lonely Villa* (1909) as described in Tom Gun-

ning's essay "Heard over the Phone: *The Lonely Villa* and the de Lorde
Tradition of the Terrors of Technology." Gunning's analysis of the film
is concerned with the role of telephone conversation both in the development of editing techniques such as crosscutting and in its relation to
an "archetype of film melodrama," wherein a woman threatened in her
home by criminals makes telephone calls to her husband, who rushes to
the rescue (1991, 188). Gunning traces this narrative to the 1901 play
Au téléphone written by André de Lorde, and connected to the Parisian
horror tradition of the Théâtre du Grand Guignol (191).

De Lorde's earlier version of the story reveals a nightmare behind
Griffith's melodrama because it features not the rescue but the brutal
murder of the woman and her child. Moreover, these deaths are experienced as a "specifically technological agony," since the father is forced
to hear the scene of distant violence and the following horrifying silence
over the telephone (190). In this ur-form of *The Lonely Villa*, Gunning
sees not only a "nightmare of masculine impotence," but a narrative of
technological anxiety that reverses the utopian claims of the telephone's
mastery of space. Rather than allowing the hero "to overcome space and
time, the telephone torments him with distance and impotence. Electronic sound on the telephone can pass to and fro instantly, but the flesh
and blood husband and father remains fixed and humiliated" (191–92).

The *Au téléphone* narrative represents the telephone apparatus primarily as a mode of point-to-point communication closely akin to the
telegraph. That is, its significance hinges on the tension between physical absence and vocal co-presence, which is brought into agonizing focus
when the father is forced to hear the sounds of his loved ones' murders.
Gunning's essay wonderfully describes how this narrative depicts anxieties about the telephone, although they are anxieties that are rooted in
a specific technological and historical context. *I Saw What You Did* illustrates a different nightmare version of the telephone shaped by a very
different telephonic environment. Unlike *The Lonely Villa*, where the
phone is experienced as a form of point-to-point communication, the terror in *I Saw What You Did* is connected to the random, anonymous telephone network in the era of automatic switching. The film taps underlying anxieties involving not so much issues of the male mastery of space,
but the dangers of the quasi-public space of the telephone network for
young women. Indeed, it is because Libby and Kit are "cruising" in
anonymous telephone space, performing a sexual masquerade as adult
women, that they find themselves in a horrifying and deadly situation.
The film thus indexes anxiety about female sexuality and, as is indicated

by the fact that the girls are left in charge of a young child, female roles. This point might become clearer through a short discussion of an urban legend that circulated at this same time, one that prominently features the telephone.

Jan Brunvand has described an urban legend he calls "The Baby-Sitter and the Man Upstairs," which has circulated in American culture since at least the 1960s. In it, a female babysitter watches TV while children sleep upstairs. The phone rings, and the sitter encounters a harassing caller who laughs maniacally. The calls continue until, in desperation, she calls the operator for help. The calls are traced, and the operator explains that they have been coming from the upstairs extension of the same line. The sitter barely escapes from the "man upstairs," who has already murdered the children. Brunvand quotes Sue Samuelson, who writes that the telephone is the "most important and emotionally-loaded item in the plot," owing to the way in which "the assailant is harassing his victim through the device that is her own favorite means of communication" (1986, 55–56).

Like Libby and Kit in *I Saw What You Did*, the girl in the legend is babysitting, what Brunvand refers to as an "important socializing experience for young women" because of how it allows them "to practice their future roles, imposed on them in a male-dominated society, as homemakers and mothers" (56). Both the legend and Castle's film, then, work on anxieties about "the most catastrophic failure any mother can suffer" (56). The "Man Upstairs" legend, along with the narrative of *I Saw What You Did*, represents a new nightmare version of the telephone that reflects changes in the experience of the telephone network in an era of automatic switching. Indeed, the narrative twist of having the calls originate from inside the house serves as a pithy demonstration of the changing experience of the telephone, since a live operator would have been able to quickly recognize the source of nuisance calls. That narrative trope succinctly reifies some of the contradictions of telephone conversation, a mode of paradoxical physical distance and intimate vocal co-presence.

The "Man Upstairs" legend was retold in numerous horror films of the 1970s, most literally in *When a Stranger Calls* (1979). As a final example of a horrific depiction of the telephone in the era of automatic switching, consider the retelling of the "Man Upstairs" legend found in a film made five years earlier: *Black Christmas* (1974). The film depicts a group of women living in a college sorority who are harassed by an obscene phone caller. In an early scene, the women stand around the receiver to listen to a call from the man they call "the Moaner" or "Super Tongue."[8] His obscene performance primarily involves the wordless expression of sheer bodily co-presence: gasps, moans, sighs, and slurps. Indeed, the trope of the telephone "heavy breather" might be seen as a perverse embodiment of the kind of intimate vocal performances of the radio crooner. As I discussed in chapter 3, crooners exploited the sensitivity of radio microphones to create a whispered, intimate style of singing in the late 1920s. A similar dynamic exists with nuisance callers who, with the help of more sensitive telephone receivers, can communicate co-presence with the sound of breathing alone.

When the calls continue and women in the house begin to disappear mysteriously, the police are called in, and they proceed to put a device on the telephone to trace the calls. While Jess (Olivia Hussey) keeps the caller on the line long enough to get a trace, the film cuts to the telephone company, where we see a technician running through banks of switches to locate the source of the calls. A decade earlier, *I Saw What You Did* had still depicted a female switchboard operator, but by the mid-1970s the workings of the telephone system were depicted as a colossal, automated grid. The scope and inhuman coldness of the grid could be harnessed to provoke a sense of uncanny horror in part because of the ease with which the killer could hide inside it. Indeed, in a clear reference to the legend of the "Man Upstairs," the police trace the source of the calls to the sorority house itself, where the killer has lodged himself in the attic. *Black Christmas* ends with the relentless ringing of the telephone, an indication that the killer is still at large. Where the *Au téléphone* narrative had ended with the horror of "the possibility of breakdown" as indexed by the silence on the line, here the ceaseless ringing signifies the impossibility of escaping the vast technological web of the telephone network.

Black Christmas, I Saw What You Did, and the "Man Upstairs" legend are narratives that represent nightmares of the telephone for an era of automatic switching. They reveal how the experience of the telephone during this time was characterized by a paradox. On the one hand, private lines and dial phones led to a certain troubling visibility since anyone could be found and reached either by chance or via the phone book ("Your name is in this book. It could happen to you!"). On the other hand, automatic switching meant that callers could remain anonymous and hidden—in the popular imagination they could even be calling from inside one's own house. Prank and nuisance calls became a potent trope of horror films because of the facts both that they were a contemporary social problem and that they brought potentially troubling aspects of everyday telephone interaction to the surface.

During the same decades when prank calling was being cast as a serious social problem, it was also becoming associated with mainstream comedy performance. For example, radio DJs of the 1950s made prank calls on the air, a practice that reflected larger changes taking place in American radio in the wake of the rise of television. The national radio networks crumbled, which gave rise to small, local radio stations that relied on local advertising. David Morton notes how radio stations at this time had to slash studio and technical personnel, substituting "disk jockeys and popular music shows for network content" (2000, 70). As radio stations increasingly dropped live performance and switched to automated equipment and the playing of records, phone pranking provided a cheap format for comedy entertainment, as well as a sense of live spontaneity—despite the fact that the shows were often on tape.

Prank calls were made as a part of televised comedy performance at this time as well. Recall that Allen Funt's greatest success with *Candid Camera* came in the early 1960s on CBS Television. Funt's use of media pranks is sometimes cited as a precursor to phone pranks. Additionally, famous comedians such as Steve Allen and Jerry Lewis made prank calls as part of their TV appearances. Some of Lewis's pranks can be heard on a CD compilation called *Phoney Phone Calls, 1959–1972* (Sin-Drome Records 2001). On one call, which was made live on the April 5, 1963, broadcast of *The Steve Allen Show,* Lewis calls a kosher restaurant in Chicago on the pretense of setting up a party, and he proceeds to deluge the clerk, Mr. Segal, with doubletalk:

> *Jerry Lewis:* Why don't we meet in the morning.
>   *Mr. Segal:* Which morning?
>   *JL:* At your place.
>   [pause]
>   *JL:* I say, why don't we meet in the morning.
>   *MS:* Which morning would you like?
>   *JL:* Well, you name it.
>   *MS:* Any morning you like.
>   *JL:* All right, what about tomorrow?
>   *MS:* Tomorrow morning, I am possible tomorrow morning.

> JL: You're possible tomorrow, well I'm impossible tomorrow my-
> self, what about tomorrow?
> MS: Tomorrow night?
> JL: In the morning.

The way in which Mr. Segal is bombarded with constant interruptions and confusing questions is typical of Lewis's style. The focus on these recordings is squarely on Lewis's fast-talking performances; the victims usually can't get a word in edgewise. Recall my discussion in the previous chapter of the issue in secret recording of whether the actor or the victim is the focus of a given prank. Funt insisted on the transparency of the former in order to highlight the latter, an approach that helped make his shows resemble social science experiments. Lewis, by contrast, was less concerned with social experimentation, and it is the caller and not the victim who takes center stage. In fact, Henry Marx, president of the record company that released the CD, called Lewis's pranks "some of the most brilliant examples of ad-lib comedy in the history of laughter."[9]

The call to Mr. Segal demonstrates how some of Lewis's pranks were made as part of television appearances, but he also made recordings of prank calls in private, using state-of-the-art audio equipment. Liner notes to the CD describe Lewis as "an avid audiophile since the early days of tape recorders," who began recording all of his performances and interviews on magnetic tape in the 1950s. Lewis even "developed a system that would allow him to tape record his telephone calls" with the help of "audio technicians at Paramount Studios." Lewis had access to cutting-edge professional audio technology that allowed him to record his pranks. For recordings of prank calls to become a grassroots media phenomenon, those sound technologies would have had to be more widely available, which is exactly what occurred in the early 1970s with the introduction of affordable home tape-recording equipment and compact cassettes. Now pranksters could easily record their calls and share dubbed cassette copies with friends. Some of these amateur, bootlegged cassettes made their way around college campuses or were passed among societies of close-knit, traveling professionals like baseball players and touring musicians to eventually became nationally known.[10]

The grassroots production and distribution of these tapes should be seen in relation to broader arguments about the uses of audio cassettes in the 1970s. For Peter Manuel, cassettes represented an important rupture with previous audio technologies: "Cassettes are a two-way medium, which can record as well as play. Cassettes and cassette players are cheaper, more durable, and more portable than records and phonographs. Recorders and players have simple power requirements and are repaired relatively easily. Most important, mass production of cassettes is incomparably easier and cheaper than pressing records, thus enabling diverse lower-income groups to enjoy access to both production as well as consumption of recorded music" (1993, 28–29). Manuel was interested primarily in the effect of cassettes on the musical cultures and industries of India, Africa, and Indonesia, where he saw cassette culture as "conducive to localized grassroots control and corresponding diversity of content" (28). Cassette technology could also be mobilized for political purposes. Annabelle Sreberny-Mohammadi and Ali Mohammadi have described the role of what they call "small media"—cassette tapes and photocopied leaflets—in the 1978–79 Iranian Revolution. Duplicated cassette tapes spread the speeches of Ayatollah Khomeini and so helped to foster participation against the shah's regime.[11] Similarly, Alexander Stille has written that the circulation of oral poetry on cassette in Somalia was an important factor in the fall of the Mohammed Siad Barre regime (2002, 182–99). Although far less dramatic, the same portability and ease of duplication that made cassette tapes a powerful political tool were a factor in the rise of prank calling as a form of media entertainment. With the ability to make anonymous calls, the idea of the prank call as comedy entertainment, and the technology to record and distribute tapes cheaply and easily, all the elements were in place for a new genre of audio entertainment: the prank call tape.

The preceding historical sketch has demonstrated how prank calls came to be understood as both a social problem and a comedy performance, a combination that imbued the practice with a certain transgressive edge. Let us now consider some specific performances more closely. What follows is a discussion of recorded pranks organized into three sections. First, I will consider calls that deal primarily with issues of impersonation and spatial infiltration. Next I turn to pranks that center on issues of masculinity. I'll end by examining recent calls that map out forms of telephone interaction that have emerged since the 1980s. The Lucius Tate and Tube Bar recordings will serve as case studies because they are some of the earliest and most influential examples of widely distributed prank tapes, and their concerns are revisited in different ways on many of the prank calls in circulation.

INFILTRATORS AND IMPERSONATORS

Many prank calls hinge on the pleasures of what I'll refer to as infiltration and impersonation. By the former I mean the telephone's ability to bring the user into spaces and interactions that could or would not be broached in person. As Lana Rakow has noted, there is a long history of both popular and academic writers heralding the telephone for its utopian potential to transcend physical space (1992, 3). As a recent example, Wurtzel and Turner write that "the boundaries of one's social reality are no longer rooted in contiguous space but in a kind of symbolic proximity that short-circuits distance into dial time and replaces the supportive nature of daily interactions with the telephone's potential for instant contact" (1977, 257). But Rakow warns that writers often make the mistake of assuming that "because the telephone *can* transcend space and time," those technical possibilities translate into actual "social practice" (1992, 4). So, for example, though the telephone could be used to "transcend" physical space and communicate across the globe, "all studies show that between 40 and 50 percent of the telephone calls originating from a household are made within a two-mile radius" (Mayer 1977, 226).

Even if one accepts that people make most of their calls within the neighborhood in which they live, there still exists in the telephone the potential to transcend spatial boundaries within towns and neighborhoods and to interact with those who live "across the tracks." That is, even though larger utopian claims of transcending space fail to match the realities of daily practice, the phone can still be used to infiltrate the spaces of economic or ethnic "Others." Along these lines, Carolyn Marvin has written that modern sound media like the telephone both allowed "lower classes" to "crash barriers otherwise closed to them" and permitted "privileged classes" to "go slumming unobserved" (1988, 86).

As one example of how telephone interaction could upset traditional ways in which social distinctions were defined and policed, recall the recurring trope in the "Cohen on the Telephone" skits in which Cohen is surprised to discover that he is talking to a social "superior," such as his landlord or the bank manager, and he quickly switches codes of speech ("if I have any more of your impertinence, I'll speak to the manager about you. I said . . . Oh, I am speaking, Oh, you are the manager? I beg your pardon, I'm much obliged.") Those records illustrate how the telephone "provided opportunities for the wrong people to be too familiar" and so posed the problem of enforcing "social distances" without face-to-face cues (88). The ability to cross social boundaries is taken up by phone pranksters who infiltrate the homes of people whose ethnicity, race, or class might typically have prevented a face-to-face interaction.

The infiltration of space on prank calls is often achieved through the vocal impersonation of ethnic, racial, and class types. Impersonation was relatively easy to achieve on the telephone, a context in which "asymmetries of dress, manner, and class that identified outsiders and were immediately obvious in face-to-face exchange were disturbingly invisible": "Reliable cues for anchoring others to a social framework where familiar rules of transaction were organized around the relative status of the participants were subject to the tricks of concealment that new media made possible" (86).

Erving Goffman's conception of the front and back regions of social interaction can provide a way to describe in more detail the impersonation heard on telephone pranks. For Goffman, the front region or "front stage" is the area of a given social activity where participants project an appropriate self-image (Goffman 1959, 110; Thompson 1995, 88). By contrast, the back region, or "backstage," is the place where "action occurs that is related to the performance but inconsistent with the appearance fostered by the performance"—that is, where "the performer can relax . . . and step out of character" (Goffman 1959, 115). Goffman characterizes backstage language and behavior as follows: "The backstage language consists of reciprocal first-naming, cooperative decision-making, profanity, open sexual remarks, elaborate griping, smoking, rough informal dress, 'sloppy' sitting and standing posture, use of dialect or sub-standard speech, mumbling and shouting, playful aggressivity and 'kidding,' inconsiderateness for the other in minor but potentially symbolic acts, minor physical self-involvements such as humming, whistling, chewing, nibbling, belching, and flatulence" (129).

John B. Thompson and Jonathan Sterne have made reference to Goffman's categories of front and back regions to explain the particularities of telephone communication. Thompson argues that "the use of communication media can have a quite profound impact on the nature of front and back regions and the relation between them": "Since mediated interaction generally involves a separation of the contexts within which the participants are situated, it establishes an interactive framework that consists of two or more front regions which are separated in space and perhaps also in time. Each of these front regions has its own back regions, and each participant in the mediated interaction must seek to manage the boundary between them" (1995, 89). This means that telephone communication entails "very small front spaces" in relation to "relatively large back spaces" when compared with face-to-face interaction, a mode in which many back-channel visual cues supplement speech (Sterne 2003, 151).

The potential for impersonation is increased on the telephone since the front stage of interaction comprises only sound and so lacks visual cues that could be used to check the claims of an imposter. I have already discussed several cases that illustrate impersonation as a tactic of prank calling since the early 1960s. Recall the groups of teenage girls tearfully informing women that their husbands had died, and Libby's impersonation of "Suzette" in *I Saw What You Did*. To get a sense of the prevalence of this kind of telephone deception, also consider descriptions of the impersonation performed on obscene phone calls from this time. In a psychological study of obscene calling from 1968, two of the three case studies involved a male caller misrepresenting himself, either as a pollster or "as a member of a fraternity in a nearby college" (Nadler 1968, 523). An article in the *Washington Post* on February 18, 1968, describes "a 54-year-old salesman who, posing as a psychiatrist, would tell a housewife that he was treating her husband and then get her to talk about her sex life" (Raspberry 1968, D1). Another *Post* article, published January 25, 1975, describes an obscene caller's remarkably elaborate ruse:

> [Passing as a police officer, the obscene phone caller] tells the woman there has been a rash of obscene phone calls in the county, and says that if she gets one she should keep the caller on the line as long as possible so that the police can trace the call. About five minutes after this call, the woman receives an obscene phone call. Believing she is aiding the police, she obligingly keeps the caller on the phone for five or 10 minutes. Shortly after she hangs up, the phony officer calls back and thanks her, and tells her the police have arrested the caller. ("Obscene Phone Caller Posed as Policeman" A17)

Finally, a 1981 case study of an obscene phone caller described a patient who would represent himself as "either a doctor or a health employee involved in a survey" and ask questions about the victim's anatomy or sexual behavior (Jenkins 1984, 150). These examples illustrate how the telephone's small front regions of interaction allowed for the impersonation of those of "sacred status, such as a doctor or a priest," what Goffman called an "inexcusable crime against communication" (1959, 67). The impersonation most frequently heard on prank calls, by comparison, is

not of doctors or therapists, but of persons of different races and eth-
nicities.

Take, for example, the calls heard on the "Lucius Tate" tape, one of
the earliest cassettes of prank calls to circulate in the 1970s, and one that
features the dynamics of infiltration and impersonation I have been describing. The calls heard on this tape feature a white man impersonating
an African American who often calls himself Lucius Tate. A Web site
dedicated to phone pranks describes the status of this tape: "The origin
of the legendary Lucius Tate calls is mysterious, (many of them were supposedly recorded as far back as the 70s) but there is no disputing their
rank as the grandaddy of all prank call recordings." More history is provided on luciustate.com: "Ever since the mid-seventies, when copies of
unmarked prank call tapes began spreading from Texas to points all over
the world, people have been asking, Who the hell was making those in-
credible prank phone calls? The answer, of course, must remain a secret.
But for the few who know the man, and for those who have made the
pilgrimmage[sic] to meet him, he has become a truly legendary figure in
the world of comedy." Tate's modus operandi is to call African Americans living in rural Texas, impersonate a black man, and provoke his victims to displays of anger.

> *Lucius Tate:* Eileen?
> *Eileen:* Uh huh.
> LT: How you doin', baby?
> E: I'm fine.
> LT: Uh, look, can you come over here and get me?
> E: Who . . . who is it? I don't know who it is yet.
> LT: This is Leon.
> E: Leon?
> LT: Yeah.
> E: Where are you at?
> LT: I ain't far from you, down here at the bus station.
> E: What's your last name?
> LT: Johnson.
> E: You must have the wrong person, do you know who you're talking to?
> LT: You Eileen, ain't ya?
> E: Yeah, I'm Eileen.
> LT: Yeah, you're my old, you're my old sweetheart.
> E: You're just a fucking liar.

> *LT:* I ain't no liar.
>
> *E:* You get off this goddamn telephone or else I'm going up here
> and call the police.
>
> *LT:* Listen, now, I want to come over there.

The call, like many others, turns into a vicious exchange of insults between Tate, Eileen, and, later, Eileen's husband. Tate incites a kind of
vocal performance that is particularly coded as black speech (verbal du-
eling with stylized insults, sometimes referred to as "the dozens"), and
then attempts to keep up.[12] This appropriation of black forms of speech
recalls the archetypal American performance of impersonation as entertainment: the minstrel show. As such, these calls represent another case
in which white performances of an African American vocal style become
entertainment for a white audience. As is true of much recorded American music, the mastery of black vocal styles is a means for a white performer to gain an aura of authenticity.

Tate's performances of black speech must be seen in relation to the
performances of his victims. After all, Tate's shtick is based on the way
in which he can coerce his victims to turn themselves into spectacle. Recall Allen Funt's technique for inciting his victims to anger and so making them legible as social types. That process worked in part by prompt-
ing a shift in the victim from a mode of standardized, front-stage speech
to a backstage mode that featured a more pronounced ethnicity. Roger
Abrahams makes a similar observation in his study of African American
ways of speaking when he notes that the language a black child learns
from her or his family tends to be "closer to creole forms" and therefore
"more 'Black.' " Those more "creole" forms are also the aspects of language that are "capable of producing a high affect" on an audience; and
so while the child's "casual or conversational code" will gravitate toward
a more standard English, "creole-like forms" will be retained as part of
a "performance repertoire" (1976, 16). Abrahams suggests that spoken
indicators of ethnicity become heightened during performance. Thus,
Lucius Tate's trick is to infiltrate a backstage interaction with his victims
and coerce them to unknowingly perform a type of particularly "black"
speech.

The relationship between Tate and his victims should be considered
in terms of the power relations of telephone conversation more generally.
One of Robert Hopper's key insights into telephone conversation has to
do with the asymmetric balance of power between caller and answerer:
what Hopper referred to as "caller hegemony." This dynamic begins

with the invasive telephone ring itself, which Hopper described as a summons.[13] As further evidence of caller hegemony, Hopper points to the
fact that answerers must speak first (thus making themselves vulnerable
to be recognized by a still-unrecognized caller), and that the caller gets
the first chance to introduce the call's initial topic (1992, 9, 34). Power
asymmetries are taken even further on phone pranks, since the prankster
often knows the name and address of the victim from the phone book
and is aware of the true framing of the situation, both factors adding to
the caller's disproportionate amount of knowledge and power.

Hopper's discussion of the power asymmetries of telephone interaction can help explain some of the ways in which the telephone has been
made to fit larger social power asymmetries. For example, Hopper asks,
"Is there a relationship between the answerer's one-down position and
the institutional deployment of women within such telephone-answering
roles as operator and receptionist?" (34). He also notes how the rich and
powerful have always been able to purchase "protection from the vul-
nerabilities of the answerer role": "People high in hierarchies hire telephone answerers—servants at home, receptionists at work—to screen
out unwanted intrusions" (202). The power asymmetries of telephone
talk are exploited on the Lucius Tate calls since the caller makes answerers perform their ethnicity in moments of spectacular threats and insults. The racism in these calls can thus be seen in part as an outgrowth
of telephone power relations.[14]

Dynamics of impersonation and infiltration are repeated endlessly on
recorded prank calls. Pranksters often infiltrate spaces such as ethnic
restaurants, religious organizations, or late-night convenience stores to
harass ethnic victims and provoke them to perform. Ethnic typing is
heard on these calls not only through the victims, but, as on Tate's,
through pranksters' delight in the vocal performances of ethnic types. Indeed, listening to prank tapes can at times recall the ethnic humor of
turn-of-the-century phonograph records and vaudeville stage performances. As I discussed in the previous chapter regarding Allen Funt's
Candid Microphone, one might assert that the sound media have tended
toward ethnic humor because of the way in which vocal accents take on
heightened importance in conveying information about performers; the
voice overcompensates in establishing character traits when it is the sole
vehicle for performance.

Impersonations of gender can also be heard on prank calls. Consider
the vocal "cross-dressing" found on a call by the pranksters "the Ball-
busters," in which a male prankster calls a strip club posing as a would-

be dancer who refers to herself as "Tricky Tracy." The gruff-voiced club owner is completely taken in by Tracy's falsetto voice and is intrigued by the range of novel acts she claims to be able to perform: "I gotta see that," he says. "When can you come down?" Tracy replies that she'll be down "as soon as possible," and she asks whether the owner would like to have "a private show." "I would love a private show," he answers enthusiastically. The prankster's reply is suddenly in his own male voice: "All right, I'll be down in twenty minutes." The owner is shocked: "What?! Who is this?" "I'll be right down," continues the male voice. "I'll show you my goods." The stunned owner catches on and barks, "Fuck you, you asshole!"

Another prankster who uses gender impersonation is Brother Russell, whose victims are the hosts of ultraconservative Christian radio call-in shows. Russell often impersonates an elderly Christian woman, and on a call titled "The Last Laugh," he poses as an elderly woman named Emily and asks for a prayer for her wayward nephew. After the prayer is performed over the radio, she and the radio preacher exchange bursts of ecstatic laughter. The title of the track becomes clear when, just as the stirring background music swells, Emily's laughter becomes both maniacal and clearly male. Brother Russell subtly reveals his act of impersonation and the depth with which he was able to infiltrate the show's religious proceedings. Both these calls feature a remarkable vocal sleight of hand when the impersonation is suddenly revealed. The sound-only environment of the telephone allows for this stunning technique, a performance somewhere between quick-change slapstick comedy and the digital morphing of 1990s cinema.

The play with flexible identities through vocal performance suggests how telephone interaction might be compared to other recent media practices. Scholars writing about new digital media have often described how identity can become fluid and flexible in the virtual space of the Internet. Much of the academic analysis of race and gender on the Internet has stressed the virtual, fragmented nature of online identity (Kolko et al. 2000, 5). This has been discussed in terms of the virtual "cross-dressing" that occurs in online chat rooms, and the fact that online multi-user games do not require users to specify their race (Kolko in Kolko et al. 2000, 216). Examples of prank and obscene phone calling reveal how a similar flexibility existed in the virtual space of telephone talk. But race has, to quote Nakamura, "a way of asserting its presence" on the Internet, "in the language users employ, in the kinds of identities they construct, and in the ways they depict themselves online, both through language and through graphic images" (2002, 31). Similarly, the fluidity of identity heard on prank calls is not used to eliminate social or racial hierarchies, but instead to bring them into even sharper focus.

FIGHTING WORDS

If impersonation and infiltration are two of the central themes of prank calls, then performances of masculinity are certainly another. This is worth noting, since the telephone has often been considered a female domain both by scholars and by the culture at large. In his social history of the telephone, Claude Fischer suggests several reasons for the association of women with telephone talk: modern women have tended to be "more isolated from adult contact during the day than men," married women's "duties have usually included the role of social manager," and North American women are "more comfortable on the telephone than are North American men because they are generally more sociable than men" (1992, 234–35). Women have been associated with the telephone through the traditional female role of the telephone operator as well. Young boys were first hired as telephone operators, but they proved to be unsuitable because of "temperamental defects" such as "swearing, beer drinking," "impudent and profane language," and "fist fighting with customers" (Green 2001, 55–56). To counter the "negative effect on business" from unruly boy operators, telephone management hired women after the 1880s, in the belief that "girls, socialized to defer on the basis of class, gender, and age, were best qualified to give the kind of service Bell envisioned" (57). Green concludes that it was "female gentility, not female docility," that accounted for their introduction into the telephone exchange (58).

In the larger context of this book, it should be noted that female operators at the turn of the century were developing a modern vocal performance style akin to the radio crooners who would become famous twenty years later. In an article in the May 1905 issue of the journal *Telephony*, William H. Kenney, a voice instructor at Emerson College of Oratory in Boston, described the female operator as the paradigm of correct telephone speaking. The operator's vocal virtues reveal the hallmarks of a modern speaking style appropriate to the telephone apparatus: low volume, precision, and direction. Note the similarity to the radio crooner in Kenney's description of the female operator: "She speaks scarcely above a whisper, and though you are standing but a few feet away you cannot follow her end of the conversation. Experience and instructions have taught her that a low tone, well directed, is sufficient to throw the voice to any point, near or distant" (1905, 428). Another article called "A Study of the Telephone Girl," in the same issue, is peppered with poetic expressions about the voice of the female operator, which is described as "musical as the woodsy voices of a summer day" and "extremely well modulated" ("Study of the Telephone Girl" 388). This article also emphasizes the quiet, professional accuracy of the operator's voice:

> That voice so sweetly distinct to the subscriber is yet so low, so carefully articulated that her neighbor, brushing against her very elbow, cannot hear her speak. Walk into a busy metropolitan exchange and the first thing by which you are struck is the decided quiet of the room. With a hundred girls, elbow to elbow, perched in a semi-circle of feminine grace before the ugly background of the board, every one of them repeating tirelessly the stock phrases of the exchange and with fingers regularly pulling out or putting in the plugs of communication, it is only after a little stay that one finally becomes aware of the faintest hum. One might think, could he shut his eyes, that it was being done by a set of automatons. (388–89)

Much could be said about this remarkable passage. In terms of the matters at hand, what is important is the way in which it reflects not only how the voices of female operators became associated with the telephone, but also how they were at the forefront of developments in modern styles of speaking that were shaped by telephone interaction.

Telephone operators were an important part of a cultural association of women with the phone that print evidence suggests extended even to pranks; in fact, most of the pranksters I have discussed through the 1960s were female. What becomes clear is that the male domination of prank calling since the 1970s represents a male invasion of a culturally defined female space, a return of the repressed, unruly boy operators. Scholars have argued that the telephone has been a site where gender is defined and performed, and on the phone pranks I examine this is largely in terms of masculinity. It should be noted that the preponderance of male pranksters and victims heard on prank tapes might be deceptive for several reasons. First, the home recording equipment used to tape calls has traditionally been a domain as rigidly defined as male as the phone has been defined female. For example, Barbara Ehrenreich has described how the *Playboy* ethic of the 1950s and 1960s was fueled in part by the entrance of men into consumer culture, and the home hi-fi was a preferred commodity for men (1983, 42–51). Second, the dominance of male victims may conceal the fact that nuisance calls to female victims often shaded into the category of the obscene call, and so they were not recorded or distributed.

If the Lucius Tate calls provided a demonstration of tendencies of impersonation found on many phone pranks, a tape of calls to a New Jersey saloon will serve as a case study for issues of masculinity. Known as either the "Tube Bar Tape" or the "Red Tape," this recording provides a stunning illustration of how cassettes of prank calls could gain cult notoriety. The calls were initially made anonymously in the mid-1970s, but the two pranksters have emerged in the light of their quasi-media celebrity, and Jim Davidson and John Elmo now release CDs under the name Bum Bar Bastards. According to a fan Web site hosted by Mike Walsh, tapes of these calls began circulating sometime in the early 1980s, "when a copy ended up in the hands of an equipment manager for the New York Mets." The tape then spread through baseball teams as well as another society of predominantly male travelers, touring rock musicians: "Bands such as Nirvana, Faith No More, and Alice in Chains . . . [include] devotees of crank classics such as the so-called Red Tapes" (Rossi 1993, 61). The Tube Bar Tape's fame grew to such a degree that it was made into a film in 1993 and even surfaced in the mainstream media on several episodes of *The Simpsons* that feature Bart prank-calling Moe's Tavern.[15] The remarkable cultural life of the Tube Bar Tape confirms some of the arguments that have been made about the potential for "small media" such as cassette tapes to allow for new modes of decentralized media production and distribution.

The pranks on the Tube Bar Tape begin with a simple premise: the caller asks to speak with someone in the bar with a preposterous name like "Al Coholic," "Pepe Roni," or "Cole Cuts." Astonishingly, the bartender, Red, falls for the gag again and again, the payoff coming when we hear him shout out each ridiculous name to the patrons of the bar.

            Red: Hello?
Bum Bar Bastard: Hello, is ah, Al there?
            Red: Al, ah, Al Berger?
           BBB: No, Kaholic.
            Red: Al who?
           BBB: Kaholic.
Red [to the bar]: Al Kaholic! Al Kaholic! . . . No, nobody by that name.
           BBB: Okay, thank you.
            Red: All right.

One thing to note about these calls is the absence of what Allen Funt called the reveal. That is, Red is not let in on the joke at the end of the prank. This makes each call feel less like a self-contained practical joke and more like one chapter in a longer, episodic narrative. In fact, the relentless procession of calls on the Tube Bar Tape plays a large part in its comedic impact: listeners often laugh at each new ring when it becomes clear that the pranksters are not yet through with Red.

After a number of such calls, Red does finally catch on to the joke, and the tape moves to its second stage, in which Red pours forth a stream of fantastically violent invective toward the callers. In call after call, Red is provoked to repeat this hyperviolent, hypermasculine performance, and the callers eventually join in, engaging in long back-and-forth exchanges of threat and insult.

Red: Yeah?

BBB: Hello, Red?

Red: Yeah?

BBB: Why don't you stick your tongue up my ass?

Red: Hmmm?

BBB: Why don't you stick your tongue up my ass, Red? Huh?

Red: Are you talking to me?

BBB: Yeah, who do you think I'm talking to?

Red: Why, you motherfucker cocksucker, why don't you come over and talk to me person to person? You . . . Why don't you go out and fuck your mother, you son of a bitch? You'd be a nice guy, ain't ya? . . . If anybody would say that to me, I'd come down and fight 'em. But you ain't got the nerve, you fucking bum.

BBB: Want me to come down and fight ya?

Red: Come on down, you son of a bitch, I'll give you fifty dollars for a reward.

BBB: I'll fight you!

Red: Come on down, you fucking bum.

BBB: I'll get my friend to fight you.

Red: Why don't you come down, you yellow son of a bitch. You motherfucking bum.

Like Lucius Tate, the Bum Bar Bastards use the telephone to infiltrate off-limits social spaces, in this case a roughneck, working-class bar, and provoke their victims to spectacular displays of anger. Again, dynamics of caller hegemony are exploited, since the callers are able to turn this potentially powerful and frightening figure into their puppet: Red is made to perform, first by calling out to the bar, and then with his fantastically violent speech.

The agonistic episodes with Red take on a strangely choreographed and ritualized cast as the calls progress. As Walter Ong has described "the ridiculously elaborate codes for the duel," this interaction suggests "the curiously formal quality of male-with-male combat" (1981, 80).[16] The Tube Bar calls demonstrate the kind of ritualized male performances that have often been a prelude to physical violence. Ong notes that a major outlet for male "agonistic drives" has tended to be verbal activity (107). Take, for example, the "fliting of heroes, in which verbal insults are hurled by heroic fighters at one another often as a prelude to physical combat" (108). Richard Martin, in his analysis of agonistic talk in Homer, also speaks of how, in order "to draw attention to his martial ability, the hero must use language well, and be criticized on his performance" (1989, 76–77). James Leary's discussion of the performative nature of barroom fights brings this analysis closer to the situation presented on the Tube Bar Tape: "Responding to audience encouragement and conscious of the conventions of past fights, fighters automatically overplay indignation, they relish the trading of insults, they enjoy being temporarily restrained so they may make a show of breaking loose to renew battle. Even brief encounters . . . [exhibit] a certain theatrical flair" (1976, 35). Leary's essay provides another demonstration of the importance of words as a prelude to physical violence, since the "exchange of words" precedes the "exchange of blows": "Actual punches generally follow talk" (31).[17]

Seen in this light, the Tube Bar Tape features ritualized performances of male strength and power through verbal display. It also demonstrates, however, the potential for new technologies and, by extension, new social formations to disrupt traditional ways of establishing male status through physical altercations or the threats thereof. That is, the telephone enables the pranksters to engage Red in a prelude to physical violence, but without actual physical co-presence this process can never move on to the next phase, which is the exchange of blows. Red is held, then, trapped in a loop of futile words that becomes more and more mechanical. His small repertoire of insults and expletives reveals a paradox: in our moments of greatest emotional excess, our verbal expressions are often the most circumscribed. One might say, following Bergson, that it is this mechanical inelasticity that makes Red a comic spectacle. A once-powerful male performance that played an important role in the formation of male hierarchies is held up like a bug on a pin.

The Bum Bar Bastards flaunt the destabilization of male hierarchies by exaggerating the contrast between their voices and Red's, which differ wildly in terms of timbre, tone, and inflection. Masculine authority is embodied by Red's voice, whose deep tone and harsh rasp seem to index his strength and physical size. Walsh writes on his Web site, "Red's voice is so far gone it's actually got the kind of resonance and distortion that noise bands spend years honing." One is reminded of Roland Barthes's description of the Russian operatic bass whose voice "directly conveys the symbolic, over and above the intelligible, the expressive: here, flung before us all in a heap, is the Father, his phallic status" (1985, 270). By contrast to Red, the pranksters are barely postadolescent young men with clear, high-pitched voices. The callers exaggerate this difference, sometimes slipping into falsetto in their taunts of Red, other times impersonating a woman or a small child. The difference in age between the callers and Red, and the violent sexual nature of many of the calls, also works to present Red as the vocal embodiment of the castrating father:

Red: Yes?

BBB: You suck my prick?

Red: Yeah, sure come on over here. I'll bite it off on you.

BBB: You cock-eating fuck.

Red: I'll bite it off on ya!

BBB: You'll bite [laughter] . . .

Red: Why don't you, buh, come over here, you yellow rat? If I . . .

BBB: I'm telling you I want to fight.

Red: If anybody were to call me the names I call you, about your mother and all that, I'd get down and fight 'em face-to-face.

BBB: Yeah, but you ain't got no guts.

Red: I ain't got no guts?

BBB: Yeah!

Red: I'll meet you any place you want, you son of a bitch. I'd . . . You know what I'm gonna do with you? I'd cut your fucking balls out if I'd see you, you son of a bitch and I'll . . . come over and I'll . . . show your face, I'll show you what I'll do to you.

Freudian undercurrents on calls such as this suggest their connection to obscene phone calling. Raoul P. Nadler, in his study of the psychodynamics of obscene phone calls, describes their similarity to acts of exhibitionism. He states that the exhibitionist seeks "reassurance against castration" by unconsciously conveying to the victim the message "Reassure me that I have a penis by reacting to the sight of it" (1968, 521). Nadler describes how both exhibitionism and obscene calling are "prompted by the desire to gain sexual pleasure by the spectacle of emotion—whether of corresponding pleasure, or of confusion, or of

horror—in a person of the opposite sex" (521).[18] Similarly, the Tube Bar
calls provoke a spectacle of emotion in their victim, in this case anger,
but that emotion is elicited from a person of the same sex, the result
being a kind of homosocial exhibitionism. Red's anger functions in part
to reassure the callers, and perhaps by extension those listening to tapes
of these calls, that they possess a certain male potency. Perhaps this un-
stated social function has something to do with the fact that the Tube Bar
Tape has gained such a cult following, becoming a blueprint for scores
of pranks whose central spectacle is futile male anger. Nadler stated that
obscene phone calls tend to be "more aggressive" than acts of exhibitionism because the former are done at a distance: "the telephonist acts
out his perversion at a greater distance but more actively" (526). Similarly, prank calls such as those heard on the Tube Bar Tape push telephone co-presence to some of its furthest extremes.[19]

TALKING BACK

I've offered the Lucius Tate and Tube Bar recordings as examples of
trends in prank phone calling that emerged in the 1970s. Dramatic
changes in the experience of the telephone occurred in the 1980s, and in
this last section I will outline some of the new telephone services that
emerged in that era and describe new types of phone pranks that have
arisen alongside them. Many of these developments were either the direct or indirect result of the breakup of AT&T, which was mandated in
January 1982 and became official on January 1, 1984. This landmark
decision ushered in a new era of phone service characterized by smaller
regional phone companies and limited regulation and competition in
areas such as long-distance service and equipment manufacture (Stone
1989, 315). One result of increased competition was the introduction of
new telephone services such as caller ID.
    Patented by Bell Labs in 1982, caller ID became a widespread service
by the end of the decade. A March 1, 1989, *New York Times* article
stated that the Nynex Corporation was making available a "caller identification system that would display the number from which an incoming call was originating before the call was answered," along with other
services such as automatic redial, call return, and a call-trace function
that could initiate "a trace of the telephone number of an obscene or unwanted call" (Sims 1989, D1). These new services were made possible by
computerized switching equipment that allowed the phone company to
"transmit information about the call separately from the actual voice

signal" (D1). In articles from this time, caller ID was referred to as being akin to a front-door peephole (King 1989, B1; Sims 1989, D21).[20] That analogy makes clear that one of the effects of services such as these would be to make anonymous phone calling much more difficult.

By extension, caller ID and call-return services such as *69 had a chilling effect on phone practices that thrived in an environment of anonymity—a fact that can be illustrated by Todd Solondz's 1998 film, *Happiness*. A self-absorbed writer, Helen Jordan (Lara Flynn Boyle), receives an obscene phone call from Allen (Philip Seymour Hoffman). Helen had just been verbally chastising herself for writing about topics such as rape while having experienced so little suffering herself, and she is stunned when Allen's abusive language closely mirrors her own. Intrigued by the synchronicity of the call, Helen pushes *69 on her phone, which allows her to reach Allen at his office instantly. Allen is shocked to find Helen on the line, telling him, "I want you to fuck me." Allen shrivels in the face of this direct confrontation and mumbles, "I . . . don't think I can do that." Helen proceeds to harass Allen by calling his home constantly, finally persuading him to come to her apartment. This leads to an emasculating meeting in which Allen is rejected. "This isn't working," Helen says as Allen awkwardly tries to make a move on her; "You're not my type." Solondz's film demonstrates how new telephone services introduced in the 1980s made anonymous obscene calling difficult, and the same held for prank calling. At the Web site for Prank Call Central, prospective pranksters are warned that "with caller ID and other devices on the market, it's an easy task to find out where specific calls originated."

In addition to their effects on anonymity, phone services such as caller ID helped to equalize the power dynamics of telephone conversation that had for so long been tilted in favor of the caller. Hopper saw a similar change occurring in the 1980s with the implementation of answering machines, another result of compact cassette technology. Hopper writes: "The telephone caller has been protected until the answering machine, but now the caller must state his or her identity and business. The machine commits to nothing. This is the most principled reversal of empowerment in telephone history. The answerer strikes back" (1992, 212). Caller ID, in its function as a telephonic "front door peephole," gave the answerer more knowledge and so more control over phone interaction. Technological developments of the 1980s such as caller ID and answering machines were changing the dynamics of telephone interaction in fundamental ways, changes that were reflected in the performances of phone pranksters.

Since it became difficult to make anonymous calls to strangers, pranksters developed comedic pranks built around "inbound calls." "The best thing about inbound calls," states the Prank Call Central Web site, "is that since they called you, you have much more free reign to get hostile in the conversation and still avoid any legality issues." Appearing as if on cue in the telephonic culture of the 1980s was a plague of inbound calls from telemarketers. Robert Hopper has noted how caller hegemony is "dramatically illustrated" in telemarketing calls, since "telemarketers exploit a conversation systemics that normally forbids unwarranted access by strangers—to gain precisely that access" (208). That systemics has to do with the typical pattern of telephone openings, a topic that has received much attention in the field of conversation analysis. Unlike a face-to-face meeting, telephone openings must be set using only the voice, which makes them particularly illustrative of the particularities of telephone talk. Hopper presents the following as a canonical telephone opening:

R	Hello.
C	Hello Ida?
R	Yeah.
C	Hi, =This is Carla.
R	Hi Carla.
C	How are you.
R	Okay:.
C	Good.=
R	=How about you.
C	Fine. Don wants to know . . . (55–56)

The phase structure of the canonical telephone opening is based around four sets of two-utterance sequences or adjacency pairs.[21] First is the summons-answer, the summons being the telephone's ring, and the answer the first "hello." The next adjacency pair is a mutual display of recognition: "In telephone calls, mutual identification must occur in-and-through speaking" (59). Short spoken sequences provide voice samples for recognition. What follows is a pair of greetings ("How are you?"), and then the initial inquiry that begins the conversation.[22] Hopper demonstrates how telemarketers use the adjacency pair sequence of telephone openings to gain a foothold in conversation: "We find ourselves held in thrall by such strategy because telemarketers exploit principles of encounter opening and adjacency sequencing to gain access to us" (210). Hopper provides this example of a telemarketer opening that exploits this system:

H: Hello

D: Mister Smalley

H: Yes

D: This is Missy Weevil, sir I'm calling you from the Ward Life Insurance company in Chicago?

H: Uh huh

D: How do you do sir.

H: Just fine.

D: Great. How was your Christmas?

H: Just fine.

D: Good . . . today we—we wanna tell y' about an important service. . . . (208–9)

In this example, the caller repeatedly prompts the answerer to respond, and so she triggers adjacency pairs that allow her to burrow deeper into interaction. Tactics such as these helped fuel the remarkably widespread and virulent resentment toward telemarketers in the American culture of the 1980s and 1990s.

Telemarketers are characterized on prank websites as a particular menace, and it is with great relish that they are made the victims of pranks. A Web site called "Telephone Solicitor's Nightmare" declares, "Whether we're in the middle of dinner, relaxing in front of the television after a hard day's day at work, or sharing quality moments with our loved ones, when we hear the phone ring we're thinking 'not another one of those annoying telephone solicitors or telemarketers again!' Well, Revenge is here!"[23] Revenge is also the central theme in the work of Tom Mabe. One of the most successful phone pranksters, Mabe has released several CDs of pranks on telemarketers, including *Revenge on the Telemarketers* (Virgin 2000). Since, as the quote above illustrates, the worst crime of telemarketers is taking up the time of answerers, it makes sense that the primary tactic for revenge is to take up as much of their time as possible. This can be heard on calls that humorously prolong the telemarketer's experience, taking them as far afield from their intended business as possible.

On Mabe's "Stand Up Comic," a telemarketer begins by using adjacency pairs to trigger the answerer's responses: "How are you doing this evening, sir?" "I'll tell you what, man," Mabe replies, "I'm a little bit nervous. Tonight they got the open stage at the Comedy Caravan and I'm, I'm thinking about getting up and doing a couple of three minutes, you know, some stand-up. . . . I would love to have an unbiased ear, could I run some of my material past ya?" Mabe proceeds to turn the tables on the telemarketer by making him perform in Mabe's act: "So I'll come out and go, 'So how are you all doing tonight?' And that's when you just go, 'All right!' So let me start all over. 'So how are you all doing tonight?' " The telemarkter half-heartedly responds, "All right." The call quickly disintegrates when it becomes clear that all of Mabe's jokes are about telemarketers. ("How many telemarketers does it take to screw in a light bulb? Six, but only one to screw an old lady out of her life savings.") Other pranks force telemarketers to sit through paranoid conspiracy theories or long, tedious descriptions of the answerer's drug experiences.

Another technique for getting revenge on telemarketers involves forcing the caller to shift from the official, front-stage act of solicitation to the backstage individual. Take, for example, a recording of a call Tom Mabe received from a cemetery:

> *TM:* How are you today?
>
> *Mabe:* Uh . . . not, not, not that good.
>
> *TM:* Oh, I'm sorry. Well, listen, the reason I'm calling you today is to offer you peace of mind through prearranged burial plots . . . and you can rest assured that all of the details, you know, can be taken care of for you. . . . Sir?
>
> *Mabe:* What's your name again?
>
> *TM:* Bob.
>
> *Mabe:* Bob, you're not going to believe this . . . I lost my job Thursday. Company closed shop, I, uh, my . . . my wife left me . . .
>
> *TM:* Oh, I'm sorry.
>
> *Mabe:* And . . . but this is so bizarre, I was sitting here just contemplating suicide, and I was praying, asking God for a sign.
>
> *TM:* Yeah, but I'm just calling you because your name is on a list.
>
> *Mabe:* No, but no, you don't understand, I, just five minutes ago, I was, I was just praying and asking God for a sign and, and you called!
>
> *TM:* Yeah, but I'm just doing my job, I—I—

Mabe, like many pranksters, undermines the project of the telemarketer by shifting to more personal, individual registers, whether sexual, personal, or spiritual. In this way telemarketer pranks show how potentially uneasy is the fit between formal, business uses and the telephone's potential for intimate co-presence.

The combination of commercialism and the intimacy of telephone conversation was also the central feature of another group of telephone entrepreneurs that emerged on the cultural scene in the 1980s. Spurred by a growth in credit-card use and toll-free 800 lines, services that either played recorded descriptions and enactments of sexual acts or allowed for a sexually explicit live phone chat debuted in New York in September 1983 (Kristof 1986, A16). Press coverage of the time made a clear connection between "dial-a-porn" services and the impending breakup of AT&T. An article in the May 9, 1983, issue of *Time* stated that dial-a-porn was "a byproduct of AT&T's recent Government-mandated breakup: the deregulators ordered local telephone companies to give up their monopoly on their sponsored Dial-It services (time, weather, Dial-A-Joke and so on). 'High Society' [an adult magazine] was one of 21 enterprises picked by lottery to get a piece of the New York Telephone action, and has since bought two more of the numbers from other lottery winners" ("Aural Sex" 39).

Dial-a-porn met with immediate and phenomenal success: the initial New York service established by the publishers of *High Society* drew 19 million calls in just the month of April 1983, and in 1986 similar services were still reporting "nearly 5 million calls each month" (Kristof 1986, A16).[24] One explanation given for the success of phone sex services has to do with concern about AIDS. An April 13, 1990, article in the *New York Times* stated that "among the staunchest defenders of the services are some gay and lesbian organizations": "They say that in an era when AIDS has made 'safe sex' essential, many homosexuals have turned to provocative conversations on the telephone lines as a means of sexual release" (Briceno 1990, B5).[25] It will come as no surprise that dial-a-porn services sparked a great deal of controversy. Indeed, dial-a-porn legislation was debated in Washington throughout the 1980s, which led to the Helms Amendment, named for its main author, Senator Jesse Helms of North Carolina, which limited access to those services.

The success of phone sex services was primarily due to the actorly vocal performances of a mostly female workforce. Female phone sex workers weren't the first telephone workers to stimulate the imagination of male clients. Consider some accounts of female telephone operators or "hello girls" from the first decades of the twentieth century. A February 1904 article in the journal *Telephony* entitled "The Telephone Girl's Voice" explained that "there is something peculiarly attractive about the telephone girl's voice. Probably because she is unseen and because the voice is mellowed and softened as it comes over the wires" ("Telephone Girl's Voice" 126). Other articles dealt with management's problem of losing female operators to marriage. A story entitled "Soft Voices Ensnare Men's Hearts," in the April 1905 issue, quotes a "Manager Clapp," who stated that "there is something about the sound of the

voice of a girl on the wire that sets a young man into a wooing mood":
"A girl who has lived through her teens without a proposal will enter a
telephone office and before she has been at the board a week some young
man will want to marry her" ("Soft Voices" 328). The sensual appeal of
the female operator's voice was harnessed for its own sake in the paid
performances of female phone sex workers.

It should be noted that phone sex services often feature aspiring or unemployed actors. "Diana," a phone sex worker, stated in a 1987 interview that "this work is part being an actress and part writing while on
your feet" (MacDonald 1987, 43). Gary Anthony, whose book, *Dirty
Talk,* describes his experience in the phone sex industry, discussed his
phone sex work in terms of acting: "When phone actors are hired, they
have to come up with all their lines, stories, and characters completely
on their own. There is no script" (1998, 46). The lines between phone
sex performance and traditional acting are explored in Spike Lee's 1996
film *Girl 6.* Judy (Theresa Randle) is an aspiring actress living in New
York, and as the film begins, we see her audition for a part in a film. The
director (Quentin Tarantino) brusquely interrupts her audition monologue, saying at one point, "Don't talk, listen." Indeed, the director is
portrayed as being concerned only with the visual aspects of performance: in regard to the part he is trying to cast, he says, "I'll know her
when I see her," and when Judy tries to reply to some of his comments,
he ostentatiously covers his face with a head shot. He is clearly unable
to listen and uninterested in listening, and he is concerned only with appearances. This becomes painfully obvious when he asks her to stand
and turn around ("Freeze, don't move, don't talk") and then to unbut-
ton her blouse so that he can see her breasts. Unable to go through with
the audition, Judy walks out. We see many of Judy's most awkward moments through the video monitor, which gives the scene a heightened
sense of voyeurism.

Later, we see Judy practicing the same monologue with her acting
coach (Susan Batson). Her delivery is completely flat and devoid of emotion, so that the coach cries out in despair: "Where is the pain? Where's
the bottom? What is this shallow shit? Drop into the pain. Acting is
about doing and feeling." Desperate for work, Judy applies for a job at
a phone sex agency (figure 15). It's notable that the workplace is an almost entirely female space, and the workers are watched over and
trained by the maternal Lil (Jennifer Lewis). At a training session it becomes clear that phone sex is a form of acting: each girl must create an
array of characters, such as the girl next door, the dominatrix, and the

Figure 15. Judy (Theresa Randle) learns about acting in Spike Lee's 1996 film *Girl 6*. Source: BFI.

transsexual. Later, in a conversation with her friend Jimmy (Spike Lee), Judy is moved to explicitly defend her new work as acting. "What does this have to do with acting?" Jimmy asks her. "You're not onstage, you're not in front of the camera, you're on the phone."

Judy's experience with phone sex begins to sour as she struggles with becoming too emotionally involved with some of her clients. When she begins taking calls in her own house, an abusive client reveals that he knows where she lives. She breaks down and hysterically threatens to kill him if he comes over, much to the enjoyment of the caller: "That's what I wanted. Why'd you hold out on me?" This disturbing incident motivates Judy to move to California and try again to pursue her acting career. The film ends with a second audition scene in California, in which Judy is again asked to remove her shirt. Again she is unwilling to do so, but this time she launches into her monologue and finishes it. When she stops, the director (Ron Silver) is noticeably impressed, and though she walks out, dropping the script on the floor, we are left thinking that her confident and intense reading may very well lead to a callback and to success on her own terms.

Girl 6 explicitly raises questions about the nature of phone sex as performance, in the end offering it as a potentially powerful though dangerous form of acting. Recalling the scene in which Judy met with her acting coach, one could suggest that her experience as a phone actor has shown her how to "drop into the pain," as well as how to use her voice to create emotionally vivid characters. The film seems to assert that the voice is, if not the crucial aspect of acting, one that commercial film directors too often forget.[26] The irony here is that the culturally debased site of phone sex provides Judy with a "truer" vocal acting training than stage or screen.

Dial-a-porn having become a booming business, it is not surprising to find that phone sex is referenced on prank call recordings in several ways. Male pranksters sometimes call phone sex lines to turn business-as-usual on its head. In an era when the anonymous harassment of random victims was difficult, phone sex workers made for safe and easy targets. But also consider the 976-Girls, one of the few groups of female pranksters, who took their name from the New York phone prefix for phone sex numbers. On their CD *PhonePhuct* (D.I.L.L.I.G.A.F. Records 1994), "Cherry" calls a male victim to say that his friends have chipped in to buy him ten minutes of phone sex. With very little convincing, she is able to get the man into the bedroom and ready for a sexual encounter. The sex talk takes a strange turn when Cherry's descriptions of the action become surreal and violent. She breathily tells him that she wants to put super-glue "between his ass cheeks and push them together really hard," and even "chop off his prick with a ginsu knife." "Oh, god," she says at one point, "I want to beat you senseless with a brick. Oh, baby, oh, you make me so horny just thinking about that!" The call ends when she brusquely declares that "time's up" and insists that he owes her $250. Cherry's violence can be seen as a reversal of the typical phone sex encounter where, as the phone actor Gary Anthony writes, the fantasies of male callers often tend to be violent or degrading to female phone actors (1998, 61).

A similar gag can be heard on a recent CD of prank calls that use digital sampling technology. The pranksters behind the "Kathy McGinty" calls lured men from Internet sex rooms to what they thought would be a phone sex session. They encountered the seductive voice of a woman calling herself Kathy, which was actually a collection of digitally sampled statements being triggered by the pranksters. On the most effective calls, "Kathy" manages to get the men very aroused with a remarkably small repertoire of come-ons. Then, in a manner similar to that of the 976-Girls, she begins to drop non sequiturs into the interaction, such as "You sound like a child molester" and "Taco Bell tastes soooo good." Though the process is often painfully slow, the prank is eventually revealed to the empurpled male victims. Kathy's male victims (like the inflexible Red in the Tube Bar pranks described above) are made to appear mechanical and ridiculous: one reviewer wrote that "the callers' come-ons and common obsessions (size, power, dominance) come to seem as mechanized as Kathy's responses" (Ridley 2002). Indeed, the Kathy McGinty calls can serve as an interesting counterpoint to the Tube Bar pranks. Where the latter exploit forms of ritualized talk that are a prelude to fighting, the Kathy calls exploit forms of ritualized talk that serve as a prelude to sex. In both cases humor arises from the inflexible behavior of the victim. Gary Anthony has described how phone sex callers are often in a "trancelike state," which can render them almost inarticulate, but which can also enhance "the sexual images that help to drive their sexual excitement forward during masturbation" (1998, 91). As was the case with male "fighting words," we find here the paradox where, in one's most ecstatic and intimate moments, one's verbal expression becomes the most mechanical.

The Kathy McGinty calls are an appropriate way to end not only this chapter but this book, since they offer something of a bookend with the example that began my first chapter: the scene featuring the laughing android David in Steven Spielberg's *A.I.* In both that scene and the Kathy calls, ecstatic vocal performances are used to explore the boundary between human and machine, and to search for the lines dividing technology, self, and performance. The case studies in each of the foregoing chapters have indicated the close connection between vocal performance styles and the technological and social networks of the sound media industries. In the case of the last section of this chapter, pranks concerned with telemarketing and phone sex lines reflect the changing nature of the culture of the telephone since the 1980s.[27] More generally, media practices that turn the telephone into a mode of performance are a rich source of information about the experience of the sound media in our everyday lives. Robert Hopper has written that the use of the telephone has tended toward "purposeful communication," and so subordinated "poetry to purpose" (1992, 191). Telephone pranksters talk back to this trend, introducing a sense of play to telephone interaction, subordinating purpose to carnivalesque poetry. Recordings of prank calls harness one of the largest sound media industries and most complex media networks in order to create grassroots comedy texts. In so doing they reveal the richness, complexity, and intimacy of vocal interaction and mediated copresence.

Conclusion

Over the course of the diverse case studies in this book, the voice has proven to be a rich topic for the consideration of the ways in which performance has developed in an era of sound media technologies. I have suggested that three aspects of modern vocal performance—flooding out, the grain of the voice, and secret recording—have important implications for the study of performance in the media more generally. The analysis of flooding out can be useful for the consideration of a range of genres, from pornography to reality television to the outtake reel—increasingly a standard DVD extra. The use of the closely held microphone to capture nuances of the voice was seen to be an important factor in many forms of acting and popular singing, and, indeed, the analysis of the timbre of the voice might serve as a model for the discussion of such things as cinematic mise-en-scène and the photogenic appeal of film stars. Finally, secret recording is a mode of production and textual pleasure that continues to proliferate and fascinate, making its origins in the sound media merit a close examination. In this final chapter, I would like to underscore four motifs that have run through this book and that can suggest further conclusions about vocal performance in the sound media.

One recurring concern of this study has involved how structures of participation are managed in the context of the modern sound media. Note that the interaction between audience and performer is a central component of performance as a mode of communication (Bauman 1986, 11). The vocal techniques described in the foregoing chapters can be understood as representing a range of performance strategies for keying the relationship between performer and auditor in the context of the modern media. Recall that keying is the communicative process whereby participants are made aware of the nature of a situation or interaction (Goffman 1974, 44). In Goffman's terms, media performance features a certain ambiguity concerning how "participation status" should be keyed: is the media consumer an audience member, a ratified participant in an intimate one-to-one exchange, an overhearer, or an eavesdropper? This ambiguity can be felt in the slipperiness of the terms used to describe the media auditor—are we talking about isolated listeners or a unified mass audience?

In the cases I have examined, the voice keys performances toward one model of participation or another, thus shaping both the formal aspects of the media text and indicating its intended mode of reception. For example, the laughing records and laugh track discussed in part 1 illustrate how media texts can be keyed to a mass audience—when one hears the laugh track, it becomes clear that the performance is not keyed to the individual listener, but to a larger audience (no matter how immediately intangible that audience might be). By contrast, vocal techniques that depended on a closely held microphone, such as melodramatic acting on the radio and singing styles such as crooning and the rasp, appropriate the semiotics of intimacy, collusion, and immediate bodily presence, and so they tend to key the performance to an individual listener. Some of the vocal performances I have examined play with the ambiguities of participation in complex ways. Consider how laughing records typically begin with a one-to-one address to a listener, which then becomes complicated by the emergence of another textual audience member, or how the blue disc *Silent George* merited closer examination because of how it balanced its address between a group audience at a tavern or party and a single overhearer. In these terms, the troubling nature of performances captured via secret recording is in part due to their lack of any clear key as a performance at all, which places the listener in the uncomfortable position of pure eavesdropper. Aspects of Allen Funt's candid format, such as the inclusion of the "provocateur," a studio audience, and voice-over narration, have the effect of rekeying secret recording as a performance made for an audience, not an overhearer. Similarly, the inclusion of a third-party eavesdropper on some blue discs served to placate listeners' anxiety about their own mediated act of eavesdropping. Clearly, the keying of structures of participation is an important way to understand how performers make use of the expressive repertoire available to them in the modern media.

While working to key the puzzling relationship to audiences, vocal performers were also influenced by the contexts of media production. In fact, many of the preceding chapters have traced types of vocal performance as they move from spaces such as the concert hall or theater to the studios where phonograph records were made or where radio and television programs were broadcast. These modern spaces played a role in shaping what was heard on sound media texts, but we have seen how sound has a particularly resonant relationship with space more generally. For example, recall how the category of timbre indicates the space through which a sound has passed. At this point one might consider the arguments of writers such as Walter Ong, who pointed out that sound can "test the physical interior of an object," and that, since sound places a person in the center of a three-dimensional perceptual environment (we can simultaneously hear sounds all around us), hearing is a particularly immersive sense: "You can immerse yourself in hearing, in sound. There is no way to immerse yourself similarly in sight" (1982, 71–72).

Another way to consider the intimate relationship between sound and space, and the resulting effect on vocal performance, is to refer to M. M. Bakhtin's concept of the chronotope. Bakhtin uses the term *chronotope* to refer to "the intrinsic connectedness" of temporal (chrono-) and spatial (tope) relationships that are artistically expressed in literature (1981, 84). For Bakhtin, chronotopes such as "the road" are the defining factor in literary genres, as well as being "the organizing centers" for narrative events since they dictate settings, characters, and types of interaction as well as a certain experience of time (250). The concept of chronotope stresses the inseparability of the spatial and temporal dimensions of experience: "Time, as it were, thickens, takes on flesh, becomes artistically visible; likewise, space becomes charged and responsive to the movements of time, plot and history" (84). In similar fashion, the category of the *sonotope* can describe the "intrinsic connectedness" of sound and space as it draws attention to the way the nexus of sound and space helps to shape performance. My conception of sonotope is similar to Rick Altman's notion of a sound's "spatial signature," which he defines as "the testimony provided by every sound as to the spatial circumstances of its production" (1992, 252). Sonotope adds to Altman's term the sense that the relationship between sound and space is reciprocal, and, further, that the nexus of sound and space can have an important influence on media texts. Thus, the concert hall can be considered a sonotope that encourages a certain kind of vocal performance: that characterized by the bel canto timbre, and, vice versa, the use of the bel canto timbre suggests the concert hall sonotope. Like Steven Connor's notion of "vocalic space," an attention to sonotope can direct our attention to the way in which voices indicate spaces and frame performance.

We might say, then, that the sound media created performance spaces that amounted to modern sonotopes that then shaped different types of performance. Emily Thompson's book *The Soundscape of Modernity* describes a soundscape that emerged in connection with sound technologies and modern methods of architecture. The modern soundscape Thompson describes was characterized by a clear, controlled sound and a lack of reverberation. Thompson argues that since reverberation is "a means by which we perceive space through time," the experience of this modern sound represented a transformation of the traditional relationship between sound and space in which, in fact, "sound was gradually dissociated from space until the relationship ceased to exist" (2002, 186–87, 2). Thompson's historical argument is persuasive, although we could say that the relationship between sound and space did not so much cease to exist as become "up for grabs": the application of reverb effects in the studio or types of performance such as the croon allowed the relationship between sound and space in the modern media to be subtly calibrated. Further, if we take this electronic soundscape as the modern sonotope that replaced spaces such as the concert hall, the vocal performances I have described often pulled against the stream of the culture of engineers described by Thompson, who focused their efforts on sonic clarity. That is, the vocal performances I have described are characterized by the presence of all kinds of vocal "noise" such as sobs, sighs, and the rasp. Here, then, is another example of how the popular uses of mass media technologies can often differ from their intended uses.

Listening even more closely to the cases in this book, one can perhaps discern several more specific sonotopes. As two examples, consider the "alone together" mass audience that is keyed by the laugh track, and the distant co-presence of point-to-point communication. Both are paradigms whereby performance is emplaced, either in the residual model of the theater or in the intimate proxemics of conversation. It is logical to place telephone conversation in the latter category, although my discussion of telephone pranks allowed us to discern a shift from experiencing telephone interaction as point-to-point communication to the social network of the telephone grid—a powerful modern sonotope of its own, as is made clear by narratives found in urban legends and horror films. Further work might be done in applying the concept of the sonotope to questions about how the electronic media shape configurations of space and time in which performance is situated, and techniques of both the voice and studio production that are calibrated to those configurations.

It is notable that, given the modern contexts of media production and the dislocation of media participation, the three aspects of vocal performance that served as the organizing topics of the sections of this book have all functioned as signs of authentic human presence. That said, it is not surprising that discourses of presence have surrounded the mediated voice, since the voice is such a potent index of identity and tends to be strongly anchored in specific spaces. Modern sound-recording devices have allowed us to perceive the world in hitherto impossible ways; they have had, like the cinema camera, scientific as well as artistic uses, as can be seen in my discussion of the social scientific uses of secret recording and the modern analysis of singing made possible both by sound recording and by Manuel García's laryngoscope. Photography's oft-discussed indexical relationship with its subject matter is true of the phonograph as well, and it became a central aspect of texts that highlight the grain of the voice, "inappropriate" modes of performances such as the laugh, or the "casual body" of the candid format.

We have seen how sound recording was often used to capture the accidental, casual, and individual—a tendency that could be in tension with styles that relied on the voice to indicate social and ethnic types. Sound media such as radio and phonography have often tended toward ethnic typing in order to convey character. Indeed, we have seen how the construction of vocal "authenticity" has often been tied to the performance of race (the rasp, laughter), class (the laughing rube), and gender (hierarchies of radio performance, male victims of telephone pranks). My study suggests that there is, however, no inherent way in which sound technologies could be used in this regard, and the voice in particular emerges as an instrument of performance with a particularly subtle give-and-take between expressing the individual and the type: another reflection of the voice's double nature as both "the intimate kernel of subjectivity" and "the axis of our social bonds" (Dolar 2006, 14). Erotic performance was another site where the issue of authentic presence could arise in a powerful way. Recall Linda Williams's claim that there can be no such thing as "hard core sound," since vocal performances of ecstasy can always be faked in a way that the visual evidence of the body cannot. That has certainly not stopped performers and audiences from trying, and indeed, the "breakthrough out of performance" is the best way to understand the structures of pleasure found on many genres of audio entertainment.

In their pursuit of the depiction of authentic presence, producers and performers in the sound media have been drawn to expressions of the body in spasm: in laughter, anger, surprise, and sexual abandon. On closer inspection, these sound media texts demonstrate how, even in such moments, the "authentic" self is always dependent on the enactment of specific social roles. Erving Goffman has argued that the performance of a given social role always allows for the expression of "something that is more embracing and enduring than the current role performance and even the role itself": "something, in short, that is characteristic not of the role but of the person—his personality, his perduring moral character, his animal nature, and so forth." Self, for Goffman, is not "an entity half-concealed behind events, but a changeable formula for managing oneself during them": "Just as the current situation prescribes the official guise behind which we will conceal ourselves, so it provides for where and how we will show through, the culture itself prescribing what sort of entity we must believe ourselves to be in order to have something to show through in this manner." Goffman pithily sums up: "Whenever we are issued a uniform, we are likely to be issued a skin" (1974, 573–75).

In light of the performances described in this book, we might also state that whenever we are issued a social language, we are also issued an individual, "authentic" voice. For example, recall the 1908 phonograph record *The Laughing Spectator* described in the introduction. When the comedian steps out of his role as a stage performer to comment on the goatlike laughter of an audience member, he exudes a sense of spontaneity and suggests the revelation of a truer self. Similarly, laughing records enact the expression of self when musicians and audience members step out of their given social roles in laughter. Finally, Allen Funt's narratives tend to involve a victim defined by a particular role (a waiter, a delivery man, and so on) who is made to deviate from his or her prescribed social script. What becomes clear is that the modern media are adept at representing what Goffman calls the "changeable formula of the self," and that the "authentic" self is always the effect of performances given in particular social, cultural, and historical contexts.

Although sound media technologies could capture the evidence of bodies in new ways, my discussion of secret recording and the grain of the voice demonstrates how a balance often had to be struck between the desire to relish that ability and the desire for traditionally recognized, formal conventions of the performance frame. Recall how Allen Funt's use of the rile and the reveal functioned to provide a potentially amorphous secret recording of conversation with a sense of closure. The trademark "Smile! You're on *Candid Camera!*" is also a paradigmatic illustration of how rekeying an event has often been a technique for giving formal shape to a performance. Also consider how, on many blue discs, a performance featuring the ongoing erotic appeal of double entendres is brought to a close by a moment of rekeying in which a character is let in on the erotic frame of the proceedings.

A similar moment of rekeying is often mobilized to provide closure to academic books. That is, I could now rekey my writing to a more poetic mode, perhaps returning to Roland Barthes's quote to the effect that there is no science that can exhaust the voice (1985, 279). Then again, I could rekey a rather detached cultural analysis to a more personal, journalistic voice, and describe how it was my own experience as a singer, working in a recording studio on digital audio workstations for the first time in the mid-1990s, that drove home to me the fascinating interactions among performance style, technology, and cultural meaning and so inspired this book. Formal conventions aside, I end with the contention that the scholarship of media studies, cultural history, and performance theory can enable us to hear voices of the mass media from the past century with fresh ears. The modern sound media have offered texts that need to be heard from these multiple positions, since the voice is always saying so many things at once—speaking of culture, identity, technology, and performance with the same fragile, complex, and beautiful tones.

Notes

CHAPTER I

1. See also my discussion of George Washington Johnson in chapter 4 of this volume.

2. The laugh can be seen as a transitional vocal performance for African American performers, one that could slide between the stylistic categories of the European bel canto style and the raspy voice identified with African American forms such as blues or gospel. I will return to these issues in chapter 4.

3. Along these lines, David Morton asserts (2000, 24) that "high culture music has had an influence in the record industry that exceeds its economic importance. The reason for this reversal of economic logic is related to the fluctuations of the popular music market, the prejudices of engineers and musicians, and the social agenda of the record companies." See also Katz on the music appreciation movement (2004, 49–66).

4. On the 1923 Edison recording *Laughing Record (Henry's Music Lesson)*, which features Sally Stembler, the woman's presence is motivated in the narrative by the fact that she is the piano accompanist in the music lesson.

5. We might also consider Brady's description of such phenomena (1999, 40) as the tendency to "personify" the phonograph machine and phonograph demonstration records that made the machine speak in the first person.

6. Patrick Feaster notes (2006b, 69) that the laughter of early talking machines was sometimes interpreted as insincerity: "On the one hand, the machine's laughter was grotesque and unnatural because of its mechanical point of origin; but on the other, it also reminded listeners of insincere laughter, whether nervous or sarcastic."

7. In Robert R. Provine's study of laughter, he describes attending an improvisational acting class at the University of Maryland–Baltimore County, where students participated in a "laughing exercise." Provine notes that "their

efforts were not impressive—most of their laughs sounded forced or artificial" and that "the struggling novice actors were announcing that laughter is under weak conscious control" (2000, 49). Indeed, the laugh seems to be an expression that is particularly hard to fake.

8. Though laughter seems to have had a limited place in the emotional vocabulary of the histrionic style, stage melodrama was nevertheless devoted to the idea of gesture as the site of truth, a topic I discuss further in chapter 3. Even so, the performed laugh would still pose certain problems for the actor. The body of the actor becomes foregrounded in the spasm of laughter and, if not placed under constraints, can threaten to draw attention from the role being played.

9. See for example, Hansen (1991, 25–28), and Musser (1990, 321–23).

10. The "Arkansas Traveler" was a combination of song and dialogue whose origins date back to the 1840s. It is the story of "the interaction between urbane sophisticate and an uncouth squatter" (Green 2001, 31). A stranger, approaching a shack on horseback, asks for directions from a fiddle-playing rube, only to be met with a string of jokes and wisecracks. On early recordings of this sketch, these jokes are accompanied by enthusiastically performed laughter and followed by a short burst of fiddle playing. The climax of the story comes in a narrative turn so famous it has acquired its own name: the Turn of the Tune. The stranger asks the rube why he won't finish the tune, and he replies that he doesn't know the second part. At this, the stranger picks up the fiddle and plays the whole thing perfectly, inspiring the rube to call him "the smartest man living," and invite him inside. Green describes this as a tale of American democratic ideals: "Neither figure achieved full victory over the other: both shared power . . . [which serves as a] metaphor for constant mediation between patrician and plebeian, aristocrat and commoner" (33). In light of the function of laughter on other, similar recordings, *Arkansas Traveler* represents another purpose of frame disintegration: a utopian democratic erasure of social frame whereby the rube can best the sophisticate in wit, but the urbane traveler can still "get down" with the common folk.

11. The stereotype of the carefree, laughing black man is, of course, ultimately the product of proslavery propaganda that implied that the slaves were happy with their brutal plantation existence. Lawrence Levine writes (1977, 300) of the problematic position of laughter within the black community, given such stereotyped depictions: "For many the sights and sounds of black laughter verged too near the vacuous, happy-go-lucky, Sambo image; black people needed to confront their problems not grin at them."

12. Bing Crosby began using Jack Mullin's Ampex magnetic tape machine to record his *Kraft Music Hall* radio show in August 1947. Mullin described (1976, 66–67) how the ease of editing radio shows on tape led to the laugh track: "One time Bob Burns, the hillbilly comic, was on the show, and he threw in a few of his folksy farm stories, which of course were not in Bill Morrow's script. Today they wouldn't seem very off-color, but things were different on radio then. They got enormous laughs, which just went on and on. We couldn't use the jokes, but Bill asked us to save the laughs. A couple of weeks later he had a show that wasn't very funny, and he insisted that we put in the salvaged laughs. Thus the laugh-track was born."

13. Other famous comedians have shared this view. Groucho Marx, in a 1967 interview, stated that humor had "fallen upon bad times in recent years," and he placed the blame on the laugh track's effect on writing: "Those phony, recorded laughs on television comedies have done more to destroy comedy than anything else. The laugh track has made it too easy for writers. They no longer have to struggle to write funny material. They know that if a joke doesn't go over, it can be covered with a laugh track" (Thomas 1967, 1). A decade later, Bob Newhart made the same argument: "To me the laugh track killed TV for a while. . . . Writers don't have too [sic] stay up half the night working on a scene to make it better. They knew they'd get a laugh from the track whether it worked or not" (Buck 1972, 16).

14. Notably, Rhodes's foil in the film is the big-hearted television writer Mel Miller (Walter Matthau).

15. A newspaper column from 1978 featured an interview with one of "Hollywood's handful of laugh track experts," John Pratt. Pratt refused to name the shows he worked on, claiming that "it's like plastic surgery. It's not the doctor's place to say who got the nose job." Pratt also stated that most of the work he did was manipulating the laughter of the studio audience: "we re-insert their own material. . . . We're . . . not adding laughs, but blending edits" (Sharbutt 1978, 9).

16. The remarkably wide range of terms used for laughter in the 1950s suggests that stage professionals perceived it in shades of nuance of an almost musical quality. Take for example a *Variety* article in which Ray Bolger describes the limited range of laughter on the laugh track: "These laugh tracks have practically put the titter and the smirk and the smile and the grin out of show business. . . . I can recall when varying shades of humor actually produced giggles and chuckles as well as guffaws. But that was before TV comedy shows were filmed. Now you hear nothing but boffs" (1954, 98).

17. Recorded loops of laughter have sometimes been used in popular music not to smooth over the mechanical nature of recording technology but to draw attention to it. For example, a number of recordings by techno artists feature the loop of a female laugh. At first, the looped laugh seems to present an authentic human expression in the context of an extremely technological musical production. But as this laugh is played and replayed, the spasm of laughter is bled of any sense of spontaneity, becoming increasingly mechanical and uncanny. See, for example, Rhythm Is Rhythm's 1987 recording "Nude Photo," a title that obliquely reestablishes the connection between the performed laugh and other mediated body genres.

18. Jack Klugman and Tony Randall, stars of the TV series *The Odd Couple,* made a much-publicized plea to remove the laugh track from the show in 1971. They announced on *The Dick Cavett Show* that a single episode would be broadcast without it and asked viewers to write in and say if they liked it better that way. Newspaper articles from the time state that ABC received 135,000 letters, of which about 112,000, or 83 percent, were against the laugh track ("Viewers Rule Out Laugh Track" 5-B).

CHAPTER 2

1. Phonographic recordings with erotic content take a variety of forms. For this chapter my main focus is on those blue discs that are descriptive sketches and not the large body of risqué songs also in circulation. I'm also not including in this study adult comedy records made in the 1960s and 1970s by performers such as Rusty Warren, Rudy Ray Moore, and Redd Foxx, who were working in a historical context that is different enough in terms of policy, technology, and culture to merit its own study.

2. The *New York Times* reported on October 14, 1897, that Comstock and detectives of the Queen's County district attorney's office made a raid, resulting in two arrests: "It is alleged that Comstock, while here on Sept. 25, discovered that improper songs were being produced in the phonograph gallery. The phonograph was seized and the two prisoners taken before Justice of the Peace Suter. . . . It is alleged that the man who sung into the phonographs the words composing the songs is in prison serving a term for doing so" ("Raid by Anthony Comstock" 3).

3. The early phonograph historian and scholar Patrick Feaster suggests that the cylinder I describe may be the work of Russell Hunting. In order to mark his records covertly and so make them more difficult to pirate, Hunting tended to include a trademark vocalization "uh" in his spoken announcements. Not only is that trademark expression heard on this risqué cylinder, but it occurs right before the word *cunting*, perhaps intended to signal the authorship by Mr. Hunting.

4. I wish to thank Jerry Fabris, the museum's curator, Patrick Feaster, and David Diehl for helping make these recordings available to me.

5. William Kenney writes that "until the commercial introduction of the Edison 'gold moulded' cylinders in 1902, the necessary technology did not exist to mass-produce copies from original recorded cylinders: the 'gold moulded' process introduced the system of a master cylinder from which copies might be made" (1999, 42). Patrick Feaster notes that by around 1903, Victor had also perfected a system of disc duplication that "vastly increased the number of copies it could make from each master" (2006a, 205). Feaster points out, however, that those masters were still liable to wear out with use.

6. The U.S. House Committee on the Judiciary noted that "reports from law-enforcement agencies indicate that the volume of shipments of 'obscene, lewd, lascivious, or filthy' phonograph records and other sound-producing and -recording devices in interstate commerce had been "on the increase" (1950, 1).

7. Reports in the popular press indicate that obscene phonograph records continued to be an issue in the late 1950s. The *Syracuse Herald-Journal* reported on April 2, 1958, that "Queens District Attorney investigators raided six Queens music shops and a Manhattan record distributing house yesterday and arrested eight men on charges of selling obscene phonograph records. Hundreds of records, some selling as high as $50 each, were seized. Frances X. Smith, assistant district attorney, said the shops sold some of the records openly to teenagers" ("N.Y. Police Seize Obscene Records" 21). Later that year a superior court judge in Newark, New Jersey, ruled that Newark's ordinance on obscenity covered

only material that can be seen, and so dismissed a municipal court conviction for the sale of a phonograph record, "although he had found its contents obscene" ("Obscene Record Legal in Newark, Judge Says" 23).

8. Rev. Warren Debenham, a noted collector of comedy records, has discussed *The Crepitation Contest,* saying that "there exist maybe 18 different editions of the same material. . . . This record probably originated as a silly improvised contest, much like a garage band—and it became part of the culture." Indeed, Debenham stated that "as kids we would play this when our parents were gone," and that "people of my generation remember it fondly; it's a part of our growing up" (Vale and Juno 1994, 144–45).

9. Legman mentions this recording (1982, 372–73).

10. Rusty Warren, an early 1960s risqué comedian famous for her "Knockers Up!" routine, described her records as always being "a shared experience": "You never sat alone and listened with earphones like people do today in the '90s. I was a 'party album' concept—you shared my records with friends at a barbecue or a party" (Vale and Juno 1994, 56). As another indication of this type of context, consider an article in the *Syracuse Post-Standard* of April 18, 1950, that describes a Chief Justice Vinson who was caught at a drinking party "which took a revolting turn when an obscene phonograph record was played thru to the last foul phrase" (Pegler 1950, 13).

11. Legman writes that "the party records of the 1940s leaned heavily on the double-entendre shop or service situation," and that they were the product of "earlier recitations and printed novelties" that were "dressed up in dialogue form" and recorded with "suitable sound effects and label names" (1982, 229).

12. Eric Schaefer describes a similar skit in the 1953 burlesque film *Naughty New Orleans* (1999, 319).

13. In Richard Bauman's terms, the moment when the woman is let in on the joke is when the fabrication is discredited. Bauman describes five main components in the structure of first-person narratives in practical jokes. First is orientation, a section that "sets out the factors that bring the participants into place for the practical joke," as well as the means "for enacting it." Second is the setup, where the engineering of the trick and "the mobilization of the means to set up the fabrication" are recounted. Third is the trick event itself: a recounting and enactment of the "actual working of the key fabrication on the dupe." Notably, this usually includes the "effect of the fabrication on the victim," such as "embarrassment, confusion, guilt, and loss of face." Following the trick event is the discrediting of the fabrication: "after the victim endures his discomfiture for a while, the fabrication frame is broken and the working of the joke is revealed." Finally, the stories close with an evaluation of "the efficacy of the practical joke" (1986, 45).

14. For a more contemporary example, see the scene in *Charlie's Angels* (2000) in which Natalie Cook (Cameron Diaz) innocently says to a well-built UPS deliveryman (Joe Duer), "Good morning. You know, I signed that release waiver, so you can just feel free to stick things in my slot."

15. Pamela Robertson Wojcik points to the influence of a tradition of female impersonators on West's double entendre–laden verbal style (2004, 31–33).

16. Amy Lawrence includes Bacall in a group of "female stars of the 1930s," like Marlene Dietrich, Greta Garbo, and Joan Crawford, who were "fetishized

for their low voices": "all sported glamorous, ambiguous images and low voices noted by critics and fans" (1991, 88). Lawrence places this trend in the context of discourses on the sound media that consistently asserted the technological "problem" of recording high-pitched female voices.

17. In fact, Weis finds that children and other outsider characters are often depicted eavesdropping in narrative film: "The eavesdropping trope thematizes the child's incomplete comprehension of the adult world, including the mystery of sexuality and the threat, real or imagined, of parental rejection" (1999, 85).

18. The quest for the evocative "breakthrough out of performance" can be described as the desire to transcend the way performative skill can "clothe" the performer, eloquently described in Roland Barthes's analysis of the striptease: "Thus we see the professionals of striptease wrap themselves in the miraculous ease which constantly clothes them, makes them remote, gives them the icy indifference of skilful practitioners, haughtily taking refuge in the sureness of their technique: their science clothes them like a garment" (1972, 86).

19. The only other blue disc I have found from this period that features extensive porno-performativity is called *Mr. Long Dick* and features African American characters.

20. I have heard multiple recordings of this same sketch, and though the versions differ in the actions of George and Mary, the introductory frame is exactly the same.

21. Gershon Legman's work on bawdy monologues makes clear that *Silent George* is part of a long-standing tradition of erotic folk recitations, many of which are told in the "first-person feminine": "A recitation in which the girl begins by repelling the man's advances, only to end by accepting everything, with various verbal ejaculations representing her orgasm" (1976, 108). I am indebted to John Mehlberg for showing me the prehistory of the *Silent George* routine.

CHAPTER 3

1. Scholars in the field of the ethnography of speaking sometimes use the term *prosody* to refer to the intonation, stress, accent, and pitch shifts of the voice (Gumperz 1992, 231).

2. Orrin Dunlap's 1936 guide to speaking on the radio stresses "naturalness, spontaneity, and sincerity" as the "three vital essentials" (1936, 33). When Gilmore and Middleton discuss microphone technique in their 1946 manual, *Radio Announcing,* they emphasize the use of "a conversational technique": "While an announcer is addressing an audience of literally millions of people, his technique should be that of conducting a one-way conversation with an individual listener or small group" (1946, 50). Later they urge the student to strive for "naturalness, sincerity, and friendliness. If an announcer will be sincere and friendly, his personality nearly always will win his audience. Voice quality is important—technique is a 'must,' but, above all, be natural, sincere, and friendly" (51). It is interesting to note that this subdued conversational style was also developing in contrast to the vocal techniques of radio advertising. John Hutchens, writing in the *New York Times* in 1942, criticized radio advertisements that featured the gushing voice ("rich, creamy, foaming soap suds"); the

snappy "hard-selling" voice ("yes, sir, men, Cuttem Razor Blades for that tough beard"); and the syrupy, insinuating voice ("ladies, is your skin always at its best?"). In contrast, Hutchens pointed to a trend toward "a controlled, resonant voice that has the ring of sincerity, distinction without affectation, and is affirmative without hawking its points" (1942b, SM26).

3. The discourse on the "good radio voice" also reveals how clearly writers and professionals of that time perceived the effect of microphone technology on the voice. Michel Chion has written that audiences from the 1920s through the 1940s were more conscious of how the voice was affected by radio technology. The discourse on the correct radio voice is thus an illustration of Chion's discussion of phonogeny: "Phonogeny refers to the rather mysterious propensity of certain voices to sound good when recorded and played over loudspeakers, to inscribe themselves in the record grooves better than other voices, in short to make up for the absence of the sound's real source by means of another kind of presence specific to the medium" (1990, 101). Chion notes that, unlike its visual analog photogenie, the concept of phonogenie has been largely forgotten. For Chion, this illustrates how audiences have often been convinced that the means of sound collection and reproduction are transparent (103).

4. Tim Gracyk notes that Spencer's performance is based on those of the actor Richard Mansfield (2002, 318).

5. Staiger describes how the Edison company in 1909 was publicizing that its films featured a subdued style of acting: "We call your attention to the absence in our dramatic productions of extravagant gesture and facial expression which frequently mar the dramatic effect of a powerful situation or climax" (1985, 20). Note the similarity between this stylistic development and Edison's aversion to vibrato in singing, which I describe in chapter 4.

6. Compare this to J. A. Hammerton's 1897 book, *The Actor's Art,* in which it was argued that "many actors, endeavoring to get nearer to nature, mistake faults for beauties, and end by becoming familiar and inartistic. The logical outcome of familiar acting would be to speak on the stage exactly as you speak in the drawing-room or in the smoking-room; that is to say, mumble and stammer, and talk so that only your tête-à-tête can hear. That, in the opinion of some, would, no doubt, be pure, unadulterated nature on the stage—it would be as near to art as the 'real water, real horses,' and 'real engines' of melodrama are" (1897, 33). Hammerton defines his stage acting in opposition both to the mumbling and stammering that microphones would soon capture and amplify, and to the spectacle of the melodramatic stage, so soon to be replaced by cinema.

7. Strasberg held that vocal exercises were "a matter of superficial skill": "It takes only time and effort. It does not take intelligence. It does not take talent. It does not even take ability. It just takes practice—literally. Technical skills are not a sign of anything except that the work on them has been done" (Strasberg 1991, 148–49). Strasberg also saw vocal training as archaic in a post-Freudian world: "Until modern psychology came into practice, we really could not understand why the actor had [certain] problems. . . . When the inspiration was not there, the best thing [he] could do was to learn voice, speech, and to train the body. These elements are not unimportant, but these elements train only the external elements of the actor . . . not the talent of the actor" (quoted in Hull

1985, 19). Strasberg's downplaying of vocal training tended to place an emphasis on gesture as the site of authentic performance: "In the theatre today we overemphasize aesthetically the word that we hear, as if hearing the word means that everything done on the stage is thereby vitalized, and not hearing the word means that what is done on the stage cannot be judged. Actually a lot of the times when you do not hear or understand the word, as happens when you go to foreign-language plays, you are by that very fact able to observe one definite area of work and to see what you really get from the actor. A good deal of the time what we think we get from the actor actually comes from the words. When we are deprived of the words, we then depend on real observation" (Strasberg 1991, 348).

8. Tyrone Guthrie, a British theater director, criticized Strasberg for his lack of interest in vocal training. "Now the actor's principal means of expression is the voice. The expression of eyes, of the whole body, is important, too; but it is on the breathstream and by means of sounds and, more particularly, the organization of sounds into, first, syllables, then words, then sentences, that the most subtle and the most articulate communication occurs between human creatures" (1957, SM112).

9. Vardac has argued that modern stage lighting was "the greatest single reason for the discontinuation of the traditional manner of theatrical production" at the turn of the century (1949, 8). Lighting would seem to be an important factor in the larger shift from an emphasis on the voice to one on gesture.

10. I am grateful to James Naremore for directing my attention to this aspect of the scene.

11. Joy Elizabeth Hayes argues that the television family sitcom has often been described as a hybrid of the live anthology drama and the variety show, and that though this description recognizes the influence of New York theater and vaudeville, it ignores television's clearest predecessor: radio (2004).

12. Critics complained that radio melodrama, like the crooners, represented an "emasculation" of the American man (Hilmes 1997, 174). A common thematic trope of the radio melodramas of the 1930s and 1940s was a physically debilitated male: "Most common were blindness and crippling diseases or accidents that left their male victims in wheelchairs; many suffered bouts of amnesia, brain injury and other mental dislocations" (173).

13. See Max Wylie's "Washboard Weepers" in *Harper's,* November 1942, and Merrill Denison's "Soap Opera" in *Harper's,* April 1940.

14. The idea that melodrama has a special connection to this type of vocal performance has become widespread in film studies since Linda Williams's famous article, "Film Bodies: Gender, Genre, and Excess." For Williams, the three "body genres," melodrama, pornography, and horror, are all represented by vocal expressions: "Excess is marked by recourse not to the coded articulations of language but to inarticulate cries of pleasure in porn, screams of fear in horror, sobs of anguish in melodrama" (1991, 4).

15. Naremore adds that "the actor is seldom called upon to register suffering alone. Usually, the film wants the woman to express some delicate, 'restrained' mixture of pain, renunciation, and spiritual goodness—a smiling though tears that leads up to a kind of acquiescence in suffering. . . . The actor's

job involves combining conventional expressions (anger or indignation are the only emotions the genre seems to rule out), so that the shot has an ambiguous effect" (1988, 112–13).

16. A 1945 article in the *Los Angeles Times* described how Audrey Totter, a "Soap Opera Queen," had to adapt in her move from radio to making movies at MGM: "Sure, a radio performer has to 'ham' it up a bit, but because your audience can't see you leering into the microphone and only hears, the overacting apparently gets by. . . . But pictures really require 'gentle' emoting, especially in close-ups. I use to act directly into the mike and probably neglected my leading men shamefully. Naturally, in pictures it's different" (Scott 1945, B1).

17. Allison McCracken notes that "in radio suspense texts, the absence of the visual shorthand of film noir—'Freudian' symbols, fetishes, expressionist lighting, 'mysterious' femme fatales—[required] that more emphasis be put on social and psychological realism. First-person narration, for example, is much more detailed on radio in terms of the character's social context and motivation" (2002, 193–94).

18. Webb talked about how *Dragnet*'s writers put "a lot of punch" into the show by "writing dialogue against the situation": "When I, as Sgt. Joe Friday, come across a corpse I report it with about as much emotion as a man finding a penny on the sidewalk, and with the same amount of preparation. It seems to work better than the big musical build-up followed by a shriek that you hear on some of the private-eye shows" (Hewes 1951, 103). Here we can see an interesting variation on the acting technique wherein the inflection of the voice serves as counterpoint to the meaning of the words.

19. Anderson notes that Webb used the same scripts for both the radio and television versions of the show, "making only minimal concessions to the opportunities provided by a visual medium," a practice that led to the show's "monotonous conversational scenes and its unintentionally Brechtian performances, often-parodied elements of a narrative world populated by seemingly emotionless automatons" (1994, 67).

20. Wexman refers to factors such as the nature of postwar corporate work, the entrance of women into the workforce, new ideas about the nature of sexuality, and the growing cultural conception of adolescence (1993, 170).

CHAPTER 4

1. Ehrenreich et al. and Douglas provide insightful analyses of Beatlemania. In "The Celebrity Legacy of the Beatles," P. David Marshall has written a penetrating essay on the Beatles in terms of media celebrity. Anthony Elliot's *The Mourning of John Lennon* is a fascinating study of themes in Lennon's solo work and the cultural reaction to his death.

2. Fales refers to the voice as the epitome of a formant-structured timbre, a term that refers to a sound that is determined by the presence and strength of formants: broad bands or clusters of high-intensity harmonics or overtones (Fales 2002, 72; Stark 1999, 46). Formant-structured timbres can be compared to "harmonically structured" sounds such as a "flute tone in a high register," whose harmonics are more narrow and restricted (Fales 2002, 72).

3. Opinions differ as to how the "singer's formant" is produced. Sundberg writes that "the larynx tube seems to be an important tool for obtaining the clustering of the higher formant frequencies needed for generating a singer's formant" (1987, 121).

4. Lind went to Paris in 1841 and performed for García, who famously told her that "It would be useless to teach you, Mademoiselle; you have no voice left." García recommended that she give her voice six weeks of perfect rest, abstain during that time from singing "even so much as one single note; and to speak as little as possible." After this period, Lind returned to García, who pronounced that she had improved sufficiently to become his student. García then agreed to give her two lessons every week, "an arrangement which set all her anxieties at rest, and for which she was deeply grateful, to the end of her life" (Holland 1893, 68–70).

5. A 1925 newspaper article recounted his discovery this way: "One day in 1854 he tied a small mirror to the end of a pencil, held it in his throat and placed another mirror in front of his mouth. It worked. He saw the glottis and was able to study it as he made sounds. He rushed from his studio to a little instrument maker around the corner, and within a few weeks the laryngoscope was perfected" ("Young García Passed Up Opera Career" 8).

6. Sterne describes developments in the understanding of perception from this era: "Each sense could be abstracted from the others; its peculiar and presumably unique functions could be mapped, described, and subsequently modeled. Physiology moved questions of hearing from morphology to function and technics. Audition became a mechanism that could be anatomically, processurally, and experientially abstracted from the human body and the rest of the senses" (2003, 62).

7. That vibrato could be so useful for studio performers makes all the more surprising Thomas Edison's crusade against it. Edison famously refused to accept the reputations of well-known musicians, and insisted on selecting artists and repertoire himself (Harvith and Harvith, 1986, 6). Edison's assessment of singers was, by his own account, mechanical, and he found fault "not on the basis of interpretation or musicianship but on what he felt to be excessive vibrato or tremolo" (7). Writing in a "Voice Demonstration Comments" notebook, Edison claimed that tremolo was "the greatest defect of the human voice" (8). Though Edison's obsession with vibrato can be understood as the idiosyncratic whim of a half-deaf demagogue, it can also be seen as another illustration of how recording represented a rupture in musical performance style from the expressive codes of the Romantic era and encouraged musical evaluation based on nuances of timbre and technique.

8. Edmund Shaftesbury, whose writing on acting I discussed in chapter 3, had this to say about the "guttural timbre": "We inherit the feeling from the dark and warlike ages of our ancestors. The timbre of hate is found most prevalent in the voices of those nations or those people whose existence has been devoted to quarrels. It is one of the defects of the voice, but has its use in depicting feelings of dislike and hatred, and for that reason should be practiced" (1891, 110). For Shaftesbury "throatiness" was "always harsh and disagreeable, and antagonizes the richness and purity of the voice" (30).

9. In his study of black culture during slavery, Philip Morgan writes that slave masters spoke of the slaves' "thick" and "hoarse" voices (1998, 578). Morgan is among writers who make a connection between the timbral complexity of African American speech and the importance of pitch in some African languages (579). Robert Palmer writes that "the Yoruba, the Akan, and many other African peoples speak pitch-tone languages in which a single syllable or word has several meanings, and one indicates the desired meaning by speaking at an appropriate pitch level, usually high, middle, or low. Among these people, speech has melodic properties, and the melodies found in music suggest words and sentences. By using generally understood correspondences between pitch configurations in speech and in music, musicians can make their instruments talk" (1982, 29). Baraka also refers to the nature of some African languages: "In African languages the meaning of a word can be changed simply by altering the pitch of the word, or changing its stress . . . significant tone . . . the combination of pitch and timbre used to produce changes of meaning in words. This was basic to the speech and music of West Africans" (1963, 26).

10. See also Palmer: "European and American visitors to Africa have often been puzzled by what they perceived as an African fondness for muddying perfectly clean sounds. African musicians will attach pieces of tin sheeting to the heads of drums or the necks of stringed instruments in order to get a noisy, rattling buzz . . . and their solo singing makes use of an extravagant variety of tonal effects, from grainy falsetto shrieks to affected hoarseness, throaty growls, and guttural grunting. This preference for what western musicology tells us are impure sounds has always been evident in black American music, from the rasp in so much folk, blues, and popular singing . . . to the gut-bucket sounds of early New Orleans jazz trumpeters, who sometimes played into brass spittoons or crammed homemade mutes made out of kazoos into the bells of their horns" (1982, 31).

11. An interviewer in a 1911 *Chicago Tribune* story on Williams was shocked to discover that he spoke with an English accent: "I gasped, 'Your accent is English.' 'Of course. I was born in West India. There they speak a literal English.'" Williams goes on to explain that he had to live in the American South for two years to "acquire a negro dialect, and it was no easy matter": "It's no more natural for me to speak with the dialect of a southern negro than it is for a Swede to talk English" (Samter 1911, B5). Williams's distance from the stereotype he portrayed served both to display his virtuosity as a performer and to underscore the racism of those stage conventions.

12. It should also be noted that a central feature of minstrel performance was choral singing, which requires a timbral approach different from that to solo singing. Sundberg notes that solo singing tends to be louder and have more overtones in the region of the singer's formant, whereas "choral singers strive to tune their voice timbre in order to mesh with the timbre of the rest of the choir" (1987, 141–43).

13. We might also consider the influence of the round tones heard on records by African American vocal quartets such as the Fisk Jubilee Singers. Brooks describes these as "the first 'serious' African American recordings to be widely distributed," and he suggests that they were quite popular among middle-class white audiences at the time (2005, 198).

14. It is interesting to note how Golden's rasp frequently appeared to emerge from an animal such as a turkey or a rabbit, as if even here the white performer needed to maintain a certain degree of distance.

15. This style can also be considered in relation to the tendency in late nineteenth-century musical performance that Rick Altman calls the "aesthetic of discontinuity," in which "divergent sound experiences alternated within a single program": "Theaters systematically supported interpolated performances of songs, dances, or variety acts entirely unrelated to the plot of the play" (2004, 51).

16. Simon Frith writes: "It was the 'vocal' qualities of the electric guitar developed by black musicians that inspired a generation of white rock stars in the 1960s" (1981, 18).

17. Indeed, Armstrong had a tendency to quote musical phrases from opera records in his trumpet solos, adding to the sense of the horn as a bel canto voice (Berrett 1999, 24–29).

18. For an insightful discussion of river imagery in the African American musical tradition, see Dyer, 1986, 87–88.

19. Gabbard defines *signifying* as "an African American term for the art of talking about, criticizing, ridiculing and/or putting one over on the audience" (1996, 138–39).

20. Lomax guessed that one reason for men's using a raspy sound was "to produce an animal-like growling or roaring sound, thus identifying with the animal world" (1968, 73).

21. As another indication of bel canto's tendency toward the transcendence of the physical body, note that bel canto is often considered to have originated with the castrati: eunuchs whose bodies were mutilated to achieve "heavenly" tones that seemed impossible to have "proceed[ed] from the throat of anything that was human" (Pleasants 1981, 42).

22. Frank Sinatra illustrates that the bel canto style could still be mobilized in 1950s popular music. Pleasants quotes Sinatra as stating, "When I started singing in the mid-1930s . . . everybody was trying to copy the Crosby style—the casual kind of raspy sound in the throat. . . . I decided to experiment a little and come up with something different. What I finally hit on was more the bel canto Italian school of singing, without making a point of it. That meant I had to stay in better shape because I had to sing more" (1974, 189). Sinatra was able to pair that bel canto sound with a conversational, individual style.

23. Simon Frith makes the great point that Presley was like his "own doo-wop act, his bass no more unnatural than his falsetto" (1996, 195).

24. Here we should note that a crucial musical influence on the Beatles, and in particular on McCartney, was Little Richard—a singer not only with a buzz-saw rasp and explosive screams, but who crossed both vocal registers and gender conventions with a similar deftness.

25. Douglas writes that Beatlemania "marked a critical point in the evolution of girl culture" (1994, 116): "they took their female audience seriously . . . perfectly fused the 'masculine' and 'feminine' strains of rock 'n' roll in their music. . . . Without ever saying so explicitly, the Beatles acknowledged that there

was masculinity and femininity in all of us, and that blurring the artificial boundaries between the two might be a big relief " (116).

26. *Sgt. Pepper*–era Beatles LPs have often been discussed as representing a moment when rock and roll was elevated in the eyes of the public at large to the status of art. The danger of this view is, of course, that it reduces all that came before this era to non-art, meaningful only as stepping stones to the moment when rock and roll is rid of its residual primitivism (read: blackness) and made artistically valid.

27. A *New York Times* article from 1971 compared a group therapy session to Method acting: "To an observer much of what happens seems absurdly artificial—most participants seem like inept zombies trying to imitate Method actors showing big emotions" (Malver 1971, SM4). In fact, cathartic therapy was actually the reverse of Method acting, since it's goals were to work not from inner emotions to outer expression, but from outer expression (the scream) to inner emotional release.

28. Storr wrote that primal therapy "contains nothing which will not be familiar to the student of psychiatric literature," and that Janov made no reference to literature on such topics as abreaction (1970, 283). Storr added: "Janov has one card up his sleeve which few of us [therapists] can match. He is absolutely sure that he is right. Again and again he makes remarks of an unbelievably dogmatic kind. Primal therapy is not only the best cure for neurosis, it is the only cure—a statement not only arrogant but demonstrably false" (1972, BR8).

29. Such screams index a certain "vocalic space," Steven Connor's term for how the voice operates in and articulates "different conceptions of space" (2000, 12). Connor suggests that the shout re-creates "the infant's archaic space" with its "reassertion of the blind imperative demand" (34). At another point Connor describes the "voice of rage" as being "a kind of projectile, a piercing, invading weapon, in order to disintegrate, and abandon itself " (37). Here is the same paradox found in Chion's thought: the raspy cry as reflective of both self-assertion and helplessness; both threatening and imploring; creating both distance and seeking to annihilate all interpersonal distance; the mark of an individual and the vehicle of a primal experience that erases the individual ego.

30. The subject matter of this song makes it ripe for psychoanalysis, and Anthony Elliot suggests that "Lennon moves back and forth across the spacings of loss, from object-loss to loss of self. Lennon's screams of pain burst forth as a redoubling of loss, reopening the gap between the lost maternal body and self-differentiation" (1999, 51).

31. Hugues Panassié wrote that "Louis has a small harsh voice and needs a mike" (1971, 54).

CHAPTER 5

1. In December 1967 the Supreme Court ruled in *Katz v. U.S.* that "the Fourth Amendment protects people, not places," and so reversed the *Olmstead* case, a ruling that "completely altered the legal context of American tapping" (Fitzgerald and Leopold 1987, 169). Legislation was soon passed to ensure that

law enforcement could continue to tap: the Omnibus Crime Control and Safe Streets Act of 1968 brought tapping under the control of courts at both the federal and state levels (170).

2. The logic of this ruling provides a window into the status of the mediated voice at this time. That is, the court's decision begs the question: where does the voice fall in the distinction between people and places? Justice Taft's comparison of telephone wires with highways suggests that his decision is based in part on an understanding of telephone interaction as a public act—a view that I will suggest in the next chapter was appropriate for an era of operator switching and party lines. Justice Brandeis, on the other hand, highlights the private, intimate nature of telephone conversation: "Discovery and invention have made it possible for the government, by means far more effective than stretching upon the rack, to obtain disclosure in court of what is whispered in the closet." The disembodied voice thus became a legal issue, and it is notable that decisions about its status hinged on the voice's uncertain relation to bodies and places.

3. Some of Brandeis's statements suggest the mysterious, disturbing quality of wiretapping at that time: "The progress of science in furnishing the government with means of espionage is not likely to stop with wire tapping. Ways may some day be developed by which the government, without removing papers from secret drawers, can reproduce them in court, and by which it will be enabled to expose to a jury the most intimate occurrences of the home. Advances in the psychic and related sciences may bring means of exploring unexpressed beliefs, thoughts and emotions."

4. A remnant of this culture of tap jitters can still be heard on every telephone answering machine. The beep heard on answering machines is a direct result of anxiety about taping conversations. In 1946 and 1947 "the FCC ruled that telephone recording devices could be attached to AT&T's lines, but the company insisted that they issue a 'beep' at regular intervals to make it clear to both parties that the call was being recorded. The vestige of this regulation is the universal use of a beep to signal the beginning of a recording on current answering devices" (Morton 2000, 126).

5. When it went on the air *Candid Microphone* had some sequences that captured a victim without Funt's shaping the proceedings. These were typically "candid portraits" of children, although the dialogue between World War II veterans described above also falls into this category.

6. For more on Bauman's analysis, see chapter 2, n. 13.

7. Funt's victims on *Candid Microphone* were typically working class, although one sketch proves to be a notable exception. In a gag called "How to Get Fired before You Get Hired," Funt answers an ad for a chauffeur. Funt tells us that the interviewer is a "gentleman of the old school," and sure enough, he chastises Funt's insolence in an urbane English accent. Again, an important part of the show seems to be structured around the presentation of a "candid portrait" of social types.

8. For example. Paul Distler writes that ethnic humor was "the mainstay of vaudeville and burlesque during the late nineteenth and early twentieth centuries" (1979, 36).

9. My argument is informed by the work of Patrick Feaster, who concludes that "ethnic caricature in phonography seems to have remained securely anchored" to intertextual conventions of other stage practices that had "made it so efficient as a vehicle of comedy in general" (2006a, 664).

10. Flagler noted that "Funt chooses his cameramen largely for their ability to zoom the lens in for a closeup at just the moment a subject begins to register some such primal emotion as surprise, dismay, or outrage" (1960, 68–70).

11. Funt also hired the playwright William Saroyan to create a drama that Funt could compare with the same scene in real life. Saroyan wrote several playlets concerning a man buying furniture on credit who finds out that his payments have been made by an anonymous benefactor. Each contained what Funt called a "heroic theme"; for example, the man refuses to accept this charity. Then Funt filmed "how real people reacted to the same situation": "I'm sad to report there were no heroic reactions of 'I want to pay it myself!' Some of the people were a bit confused, but all of them accepted credit from the unknown benefactor and beat a hasty retreat out of the store. That experiment taught me that even as talented a playwright as William Saroyan would find it difficult to predict the behavior of real people. And for my taste, the 'Candid' scenes were vastly more entertaining than the scripted drama" (1994, 50–51).

12. Funt's film is both a celebration and denial of sexual liberation, seemingly championing a new, more enlightened sexual freedom but in the end rejecting it. For example, a recurring dynamic of the film is to juxtapose reactions of outrage or shock at "liberated" sexuality with a youthful openness to nudity and sex. At the same time, the film ends with images of naked children playing on a sunny lawn, seeming to suggest a presexual utopia. The film thus stays on the fence, offering casual or liberated sex as tantalizing but potentially corrupting.

13. In an interesting parallel to Funt's show, Joseph describes how one of the primary functions of police surveillance in the 1950s and 1960s "was the recording and suppression of the supposedly 'deviant' practices of homosexual men": "the fastest growing application of police film and TV surveillance is in investigations of the activities of sexual deviates, usually homosexual solicitations or acts committed in 'public' restrooms. California police have used camera surveillance in toilet booths at department stores and amusement parks" (2002, 244). The technique used by law enforcement is strikingly similar to Funt's: "A two-way mirror was installed in a towel dispenser on a door in which a hole had been cut so that the officers could observe the restroom area from a concealed position" (244). Joseph discusses the economics of surveillance as being a determining factor on the targeting of the homosexual community: "The cost of total surveillance of every member of the population would be prohibitively expensive," and so those in power had to "focus on the minority of deviants" (244). Both this police surveillance and Funt's reveal focused on male sexuality, though in the former case, it is the minority of "deviants," and in the latter, the dominant heterosexual male population.

14. Funt described his experience as the keynote speaker at the 1991 meeting of the Western Psychological Association, where he discussed his show in terms of "cognitive dissonance" (1994, 220).

15. White argues that these shows mobilize "a ready-made and familiar narrative trajectory: the eruption of a problem leads to confession and diagnosis and then to a solution or cure" (1992, 117). The narrative trajectory of White's model, however, does not apply to *Candid Camera* gags. Instead of a narrative pattern featuring problem, confession, diagnosis, and cure, we get a problem (the gag), perhaps the inadvertent confession of a victim "caught in the act," but then the reveal functions as a kind of deus ex machina, where, in effect, the author of the play runs on to the stage just before the narrative climax. There is no diagnosis and no cure; instead, there is the pleasurable bursting of frames and accompanying anxious laughter.

16. Six weeks after the September 11, 2001, attacks, Congress passed the Patriot Act, which reduced the checks and balances on government surveillance. Under the Patriot Act, the FBI can secretly conduct a physical search or wiretap on American citizens to obtain evidence of crime without proving probable cause. Though the law was renewed in 2005, central aspects of it were declared unconstitutional by a U.S. district judge in September 2007.

CHAPTER 6

1. Steinberg adds that "a prank must have some sort of wit, some sort of sense of hubris punctured or justice restored. Cruelty ruins a prank" (1992, xi).

2. A fascinating example of the changing use of the word *phony* can be found in a series of editorial cartoons made for the *Chicago Tribune* in 1916 by the silent film comedian Charles Bowers. Entitled "Life's Little Phonies," each cartoon presented someone on the phone making a statement that was contradicted by her or his actual surroundings: for example, a woman lies in bed while saying into the telephone, "Oh, I've been up for hours—beds all made—house in order and I'm dressed now to go out!" (These were brought to my attention by King 2007.)

3. Gunning writes that "Lang's editing models itself on the telephone's ability to carry instantaneous messages across space, and on a new temporality founded on instants and synchronization" (2000, 98).

4. Jean Gottman asserts that since the telephone "allowed geographical separation between office work and the other stages of business it administered, such as production, warehousing, and shipping of goods," telephone networks were as important for the development of "lofty, dense skylines" as the elevator (1977, 309).

5. In an article in the *Brooklyn Eagle* from 1890, female operators reported that they had "lots of trouble" from the "eastern district": "There are too many foreigners there who talk fragmentary English, but think their pronunciation is perfect. Many of them we can't understand at all, and they fly in a tremendous rage and then all we hear are bellowings and roarings and sounds as if fifty people were sneezing at once" ("A Talk over the 'Phone" 9).

6. Sterne suggests that "people had to be convinced that telephony was simply a mediation of a face-to-face interaction" (2003, 265). A Bell Telephone ad that Sterne provides as evidence demonstrates one of the reasons that callers would not approach early telephony as a form of face-to-face interaction: the

presence of others on the line. The ad refers to telephone interaction as a three-party, quasi-public form of communication: "In every use of the telephone system, three human factors are brought into action—one at each end, one or both anxious and probably impatient, another at the central office, an expert, at least as intelligent and reliable as the best stenographers or bookkeepers. . . . Perfect service depends upon the perfect co-ordinate action of all three factors—any one failing, the service suffers" (265). Here, perhaps, is an explanation for why callers "might not have automatically assumed that face-to-face conversation and conversation on the telephone were comparable or two species of the same thing" (266).

7. That said, it is notable that a live switchboard operator is shown once in the film. Libby's parents can't get through to the girls and so contact the operator to check the line. We see the female operator sitting at her switchboard. The operator, however, proves to be powerless and can only confirm that the line is busy.

8. On this theme, see also Wes Craven's *Nightmare on Elm Street* (1984), in which the phone literally becomes a tongue.

9. It is important when considering texts of secret recording to be clear about the respective performances of the actor-prankster and the victim-answerer. A subtle change in emphasis between these two performances can have important ramifications for the ways in which the prank is framed. Many pranks take a tack similar to Funt's, as this advice from the Prank Call Central Web site illustrates: "It doesn't sound normal, or even that funny, when it's just the prank caller doing all the chattering. Encouraging responses from the call victim makes the call flow more smoothly, sounds more natural and real, and you can then play off their responses to add even more hilarity to your calls. You'll find that some of the funniest prank calls out there are the ones where the caller plays the straight man, and through pushing the right buttons, elicits funny replies or verbal abuse from the call victim. You will find much more success this way than yourself trying to be a comedian on the phone or unleashing a torrent of verbal abuse yourself, which usually just results in a quick hang-up by the other person. I find the best prank calls are those where the other person is so frustrated and irate that they are the one who is doing all the swearing." Despite the fact that they are in wildly different information states and understand the situation in profoundly different ways, the prankster and the victim are still best understood as a comedic team. Indeed, in an essay on the legal aspects of prank calling found at Prank Call Central, calls are defined as "joint works," and pranksters are warned that victims could legally demand payment if recordings of their interactions are commercially released.

10. Indeed, my introduction to this form came during long van rides as a touring musician, and tapes of prank calls are a common item at highway truck stops.

11. Sreberny-Mohammadi and Mohammadi write that Khomeini kept two tape machines running in his rented home in France, "recording his speeches and announcements and duplicating them for transmission or transportation to Iran" (1994, 120). Audio cassettes could catch not only the nuances of the cleric's style, but the reactions of the audience as well: many influential recordings

were recorded at public events, and so "captured the sounds of the public lamentation and prayers" (121).

12. I am reminded of comments made by Michael Jarrett (2004) concerning the Eminem star vehicle *8 Mile* (2002): "Seeing a white guy rock a house party at the drop of a hat? And seeing a white guy make an ocean of black bodies sway to an invented script? That's validation of the most transcendent and irrefutable sort. . . . Seeing that same white guy kick serious black ass . . . whip black guys at a black man's game? What's that? That's rock 'n' roll, pure and simple."

13. Marshall McLuhan points to the power of the telephone ring as a summons when he asks, "Why should we feel compelled to answer a ringing public phone when we know the call cannot concern us? Why does a phone ringing on the stage create instant tension?" His answer is that "the phone is a participant that demands a partner" (1964, 235).

14. The following offensive poem is included in the Tate CD packaging: "He was born / in a watermelon patch / His momma was pitchin' melons / when he fell out of her nasty old snatch." Indeed, although the Tate tapes are widely recognized among producers and fans of prank calls as early and influential, opinions differ about the appropriateness of these calls. On one prank Web site, the Tate calls are criticized in terms of power dynamics: "Some creep in Texas calls up impoverished rural blacks and makes their lives even more miserable than they already are. This recording supports [our] theory that pranks ought to be only aimed at the powerful, the spoiled, wealthy arrogant bullies, and all others who have never had to struggle."

15. Bart Simpson's calls to Moe's Tavern nicely encapsulate the main features of the Tube Bar calls. In the episode entitled "One Fish, Two Fish, Blow Fish, Blue Fish," Bart calls Moe's Tavern and asks, "Is Seymore there? Last name, Butts?" Moe calls out to the bar, "I wanna Seymore Butts," but then catches on to the prank, shouting into the phone: "Listen, you little scum-sucking pus-bucket. When I get my hands on you, I'm gonna pull out your eyeballs with a corkscrew!"

16. Ong suggests that the formal, ritual, and abstract nature of male combat is tied to the fact that "it is not always focused simply on relations between individuals, but on territory" (1981, 59). On these recordings the territory in question (the Tube Bar) was an explicitly masculine space. In fact, Mike Walsh notes on his fan Web site that the Tube Bar did not allow female patrons until the mid-1970s.

17. If these calls freeze Leary's structure of fights in the second phase (exchange of words), then not only do the interactants never move on to the third phase (exchange of blows), but they also never move to the remaining phases: audience interaction, emergence of a victor, and reconciliation. By eliding this final phase, the calls also present a short-circuiting of a ritualized performance of male bonding.

18. Indeed, in popular press coverage, the most frequent piece of advice is for victims to avoid any kind of vocal hysterics. Ann Landers wrote in a 1968 advice column that "the best way to deal with an obscene phone call is to hang up immediately. This deprives the caller of the thing he wants most—an audience. . . . The person who is being harassed should never—repeat, never—

express fear, disgust or anger. This will delight the caller and encourage him to keep calling" (1968, C5). Similarly, E. V. McCarthy wrote in 1965 that "women who cry or 'carry on' are those most often called back" (1965, E8).

19. A recent technique of prank calling demonstrates the continuing connection between phone pranks and performances of masculine potency. "Celebrity Sound Boards" are prank calls that are made by digitally sampling the dialogue of film actors and triggering those sampled statements in phone interactions. Some Web sites make samples of celebrity dialogue available to download. The pranks made with sound boards demonstrate the jarring results of ignoring standard telephone openings, beginning with startling statements such as Al Pacino's "Guess who?" Bruce Willis's "Who the fuck is this?" and Arnold Schwarzenegger's "I'm going to ask you a bunch of questions, and I want them answered immediately!" Notably, hyperbolically masculine action heroes are most typically used; they thus become a prosthetic surrogate voice for the male prankster.

20. Caller ID could also raise questions about privacy: "Many consumer advocates warn that in its present form the caller identification system could pose an invasion of privacy because it discloses an unpublished telephone number without the caller's consent. . . . Callers [are] . . . less likely to use confidential telephone services like hot lines for AIDS, child abuse or suicide that require the disclosure of sensitive information" (Sims 1989, D21).

21. Hopper uses telephone talk to illustrate how "speech actions are performed across sequences of utterances, especially two-utterance sequences" (1992, 17). Telephone interaction shows how speech acts are more accurately described as sequences (for example, question-answer, request-response).

22. Hopper points out that there are many situational and cross-cultural variations on this canonical norm, noting, for instance, how the "telephone openings of strangers are reduced in format compared to those of acquaintances" (1992, 78):

D: Mid-City Emergency

C: Um yeah (.) somebody jus' vandalized my car,

D: What's your address.

C: Thirty three twenty two: Elm (78).

In another variation, intimates also reduce the stages of the canonical telephone opening:

F: Hello?

M: Hey!

F: Hi

M: Are you *ready yet?* (82)

23. One gets the feeling that phone pranksters might protest about telemarketers a bit too much since, in fact, pranksters and telemarketers have a lot in common: both develop techniques to keep answerers on the phone for as longs as possible in order to achieve their goals. In advice that could apply equally well to telemarketers, an essay on the Prank Call Central Web site states that "the idea is to keep the other person on the phone long enough to get everything you

wanted to do in the call completed. If they hang-up after five seconds because you're acting like an idiot then you will not have accomplished what you set out to do."

24. It should be noted that the telephone companies were often the biggest beneficiaries of these services: "The New York Telephone Company . . . receives an average of 16.6 cents for one of these calls, while the provider of the service receives 2 cents to 2.5 cents" (Kristof 1986, A16).

25. Briceno adds that some phone lines that "cater specifically to homosexuals, serve as a kind of meeting place where homosexuals who may feel threatened or isolated can find and communicate with others" (1990, B5).

26. Also consider Robert Altman's *Short Cuts* (1993), which presents the contrast between the front and back stage in phone sex. A working-class mother, Lois Kaiser (Jennifer Jason Leigh) spends her days working on phone sex lines, breathily describing explicit sexual actions while changing her baby's diaper. Pranksters also play with this stark dichotomy by, for example, calling phone sex lines and describing the superhero underwear they have on. Indeed, the ease with which callers can forget the backstage realities of phone sex workers sitting in well-lit cubicles is a striking demonstration of the power of mediated co-presence. As is the case with the "heavy breather" heard on obscene phone calls, phone sex involves making a fetish of the raw co-presence of telephone conversation, as well as illustrating the importance of verbal exchange in preludes to sexual action.

27. The explosion in the use of cellular phones has made the technological web exponentially denser, further extending occasions for speaking. Some phone pranks work to bring into high relief new kinds of telephone connectivity between strangers. This can be seen in a subgenre of calls that exploit cell phones' paging functions. A random number is dialed, and when the victim answers the phone, the caller demands to know why he has been paged. Of course, the victim denies paging the caller. In some instances this device is used to spark displays of anger and frustration, but in others the callers insinuate themselves into long encounters with strangers.

Bibliography

Abrahams, Roger D. 1976. *Talking Black.* Rowley, Mass.: Newbury House.

Ace, Goodman. 1954. "Can the Laughs." *Saturday Review,* March 6, 28.

"An Afternoon at the Waxworks." 1947. *Variety,* July 9, 37.

Alkin, E. G. M. 1973. *Sound with Vision: Sound Technique for Television and Film.* New York: Crane, Russak.

Allen, Robert C. 1985. *Speaking of Soap Operas.* Chapel Hill: University of North Carolina Press.

———. 1991. *Horrible Prettiness.* Chapel Hill: University of North Carolina Press.

Altman, Rick. 1987. *The American Film Musical.* Bloomington: Indiana University Press.

———, ed. 1992. *Sound Theory, Sound Practice.* London: Routledge.

———. 1996. "Deep-Focus Sound: *Citizen Kane* and the Radio Aesthetic." In *Perspectives on Citizen Kane,* ed. Ronald Gottesman. New York: Simon and Schuster.

———. 2004. *Silent Film Sound.* New York: Columbia University Press.

Ames, Walter. 1951. " 'Dragnet' Wins Top Mystery Writers Award." *Los Angeles Times,* May 2, 28.

Anderson, Christopher. 1994. *Hollywood TV.* Austin: University of Texas Press.

Anthony, Gary, with Rocky Bennett. 1998. *Dirty Talk.* Amherst, N.Y.: Prometheus.

"Aural Sex." 1983. *Time,* May 9, 39.

Bakhtin, M. M. 1981. *The Dialogic Imagination.* Austin: University of Texas Press.

Baldwin, Hanson W. 1966. "Crank Calls Harass Families of G.I.'s Serving in Vietnam." *New York Times,* April 4, 4.

Baraka, Amiri [LeRoi Jones]. 1963. *Blues People.* New York: Quill.

Barclay, Dorothy. 1956. "The Telephoning Teens." *New York Times,* May 20, 245.

Barnes, Andrew. 1966. "Police Report Obscene Phone Calls to Mothers, Threatening Daughters." *Washington Post,* April 23, B3.

Barnouw, Erik. 1974. *Documentary.* New York: Oxford University Press.

Barrett, Lindon. 1999. *Blackness and Value.* Cambridge: Cambridge University Press.

Barthes, Roland. 1972. *Mythologies.* New York: Hill and Wang.

———. 1985. *The Responsibility of Forms.* Berkeley: University of California Press.

Bauman, Richard. 1986. *Story, Performance, and Event.* Cambridge: Cambridge University Press.

"Beacon Hill." 1943. *Berkshire Evening Eagle (Pittsfield, Mass.),* April 22, 13.

Bellamy, Edward. 1898. "With the Eyes Shut." In *The Blindman's World and Other Stories.* Boston: Houghton, Mifflin.

Bergson, Henri. 1956. "Laughter." In *Comedy,* ed. Wylie Sypher. Baltimore: Johns Hopkins University Press.

Berrett, Joshua, ed. 1999. *The Louis Armstrong Companion.* New York: Schirmer.

"Bill on Obscene Records Signed." 1950. *New York Times,* May 27, 46.

Blanc, Mel, and Philip Bashe. 1988. *That's Not All Folks.* New York: Warner Books.

Boddy, William. 1990. *Fifties Television.* Urbana: University of Illinois Press.

Bolger, Ray. 1954. "The Last Laugh Track." *Variety,* July 28, 98.

Brackett, David. 1995. *Interpreting Popular Music.* Cambridge: Cambridge University Press.

Brady, Erika. 1999. *A Spiral Way: How the Phonograph Changed Ethnography.* Jackson: University of Mississippi Press.

Briceno, Carlos. 1990. " 'Dial-a-Porn' Industry Battles U.S. Restrictions." *New York Times,* April 13, B5.

Briggs, Charles, and Richard Bauman. 1992. "Genre, Intertextuality, and Social Power." *Journal of Linguistic Anthropology* 2, no. 2:131–72.

Brooks, Peter. 1985. *The Melodramatic Imagination.* New York: Columbia University Press.

Brooks, Tim. 1979. "What's So Funny?" *Antique Phonograph Monthly* 5, no. 10:3.

———. 2004. "George W. Johnson: The First African-American Recording Star." *ARSC Journal* 35 (Fall): 37–87.

———. 2005. *Lost Sounds: Blacks and the Birth of the Recording Industry.* Urbana: University of Illinois Press.

Brown, Penelope, and Stephen Levinson. 1987. *Politeness.* Cambridge: Cambridge University Press.

Brown, Waln K. 1973. "Cognitive Ambiguity and the 'Pretended Obscene Riddle.' " *Keystone Folklore* 18:89–101.

Brunvand, Jan H. 1986. *The Study of American Folklore.* New York: Norton.

Buck, Jerry. 1966. "Cranks Turn Telephone into Instrument of Terror." *Ironwood (Mich.) Daily Globe,* May 18, 11.

———. 1972. "Newhart Fears Another Series for Good Reason." *Newark (Ohio) Advocate*, September 8, 16.

Bulman, Joan. 1956. *Jenny Lind*. London: James Barrie.

"The Busy Wiretappers." 1955. *Newsweek*, March 7, 31–34.

Calvert, Louis. 1918. *Problems of the Actor*. New York: Henry Holt.

"Can the Laughter." 1957. *Time*, February 18, 38–40.

"Candid Microphone" [review]. 1947. *Variety*, July 9, 35–36.

Cante, Rich, and Angelo Restivo. 2001. "The Voice of Pornography." In *Keyframes*, ed. Matthew Tinkcom and Amy Villarego. New York: Routledge.

Casriel, Daniel. 1972. *A Scream Away from Happiness*. New York: Grosset and Dunlap.

Castle, William. 1976. *Step Right Up!* New York: Pharos.

Chanan, Michael 1995. *Repeated Takes*. London: Verso.

Charters, Ann. 1970. *Nobody: The Story of Bert Williams*. New York: Macmillan.

Cherry, Colin. 1977. "The Telephone System: Creator of Mobility and Social Change." In *The Social Impact of the Telephone*, ed. Ithiel de Sola Pool. Cambridge: MIT Press.

Chion, Michel. 1990. *Audio Vision*. New York: Columbia University Press.

———. 1991. "Quiet Revolution . . . and Rigid Stagnation." *October* 58 (Fall): 69–80.

———. 1999. *The Voice in Cinema*. New York: Columbia University Press.

Clark, Katrina, and Michael Holquist. 1984. *Mikhail Bakhtin*. Cambridge: Belknap Press of Harvard University Press.

Collier, James Lincoln.1983. *Louis Armstrong*. New York: Oxford University Press.

Collins, Jim. 1995. *Architectures of Excess*. New York: Routledge.

"Comedy Crisis Worries Comics." 1957. *Life*, April 15, 38.

Comstock, Anthony, and John S. Sumner, eds. 1897. Annual Report, New York Society for the Suppression of Vice. Kinsey Institute Collection, Indiana University.

"Comstock Arrests an Actor; Hunting Charged with Making Improper Use of Phonographs." 1896. *New York Times*, June 26, 3.

Connor, Steven. 2000. *Dumbstruck*. Oxford: Oxford University Press.

Corenthal, Michael G. 1984. *Cohen on the Telephone: A History of Jewish Recorded Humor and Popular Music, 1892–1942*. Milwaukee: Yesterday's Memories.

Corner, John. 1999. *Critical Ideas in Television Studies*. Oxford: Clarendon Press.

———. 2002. "Performing the Real: Documentary Diversions." *Television and New Media* 3, no. 3 (August): 255–69.

"Could Not See the Joke." 1900. *Brooklyn Eagle*, February 26, 5.

Cousins, Norman. 1979. *Anatomy of an Illness*. New York: Bantam.

Cowan, Louis G. 1947. "Disk Shows Win Their 'D.' " *Variety*, July 9, 37.

Cowie, Elizabeth. 1993. "Pornography and Fantasy." In *Sex Exposed*, ed. Lynne Segal and Mary McIntosh. New Brunswick: Rutgers University Press.

Crafton, Donald. 1997. *The Talkies*. New York: Charles Scribner's Sons.

Cray, Ed. 1999. *The Erotic Muse.* Urbana: University of Illinois Press.

Crisell, Andrew. 1994. *Understanding Radio.* New York: Routledge.

Crouch, Stanley. 1978. "Laughin' Louis." *Village Voice,* August 14, 45.

Curry, Ramona. 1996. *Too Much of a Good Thing.* Minneapolis: University of Minnesota Press.

Curtis, Scott. 1992. "The Sound of the Early Warner Bros. Cartoons." In *Sound Theory, Sound Practice,* ed. Rick Altman. London: Routledge.

Daniels, Marc. 1953. "Approximating Live TV." *Variety,* July 29, 37.

Dash, Samuel. 1959. *The Eavesdroppers.* New Brunswick: Rutgers University Press.

"The Debate on Wiretapping." 1954. *Time,* January 4, 12–13.

deCordova, Richard. 2001. *Picture Personalities.* Urbana: University of Illinois Press.

De Sola Pool, Ithiel, ed. 1977. *The Social Impact of the Telephone.* Cambridge: MIT Press.

"Diminutive Stage Star Shines in New Series." 1937. *Washington Post,* March 7, TR5.

Distler, Paul Antonie. 1979. "Ethnic Comedy in Vaudeville and Burlesque." In *American Popular Entertainment,* ed. Myron Matlaw. Westport, Conn.: Greenwood Press.

Doane, Mary Ann. 1987. *The Desire to Desire: The Woman's Film of the 1940s.* Bloomington: Indiana University Press.

———. 1999. "The Voice in the Cinema: The Articulation of Body and Space." In *Film Theory and Criticism,* 5th ed., ed. Leo Braudy and Marshall Cohen. New York: Oxford University Press.

Dolar, Mladen. 2006. *A Voice and Nothing More.* Cambridge: MIT Press.

Douglas, Susan J. 1994. *Where the Girls Are.* New York: Times Books.

Du Bois, W. E. B. 1903. *The Souls of Black Folk.* Rept., New York: Modern Library, 2003.

Dunlap, Orrin E. 1936. *Talking on the Radio.* New York: Greenberg.

Dyer, Richard. 1986. *Heavenly Bodies.* New York: St. Martin's Press.

Dygert, Warren.1939. *Radio as an Advertising Medium.* New York: McGraw-Hill.

Ehrenreich, Barbara. 1983. *The Hearts of Men.* Garden City, N.Y.: Anchor.

Ehrenreich, Barbara, Elizabeth Hess, and Gloria Jacobs. 1992. "Beatlemania: Girls Just Want to Have Fun." In *The Adoring Audience,* ed. Lisa A. Lewis. New York: Routledge.

Ehrlich, Dimitri. 1995. "The Jerky Boys Parlay Crank Calls into Big Bucks." *New York Times,* March 5, H28.

Eicholz, Jack, and Louise Allen. 1963. "Crackdown on the Telephone Crank." *Mansfield (Ohio) News Journal,* August 18, 63.

Eisenberg, Evan. 1987. *The Recording Angel.* New York: Penguin.

Elliot, Anthony. 1999. *The Mourning of John Lennon.* Berkeley: University of California Press.

Elsaesser, Thomas. 1987. "Tales of Sound and Fury." In *Home Is Where the Heart Is: Studies in Melodrama and the Woman's Film,* ed. Christine Gledhill. London: BFI.

Ely, Melvin Patrick. 1991. *The Adventures of Amos 'n' Andy*. New York: Free Press.

Engel, Margaret. 1986. "Sex and Your Telephone." *Washington Post,* March 9, C1.

Fales, Cornelia. 2002. "The Paradox of Timbre." *Ethnomusicology* 46, no. 1 (Winter): 56–95.

Fales, Cornelia, and Stephen McAdams. 1994. "The Fusion and Layering of Noise and Tone: Implications for Timbre in African Instruments." *Leonardo Music Journal* 4:69–77.

"F.C.C. Opens Inquiry on 'Sex Talk' Phone Service." 1983. *New York Times,* September 11, 59.

Feaster, Patrick. 1999a. "Cal Stewart and the Phonographic Text." Unpublished manuscript.

———. 1999b. "Extemporization in Cal Stewart's 'Uncle Josh' Recordings." Unpublished manuscript.

———. 2001. "Framing the Mechanical Voice: Generic Conventions of Early Phonograph Recording." *Folklore Forum* 32, nos.1/2:57–102.

———. 2006a. "The Following Record: Making Sense of Phonographic Performance, 1877–1908." Ph.D. dissertation, Indiana University.

———. 2006b. "A Talking and Singing Machine." Unpublished manuscript.

"Fights Obscene Recordings." 1942. *New York Times,* November 1, 49.

Finnegan, Ruth. 1988. *Literacy and Orality*. Oxford: Basil Blackwell.

Fischer, Claude. 1992. *America Calling*. Berkeley: University of California Press.

Fitzgerald, Patrick, and Mark Leopold. 1987. *Stranger on the Line: The Secret History of Phone Tapping*. London: Bodley Head.

Flagler, J. M. 1960. "Student of the Spontaneous." *New Yorker,* December 10, 59–92.

Foster, Ernest. 1942. "Hollywood Film Shop." *Valparaiso (Ind.) Vidette-Messenger,* June 22, 4.

Freud, Sigmund. 1916. *Wit and Its Relation to the Unconscious*. New York: Moffat, Yard and Company.

———. 1997. *Writings on Art and Literature*. Stanford: Stanford University Press.

Friedman, James, ed. 2002. *Reality Squared*. New Brunswick: Rutgers University Press.

Friedwald, Will. 1990. *Jazz Singing*. New York: Charles Scribner's Sons.

Frith, Simon. 1981. *Sound Effects*. New York: Pantheon.

———. 1996. *Performing Rites*. Cambridge: Harvard University Press.

Funt, Allen. 1952. *Eavesdropper at Large*. New York: Vanguard Press.

———. 1994. *Candidly, Allen Funt*. New York: Barricade.

"Funt's Fun." 1948. *Newsweek,* September 20, 62.

Gabbard, Krin. 1996. *Jammin' at the Margins*. Chicago: University of Chicago Press.

Gaisberg, F. W. 1942. *The Music Goes Round*. New York: Macmillan.

Garcia, Gustave. 1882. *The Actor's Art*. London: T. Pettitt.

García, Manuel, II. 1975. *A Complete Treatise on the Art of Singing: Part One*, ed. and trans. Donald V. Paschke. New York: Da Capo Press.

———. 1984. *A Complete Treatise on the Art of Singing: Part Two,* ed. and trans. Donald V. Paschke. New York: Da Capo Press.

"García a Centenarian." 1905. *New York Times,* March 18, 7.

Garfinkel, Harold. 1984. *Studies in Ethnomethodology.* Cambridge, U.K.: Polity Press.

Gates, Henry Louis, Jr. 1988. *The Signifying Monkey.* New York: Oxford University Press.

Gelbart, Larry. 1984. Seminars at the Museum of Broadcasting. October.

———. 1998. *Laughing Matters.* New York: Random House.

Genovese, Eugene D. 1974. *Roll, Jordan, Roll.* Rept.: New York: Vintage Books, 1976.

Giddins, Gary. 1988. *Satchmo.* New York: Doubleday.

Gilmore, Art, and Glenn Y. Middleton. 1946. *Radio Announcing.* Hollywood: Hollywood Radio Publishers.

Gledhill, Christine. 1991. "Signs of Melodrama." In *Stardom: Industry of Desire,* ed. Christine Gledhill. London: Routledge.

Goffman, Erving. 1959. *The Presentation of Self in Everyday Life.* Rept., London: Penguin Books, 1990.

———. 1974. *Frame Analysis.* New York: Harper Colophon.

———. 1981. *Forms of Talk.* Philadelphia: University of Pennsylvania Press.

Goldstein, E. Bruce. 1999. *Sensation and Perception.* 5th ed. Pacific Grove, Calif.: Brooks/Cole.

Gottmann, Jean. 1977. "Megalopolis and Antipolis: The Telephone and the Structure of the City." In *The Social Impact of the Telephone,* ed. Ithiel de Sola Pool. Cambridge: MIT Press.

Gould, Glenn. 1984. "The Prospects of Recording." In *The Glenn Gould Reader,* ed. Tim Page. Rept., New York: Vintage, 1990.

Gould, Jack. 1946a. "They Say the Right Thing at the Wrong Time." *New York Times,* March 24, 100.

———. 1946b. Untitled article. *New York Times,* September 15, 20.

———. 1948. "How Comic Is Radio Comedy?" *New York Times,* November 21, SM22.

———. 1951. "Radio and Television." *New York Times,* December 19, 48.

———. 1956. "Live TV vs. Canned." *New York Times Magazine,* February 5, 27.

———. 1959. "CBS Revises TV Policy to End Program 'Deceits.'" *New York Times,* October 20, 1, 42.

———. 1960. "CBS Lifting Lid on Canned Laughs." *New York Times,* March 22, 75.

Gracyk, Theodore. 1996. *Rhythm and Noise: An Aesthetics of Rock.* Durham: Duke University Press.

Gracyk, Tim. 2002. *Popular American Recording Pioneers, 1895–1925.* New York: Haworth Press.

Green, Archie. 1985. "The Visual Arkansas Traveler." *JEMF Quarterly* 21, nos. 75–76:31–46.

Green, Venus. 2001. *Race on the Line.* Durham: Duke University Press.

Grutzner, Charles. 1948. "Judges Are Divided on Wire Tap Issue." *New York Times,* September 28, 30.

Gumperz, John J. 1992. "Contextualizing and Understanding." In *Rethinking Context,* ed. Alessandro Duranti and Charles Goodwin. Cambridge: Cambridge University Press.

Gunning, Tom. 1991. "Heard over the Phone: *The Lonely Villa* and the de Lorde Tradition of the Terrors of Technology." *Screen* 32, no. 2 (Summer): 184–96.

———. 1995. "Tracing the Individual Body: Photography, Detectives, and Early Cinema." In *Cinema and the Invention of Modern Life,* ed. Leo Charney and Vanessa R. Schwartz. Berkeley: University of California Press.

———. 2000. *The Films of Fritz Lang.* London: British Film Institute.

———. 2001. "New Thresholds of Vision." In *Impossible Presence,* ed. Terry Smith. Chicago: University of Chicago Press.

Guthrie, Tyrone. 1957. "Is There Madness in 'The Method'?" *New York Times,* September 15, SM112.

Hammerton, J. A. 1897. *The Actor's Art.* London: George Redway.

Hansen, Miriam. 1991. *Babel and Babylon.* Cambridge: Harvard University Press.

Harvith, John, and Susan Edwards Harvith. 1986. *Edison, Musicians, and the Phonograph.* New York: Greenwood Press.

Hayes, Joy Elizabeth. 2004. "The Sound of Whiteness: Race, Masculinity, and Class in Golden Age Radio Drama." Paper presented at the International Communication Association Conference, New Orleans, April 27–31.

Hays, Constance L. 1991. "Ruling Backs Enforcing 'Dial a Porn' Law." *New York Times,* July 16, B1.

Heritage, John. 1984. *Garfinkel and Ethnomethodology.* Cambridge, U.K.: Polity Press.

Hewes, Henry. 1951, "Radio: Realistic 'Cops and Robbers' Saga." *New York Times,* June 3, 103.

Hilmes, Michele. 1990. *Hollywood and Broadcasting.* Urbana: University of Illinois Press.

———. 1997. *Radio Voices: American Broadcasting, 1922–1952.* Minneapolis: University of Minnesota Press.

Hirsch, Foster. 1984. *A Method to Their Madness.* Cambridge, Mass.: Da Capo Press.

Hobson, Dick. 1966a. "The Hollywood Sphinx and His Laff Box." *TV Guide,* July 2, 3–6.

———. 1966b. "Help! I'm a Prisoner in a Laff Box!" *TV Guide,* July 9, 20–23.

Holland, Henry Scott. 1893. *Jenny Lind the Artist.* London: John Murray.

Hoover, Eleanor Links. "The Great 'Group' Binge." *Los Angeles Times,* January 8, L8.

Hopper, Robert. 1992. *Telephone Conversation.* Bloomington: Indiana University Press, 1992.

Hornellsville (N.Y.) Tribune. 1871. Untitled article, July 28, 3.

"The Hot Wire-Tapping Debate." 1954. *Newsweek,* January 11, 21–22.

"How Wiretap Is Worked." 1955. *Life,* March 7, 45.

Hull, Loraine. 1985. *Strasberg's Method as Taught by Lorrie Hull.* Woodbridge, Conn.: Ox Bow, 1985.

Hullum, Jan. 1972–73. "The 'Catch' Riddle: Perspectives from Goffman and Metafolklore." *Folklore Annual* 4–5:52–59.

Hutchens, John K. 1942a. "Serious Business, This Radio Humor." *New York Times,* March 15, SM16.

———. 1942b. "The Secret of a Good Radio Voice," *New York Times,* December 6, SM26.

———. 1943. "Are Soap Operas Only Suds?" *New York Times,* March 28, SM19.

Hymes, Dell. 1975. "Breakthrough into Performance." in *Folklore: Performance and Communication,* ed. Dan Ben-Amos and Kenneth S. Goldstein. The Hague: Mouton.

Ickes, Harold L. 1950. "A Dirtier 'Dirty Business.'" *New Republic,* January 9, 17.

"'Indecent' Records Eligible for Mails." 1949. *Berkshire Evening Eagle* (Pittsfield, Mass.), June 2, 19.

"Is Candid Camera Just Good Clean Fun?" 1961. *TV Guide,* February 25–March 3, 12–16.

Jakobson, Roman. 1980. *The Framework of Language.* Ann Arbor: University of Michigan, Michigan Studies in the Humanities.

Janov, Arhtur. 1970. *The Primal Scream.* New York: Putnam.

Jarrett, Michael. 1998. *Sound Tracks.* Philadelphia: Temple University Press.

———. 2004. "Eminem Versions an Old Song." Paper presented at Society for Cinema and Media Studies Conference, Atlanta, March.

Jefferson, Gail. 1979, "A Technique for Inviting Laughter and Its Subsequent Acceptance Declination." In *Everyday Language: Studies in Ethnomethodology,* ed. George Psathas. New York: Irvington Publishers.

Jenkins, Henry. 1992. *Textual Poachers.* New York: Routledge.

Jenkins, Peter. 1984. "Case Report: Obscene Telephone Calls." *British Journal of Sexual Medicine* 11, no. 18 (August–September): 150–53.

Jones, Andrew F. 2001. *Yellow Music.* Durham: Duke University Press.

Jones, Gerard. 1993. *Honey, I'm Home.* New York: St. Martin's Press.

Jordan, Winthrop D. 1986. *White over Black: American Attitudes toward the Negro, 1550–1812.* New York: Norton.

Joseph, Branden W. 2002. "Nothing Special: Andy Warhol and the Rise of Surveillance." In *CTRL [SPACE]: Rhetorics of Surveillance from Bentham to Big Brother,* ed. Thomas Y. Levin, Ursula Frohne, and Peter Weibel. Cambridge: MIT Press.

Katz, Mark. 2004. *Capturing Sound.* Berkeley: University of California Press.

Kenney, William H. 1905. "Telephone Has Improved American Voice." *Telephony* 9, no. 5 (May): 428.

Kenney, William Howland. 1999. *Recorded Music in American Life.* New York: Oxford University Press, 1999.

King, Rob. 2007. " 'The Camera Is a Monumental Liar': From Slapstick to Stop-Motion and Back Again in the Films of Charlie Bowers." Paper presented at the Society for Cinema and Media Studies Conference, Chicago, March.

King, Wayne. 1989. "Number, Please: Adieu Anonymity on the Telephone." *New York Times,* April 14, B1.

Kirshetblatt-Gimblett, Barbara, ed. 1976. *Speech Play.* University of Pennsylvania Press.

Klein, Hermann. 1923. *The Bel Canto*. London: Oxford University Press, 1923.

Klinger, Barbara. 2006. *Beyond the Multiplex*. Berkeley: University of California Press.

Knabb, Ken, ed. 1981. *Situationist International: Anthology*. Berkeley: Bureau of Public Secrets.

Koestenbaum, Wayne. 1993. *The Queen's Throat*. New York: Poseidon Press.

Kolko, Beth E. 2000. "Erasing @race: Going White in the (Inter)Face." In *Race in Cyberspace*, ed. Beth E. Kolko, Lisa Nakamura, and Gilbert B. Rodman. New York: Routledge.

Kolko, Beth E., Lisa Nakamura, and Gilbert B. Rodman, eds. 2000. *Race in Cyberspace*. New York: Routledge.

Kovitz, Ray. 1952. "Authenticity Themes Dragnet." *Los Angeles Times*, August 21, 26.

Kozloff, Sarah. 1988. *Invisible Storytellers: Voice-Over Narration in American Fiction Film*. Berkeley: University of California Press.

Kristof, Nicholas D. 1986. "Court Test Is Likely as Dial-a-Porn Services Grow." *New York Times*, October 15, A16.

Landers, Ann. 1968. "Obscene Phone Call? Don't Talk, Hang Up." *Washington Post*, August 22, C5.

Lastra, James. 2000. *Sound Technology and the American Cinema*. New York: Columbia University Press.

"Laugh Suit Lost by Radio Comedian." 1949. *Los Angeles Times*, October 4, B6.

Lawrence, Amy. 1991. *Echo and Narcissus: Women's Voices in Classical Hollywood Cinema*. Berkeley: University of California Press.

Leary, James P. "Fists and Foul Mouths: Fights and Fight Stories in Contemporary Rural American Bars." *Journal of American Folklore* 89, no. 351 (January 1976): 27–39.

Legman, Gershon. 1976. "Bawdy Monologues and Rhymed Recitations." *Southern Folklore Quarterly* 40:59–122.

———. 1982. *No Laughing Matter*. Bloomington: Indiana University Press.

Levin, Eric. 1978. "It's a Big Black Box That Yuks and Guffaws on Demand." *TV Guide*, April 8, 33–36.

Levine, Lawrence W. 1977. *Black Culture and Black Consciousness*. New York: Oxford University Press.

Lewis, Jon. 2000. *Hollywood v. Hard Core*. New York: New York University Press.

Lewisohn, Mark. 1988. *The Beatles: Recording Sessions*. New York: Harmony.

Lhamon, W. T. 1998. *Raising Cain*. Cambridge: Harvard University Press.

Liebman, Max. 1961. "Laugh? I Thought I'd Die." *Variety*, January 4, 86.

"Life in 'One Man's Family' Will Continue over Air Waves for Seven More Years." 1939. *Newsweek*, February 6, 33.

Lomax, Alan. 1968. *Folk Song Style and Culture*. Washington, D.C.: American Association for the Advancement of Science.

Lott, Eric. 1993. *Love and Theft*. New York: Oxford University Press.

Lundberg, Madeleine. 1970. "Encounter Groups Are Everywhere." *Washington Post*, July 5, 171.

Maas, James B., and Kathleen M. Toivanen. 1978. "Candid Camera and the Be-
havioral Sciences." *Teaching of Psychology* 5, no. 4:111–17.
MacDonald, Cynthia. 1987. "The Girls of Dial-A-Porn." *Penthouse Forum*,
April, 40–46.
Mackinlay, M. Sterling. 1908. *Garcia the Centenarian and His Times*. London:
William Blackwood and Sons.
Majumdar, Neepa. 2001. "The Embodied Voice: Song Sequences and Stardom
in Popular Hindi Cinema." In *Soundtrack Available: Essays on Film and Pop-
ular Music, ed. Pamela Wojcik and Arthur Knight*. Durham: Duke University
Press.
Maloney, Martin. 1949. *The Radio Play: A Workbook in Radio Dramatic Writ-
ing*. Evanston, Ill.: Student Book Exchange.
Malver, Bruce L. 1971. "Encounter Groupers Up against the Wall." *New York
Times*, January 3, SM4.
Manuel, Peter. 1993. *Cassette Culture*. Chicago: University of Chicago Press.
Marshall, P. David. 2000. "The Celebrity Legacy of the Beatles." In *The Beat-
les, Popular Music, and Society*, ed. Ian Inglis. Basingstoke, U.K.: Macmillan.
Martin, Richard P. 1989. *The Language of Heroes*. Ithaca: Cornell University
Press.
Marvin, Carolyn. 1988. *When Old Technologies Were New*. Oxford: Oxford
University Press.
Maurice, Alice. 2002. " 'Cinema at Its Source': Synchronizing Race and Sound
in the Early Talkies." *Camera Obscura* 17, no. 1 (49): 31–71.
Mayer, Martin. 1977. "The Telephone and the Uses of Time." In *The Social Im-
pact of the Telephone*, ed. Ithiel de Sola Pool. Cambridge: MIT Press.
McCarthy, Anna. 2000. "The Front Row Is Reserved for Scotch Drinkers: Early
Television's Tavern Audience." In *Television: The Critical View*, ed. Horace
Newcomb. New York: Oxford University Press.
———. 2004. "Stanley Milgram, Allen Funt, and Me." In *Reality TV: Remak-
ing Television Culture*, ed. Susan Murray and Laurie Ouellette. New York:
New York University Press.
McCarathy, E. V. 1965. "Dirty Voices in the Night." *Los Angeles Times*, March
21, E8.
McConachie, Bruce. 2003. *American Theater in the Culture of the Cold War*.
Iowa City: University of Iowa Press.
McCracken, Allison. 2001. "Real Men Don't Sing Ballads: The Radio Crooner
in Hollywood, 1929–1933." In *Soundtrack Available: Essays on Film and
Popular Music.*, ed. Pamela Wojcik and Arthur Knight. Durham: Duke Uni-
versity Press.
———. 2002. "Scary Women and Scarred Men." In *Radio Reader*, ed. Michele
Hilmes and Jason Loviglio. New York: Routledge.
McLuhan, Marshall. 1964. *Understanding Media*. New York: Signet.
Mehlinger, Kermit. 2003. "The Sexual Revolution." In *Sexual Revolution*, ed.
Jeffrey Escoffier. New York: Thunder's Mouth Press.
Mellin, William J. 1949. "I Was a Wire Tapper." *Saturday Evening Post*, Sep-
tember 10, 19–21, 46, 48, 54, 57, 58, 60, 62–63.

Millard, Andre. 1995. *America on Record*. Cambridge: Cambridge University Press.

Minsky, Morton, and Milt Machlin. 1986. *Minsky's Burlesque*. New York: Arbor House.

Modleski, Tania. 1982. *Loving with a Vengeance*. Hamden, Conn.: Archon, 1982.

Moran, William R., ed. 1990. *Herman Klein and the Gramophone*. Portland, Ore.: Amadeus Press.

"More Than a Stage Whisper." 1999. *BBC News Online*, March 31, http://news.bbc.co.uk/1/hi/entertainment/308905.stm.

Morgan, Philip D. 1998. *Slave Counterpoint*. Chapel Hill: University of North Carolina Press.

Morse, Carlton E. 1988. *The One Man's Family Album*. Woodside, Calif.: Seven Stones Press.

Morton, David. 2000. *Off the Record*. New Brunswick: Rutgers University Press.

" 'Most Heard' Man." 1947. *Washington Post*, April 27, S8.

Moyer, Daniel, and Eugene Alvarez. 2001. *Just the Facts, Ma'am*. Santa Ana, Calif.: Seven Locks.

"Mrs. Choremi Guilty, Magistrate Finds." 1948. *New York Times*, July 9, 36.

Mullin, John T. 1976. "Creating the Craft of Tape Recording." *High Fidelity*, April, 62–67.

Murch, Walter. 1995. *In the Blink of an Eye*. Los Angeles: Silman-James.

Murray, Frank, and Lynda Beran. 1968. "A Survey of Nuisance Calls Received by Males and Females." *Psychological Record* 18:107–9.

Murray, Matthew. 1997. "Broadcast Content Regulation and Cultural Limits, 1920–1962," Ph.D. dissertation, University of Wisconsin, Madison, 1997.

Musser, Charles. 1990.*The Emergence of Cinema*. New York: Scribner.

———. 1991. *High-Class Moving Pictures*. Princeton: Princeton University Press.

"N.Y. Police Seize Obscene Records." 1958. *Syracuse Herald-Journal*, April 2, 21.

Nadler, Raoul P. 1968. "Approach to Psychodynamics of Obscene Telephone Calls." *New York State Journal of Medicine* 68, no. 4 (February 15): 521–26.

Nakamura, Lisa. 2002. *Cybertypes*. New York: Routledge.

Naremore, James. 1988. *Acting in the Cinema*. Berkeley: University of California Press.

"Negroes as Singers." 1903. *Washington Post*, April 25, 6.

Nichols, Bill. 1991. *Representing Reality*. Bloomington: Indiana University Press.

Nichols, Michael P., and Melvin Zax. *Catharsis in Psychotherapy*. New York: Gardner Press.

Nowell-Smith, Geoffrey. 1991. "On Kiri Te Kanawa, Judy Garland, and the Culture Industry." In *Modernity and Mass Culture*, ed. James Naremore and Patrick Brantlinger. Bloomington: Indiana University Press.

"Obscene Phone Caller Posed as Policeman." 1975. *Washington Post*, January 25, A17.

"Obscene Record Legal in Newark, Judge Says." 1958. *New York Times*, October 1, 23.

"Obscene Record Maker Indicted." 1950. *Mansfield (Ohio) News-Journal*, April 14, 2.

"Obscene Record Ruling." 1949. *New York Times*, June 1, 42.

"Obscene Records Banned." 1950. *New York Times*, May 16, 2.

"Obscene Records Cause of Arrest." 1948. *Nebraska State Journal*, October 1, 13.

Ong, Walter. 1981. *Fighting for Life*. Ithaca: Cornell University Press.

———. 1982. *Orality and Literacy*. London: Routledge.

"Owner of Voice Vainly Sought." 1909. *Los Angeles Times*, March 11, H10.

Palmer, Robert. 1981. *Deep Blues*. New York: Viking.

Panassié, Hugues. 1971. *Louis Armstrong*. New York: Scribners.

Pear, T. H. 1931. *Voice and Personality as Applied to Radio Broadcasting*. New York: John Wiley and Sons.

Pearson, Roberta E. 1992. *Eloquent Gestures*. Berkeley: University of California Press.

Pegler, Westbrook. "Judicial Dignity?" 1950. *Syracuse Post-Standard*, April 18, 13.

Penley, Constance. 1997. "Crackers and Whackers: The White Trashing of Porn." In *White Trash: Race and Class in America*, ed. Matt Wray and Annalee Newitz. New York: Routledge.

Peterson, Richard A. 1997. *Creating Country Music*. Chicago: University of Chicago Press.

Place, Janey. 1998. "Women in Film Noir." In *Women in Film Noir*, ed. E. Ann Kaplan. London: BFI.

Pleasants, Henry. 1974. *The Great American Popular Singers*. New York: Simon and Schuster.

———. 1981. *The Great Singers*. New York: Simon and Schuster.

"Pool-Sellers Robbed Again." 1883. *New York Times*, October 18, 1.

Provine, Robert R. 2000. *Laughter: A Scientific Study*. New York: Viking.

"Radio Comic Asks Damages." 1948. *Los Angeles Times*, July 14, 16.

"Raid by Anthony Comstock; Improper Songs Given in Phonographs at College Point." 1897. *New York Times*, October 14, 3.

Rakow, Lana F. 1988. "Women and the Telephone: The Gendering of a Communications Technology." In *Technology and Women's Voices*, ed. Cheris Kramarae. New York: Routledge and Kegan Paul.

———. 1992. *Gender on the Line: Women, the Telephone, and Community Life*. Urbana: University of Illinois Press.

Raphael, Chad. 2004. "The Political Economic Origins of Reali-TV." In *Reality TV: Remaking Television Culture*, ed Susan Murray and Laurie Ouelette. New York: New York University Press.

Raspberry, William. 1968. "Crank Calls Plague Area Residents." *Washington Post*, February 18, D1.

Ray, Robert B. 1995. *The Avant-Garde Finds Andy Hardy*. Cambridge: Harvard University Press.

———. 2001. *How a Film Theory Got Lost*. Bloomington: Indiana University Press.

Ree, Jonathan. 1999. *I See a Voice*. London: HarperCollins.

Ridley, Jim. 2002. Review. *Nashville Scene*, February, http://archives.nashville scene.com (accessed November 2002).

Robertson, Pamela. 1996. *Guilty Pleasures*. Durham: Duke University Press.

Rogin, Michael. 1996. *Blackface, White Noise*. Berkeley: University of California Press.

Rose, Tricia. 1994. *Black Noise*. Hanover, N.H.: Wesleyan University Press.

Rosen, Jody. 2002. *White Christmas: The Story of an American Song*. New York: Scribner.

Rosenbaum, Jonathan. 2001. "The Best of Both Worlds." *Chicago Reader*, July 13, 32.

Ross, Andrew. 1989. *No Respect*. New York: Routledge.

Rossi, Melissa. 1993. "Prince Albert, Still in the Can." *Newsweek*, June 21, 61.

Sadie, Stanley, and John Tyrrell, eds. 2001. *The New Grove Dictionary of Music and Musicians*. 2nd ed. London: Macmillan.

Samter, Thyra. 1911. "Mr. Williams Has English Accent." *Chicago Tribune*, September 10, B5.

Scannell, Paddy. 1996. *Radio, Television, and Modern Life*. Oxford: Blackwell.

Schaefer, Eric. 1999. *Bold! Daring! Shocking! True!* Durham: Duke University Press.

Schulberg, Budd. 1953. "Your Arkansas Traveler." In *Some Faces in the Crowd*, by Budd Schulberg. New York: Random House.

Schuller, Gunther. 1968. *Early Jazz*. New York: Oxford University Press.

Sconce, Jeffrey. 2004. "See You in Hell, Johnny Bravo!" In *Reality TV: Remaking Television Culture*, ed. Susan Murray and Laurie Ouellette. New York: New York University Press.

Scott, John L. 1945. "New Film Star Rises from Radio." *Los Angeles Times*, May 27, B1.

Seldes, Gilbert. 1956. *The Public Arts*. New York: Simon and Schuster.

Shaftesbury, Edmund. 1889. *Lessons in the Art of Acting*. Washington, D.C.: Martyn College Press, 1889.

———. 1891. *Lessons in Voice Culture*. Washington, D.C.: Martyn College Press.

Sharbutt, Jay. 1978. "Radio and Television." *Marysville (Ohio) Journal-Tribune*, February 1, 9.

Shaw, George Bernard. 1931. *Music in London, 1890–94*. Vol. 2 of *Collected Works*. New York: Wm. H. Wise and Company.

Shayon, Robert Lewis. 1959. "Laugh, Soundman, Laugh." *Saturday Review*, April 18, 44.

Siefert, Marsha. 1995. "Image/Music/Voice: Song Dubbing in Hollywood Musicals." *Journal of Communication* 45, no. 2 (Spring): 44–64.

Silverman, Kaja. 1988. *The Acoustic Mirror: The Female Voice in Psychoanalysis and Cinema*. Bloomington: Indiana University Press.

Sims, Calvin. 1989. "How to Tell Who Rings Your Phone." *New York Times*, March 1, D1.

Singer, Ben. 2001. *Melodrama and Modernity*. New York: Columbia University Press.

Slawson, Wayne. 1987. *Sound Color*. Berkeley: University of California Press.

Smith, Mark M. 2001. *Listening to Nineteenth-Century America*. Chapel Hill: University of North Carolina Press.

"Soft Voices Ensnare Men's Hearts." 1905. *Telephony* 9, no. 4 (April): 328.

Solomon, Matthew. 1997. "Adapting 'Radio's Perfect Script': 'Sorry Wrong Number' and *Sorry, Wrong Number*." *Quarterly Review of Film and Video* 16, no. 1:23–40.

————. 2000. "Twenty-five Heads under One Hat." In *Meta-Morphing*, ed. Vivian Sobchack. Minneapolis: University of Minnesota Press.

Sousa, John Philip. 1906. "The Menace of Mechanical Music." *Appleton's Magazine*, September, 278–84.

Southern, Eileen, ed. 1983. *Readings in Black American Music*. New York: Norton.

Sreberny-Mohammadi, Annabelle, and Ali Mohammadi. 1994. *Small Media, Big Revolution*. Minneapolis: University of Minnesota Press, 1994.

Staiger, Janet. 1984. "The Eyes Are Really the Focus: Photoplay Acting and Film Form and Style." *Wide Angle* 6, no. 4:14–23.

Staples, Robert E. 1967. "The Mystique of Black Sexuality." *Liberator* 7, no. 3 (March): 8–10.

Stark, James. 1999. *Bel Canto: A History of Vocal Pedagogy*. Toronto: University of Toronto Press.

Stein, Sonia. 1951. "That 'Kissin' Stuff' Is Now on the TV." *Washington Post*, January 18, B13.

Steinberg, Neil. 1992. *If at All Possible, Involve a Cow*. New York: St. Martin's Press.

Sterne, Jonathan. 2003. *The Audible Past*. Durham: Duke University Press.

Stewart, Jacqueline. 2004. "What Happened in the Transition? Reading Race, Gender, and Labor between the Shots." In *American Cinema's Transitional Era*, ed. Charlie Keil and Shelley Stamp. Berkeley: University of California Press.

Stewart, R. W. 1947. "Can't You Take a Practical Joke?" *New York Times*, November 23, 85.

Stille, Alexander. 2002. *The Future of the Past*. New York: Farrar, Straus and Giroux.

Stone, Alan. 1989. *Wrong Number: The Breakup of AT&T*. New York: Basic Books.

Storr, Anthony. 1970. "A Short Course in Brainwashing." *Washington Post*, May 24, 283

————. 1972. "The Primal Revolution." *New York Times*, November 5, BR8.

Strasberg, Lee. 1991. *Strasberg at the Actors Studio*. Ed. Robert H. Hethmon. New York: Theater Communications.

"Strictly for Laughs." 1955. *Newsweek*, January 10, 46.

"A Study of the Telephone Girl." 1905. *Telephony* 9, no. 5 (May): 388.

Sundberg, Johan. 1987. *The Science of the Singing Voice*. Dekalb: Northern Illinois University Press.

"Supt. Calder Angry over a Mean Trick." 1902. *Brooklyn Eagle*, July 19, 2.

Susman, Warren I. 1984. *Culture as History*. New York: Pantheon.

"A Talk over the 'Phone." 1890. *Brooklyn Eagle,* November 30, 9.

Tamony, Peter. 1990. "The Origin of 'Phoney.'" In *Dictionaries.* Terre Haute, Ind.: Dictionary Society of America, 101–5.

Taussig, Michael. 1993. *Mimesis and Alterity.* New York: Routledge.

"The Telephone Girl's Voice." 1904. *Telephony* 7, no. 2 (February): 126.

"Terror on the Telephone." 1961. *Los Angeles Times,* July 9, TW7.

Thomas, Bob. 1967. "Groucho Marx Besieged with Offers of Jobs." *Gettysburg Times,* December 13, 1.

Thompson, Emily. 2002. *The Soundscape of Modernity.* Cambridge: MIT Press.

Thompson, John B. 1995. *The Media and Modernity.* Stanford: Stanford University Press.

"3 Indicted in Shipment of Pornographic Disks." 1950. *Variety,* May 3, 41.

"Tightening Controls over Sales by Phone." 1988. *New York Times,* June 25, 52.

Toles, George. 2004. "Auditioning Betty in *Mulholland Drive.*" *Film Quarterly* 58, no. 1 (Summer): 2–13.

Toll, Robert. 1974. *Blacking Up.* New York: Oxford University Press.

Turkle, Sherry. 1995. *Life on the Screen.* New York: Touchstone.

"Two Girls Play Telephone Joke." 1924. *Los Angeles Times,* June 29, E10.

U.S. Congress. 1950. *Obscene Matters—Importation or Transportation.* Public Law 81–531 (May 27), 64 Stat. 194.

———. 1951. *United States Code, Congressional Service.* 81st Cong., 2nd sess. Vol. 2, *Legislative History.* St. Paul: West Publishing Co.

U.S. House of Representatives, Committee on the Judiciary. *Transportation of Obscene Matters (to accompany S.2811).* (H. Rpt. 2017). Washington, D.C.: Government Printing Office, 1950.

Vale, V., and Andrea Juno. 1993. *Incredibly Strange Music.* Vol. 2. San Francisco: Re/Search Publications.

Vardac, A. Nicholas. 1949. *Stage to Screen.* Cambridge: Harvard University Press.

"Viewers Rule Out Laugh Track." 1971. *Coshocton (Ohio) Tribune,* May 3, 5-B.

Walsh, Jim. 1944. "Favorite Pioneer Recording Artists." *Hobbies,* June, 25–27.

———. 1950. "Favorite Pioneer Recording Artists: Bert Williams, a Thwarted Genius, II." *Hobbies,* October, 19–20.

Walsh, Mike. Tube Bar homepage: www.missioncreep.com/mw/tubebar/index.html.

"Wedding Feast Not Wanted." 1904. *Los Angeles Times,* April 28, A1.

Weibel, Peter. 2002. "Pleasure and the Panoptic Principle." In *CTRL [SPACE]: Rhetorics of Surveillance from Bentham to Big Brother,* ed. Thomas Y. Levin, Ursula Frohne, and Peter Weibel. Cambridge: MIT Press.

Weis, Elisabeth. 1999. "Eavesdropping: An Aural Analogue of Voyeurism?" In *Cinesonic: The World of Sound in Film,* ed. Phillip Brophy. Sydney, Australia: Southwood Press.

Wexman, Virginia Wright. 1993. *Creating the Couple.* Princeton: Princeton University Press.

White, Mimi. 1992. *Tele-Advising.* Chapel Hill: University of North Carolina Press.

Williams, Linda. 1989. *Hard Core.* Berkeley: University of California Press.

———. 1991. "Film Bodies: Gender, Genre and Excess." *Film Quarterly* 44, no. 4 (Summer): 2–13.

———. 2006. "Jane Fonda's Orgasms: Bad Sex and Good Sex in the New Hollywood." Paper presented at Society for Cinema and Media Studies Conference, Vancouver, B.C.

"Wire-Tapping Mystery." 1949. *Life,* March 28, 34.

Wojcik, Pamela Robertson. 2004. "Typecasting." In *Movie Acting: The Film Reader,* ed. Pamela Robertson Wojcik. New York: Routledge.

Wright, Robert A. 1971. "For Privacy from Cranks, Creeps and Crooks, Millions Getting Unlisted Phone Numbers." *New York Times,* December 22, 18.

Wurtzel, Alan H., and Colin Turner. 1977. "Latent Functions of the Telephone." In *The Social Impact of the Telephone,* ed. Ithiel de Sola Pool. Cambridge: MIT Press.

Yankah, Kwesi. 1985. "Risks in Verbal Art Performance." *Journal of Folklore Research* 22, nos. 2–3:133–53.

"Young García Passed Up Opera Career, but Won Fame Teaching Vocal Tricks." 1925. *Indiana Evening Gazette,* November 13, 8.

Zimbardo, Philip. 1985. "Laugh Where We Must, Be Candid Where We Can." *Psychology Today,* June, 43–47.

Ziv, Frederic W. 1947. "Doin' What Comes Naturally—By Transcripton." *Variety,* July 9, 37.

Index

Text: 10/13 Sabon
Display: Sabon
Compositor: Binghamton Valley Composition
Printer and binder: Thomson-Shore, Inc.